POLITICS IN THE ALTIPLANO
The Dynamics of Change in Rural Peru

Latin American Monographs, No. 15
Institute of Latin American Studies
The University of Texas

POLITICS
IN THE
ALTIPLANO

The Dynamics of Change in Rural Peru

By EDWARD DEW

PUBLISHED FOR THE INSTITUTE OF LATIN AMERICAN STUDIES
BY THE UNIVERSITY OF TEXAS PRESS, AUSTIN AND LONDON

Permission to quote from the following publications is gratefully acknowledged:

François Bourricaud. *Changements à Puno: Étude de Sociologie Andine.* Paris: Institut des Hautes Études de l'Amerique Latine, 1962.
Henry F. Dobyns, Paul L. Doughty, and Allan R. Holmberg. *Peace Corps Program Impact in the Peruvian Andes: Final Report.* Ithaca: Cornell University, 1966.
Héctor Martínez. *Las Migraciones Altiplánicas y la Colonización del Tambopata.* Lima: Ministerio de Trabajo y Asuntos Indígenas, 1961.
Frederick B. Pike. *The Modern History of Peru.* New York: Praeger, 1967.
Emilio Romero. *Monografía del Departamento de Puno.* Lima: Imprentas Aguirre, 1928.
Richard P. Schaedel. *La Demografía y los Recursos Humanos del Sur del Perú.* Mexico City: Instituto Indigenista Interamericano, 1967.

Type set by G&S Typesetters, Austin
Printed by Von Boeckmann-Jones Company, Austin
Bound by Universal Bookbindery, Inc., San Antonio

ACKNOWLEDGMENTS

Research in the problems of development has been given an enormous boost by the dispersion of countless alert and capable young Americans into the sensitive and troubled zones of change in the world. The Peace Corps has received many well-earned accolades for its contributions to social, economic, and political development. Increasingly, it will be acknowledged as an unprecedented channel for furthering American knowledge about conditions in this "third world."

The volunteers and staff of the Peace Corps in Peru, and particularly those in Puno, deserve special recognition for their help and for their stimulus for this study. The Peace Corps slogan, "What are you doing in the world?" can be a haunting refrain, whether one is a researcher, Peace Corps volunteer, politician, or peasant. In particular, I would like to express my boundless gratitude to volunteers Ralph Bolton, William Hutchinson, Ann and Peter Lara, and Julia and Irwin Zagar. Thanks are also due to staff members Samuel Guarnaccia, Eugene Baird, Thorburn Reid, Gino Baumann, and James Lay. Later, when this material was being revised and brought up to date, valuable comments and encouragement were received from Steve Hartwell and Cap Phillips, in Peace Corps/Washington.

My debt is great to the many Peruvian informants whose cooperation made this study possible. In particular, I must express special thanks to Ingeniero Oscar Espinoza, Dr. Róger Cáceres, Pedro Cáceres, and Dr. Samuel Frisancho, for their unfailing patience and good will extending through many hours of interviewing on repeated occasions. I am grateful to the staffs of the Puno newspapers, *Los Andes* and *El Tiempo* (now defunct), for their considerable assistance.

Dr. Earl Smith, Dr. David Brown, and Russell Scarato, of the United States A.I.D. mission in Peru, deserve thanks for the advice and help they offered me in the field. In the revision stage I was aided by the constructive comments of Gerritt Huizer, of the Inter-American Committee on Agricultural Development of the Pan American Union. Needless to say, the views expressed in this study do not reflect the "positions" of any of the above-mentioned organizations.

For their suggestions and useful criticisms of this study in its preliminary stages, I am indebted to Professors Michael F. Lofchie, James F. Guyot, John C. Bollens, Henry J. Bruman, and James N. Hill, of the University of California at Los Angeles, and Professor Russell Fitzgibbon, of the University of California at Santa Barbara. Dorothy Fialkoff and Marie Dengenis helped in my races against the clock with their typing of the manuscripts, the final draft facilitated with a grant from Fairfield University.

I should also like to thank the following people for their help in making the final manuscript more pertinent, readable, and available for the reader's scrutiny: Richard N. Adams, Thomas McGann, and Nena Bentley, of the Institute of Latin American Studies at The University of Texas, and Vaughn Bryant, Jr., of The University of Texas (who drafted the final maps).

Finally, to my wife, Anke, who made my preliminary maps and kept me from getting lost, all I can say is, when I'm down and out, lift up your head and shout, "Zorba the Greek!" It surely works, doesn't it?

To my parents, for their encouragement and help

CONTENTS

MAPS

TABLES

INTRODUCTION

At dawn on November 4, 1965, a mass of people gathered in the town of Juliaca, in the province of San Román, on the desolate high Andean plain called the altiplano, in southern Peru. The day was the two-hundred-ninety-seventh anniversary of the founding of Puno, a nearby town on the shore of Lake Titicaca, which serves as the capital of the department of Puno, encompassing the entire altiplano region of southern Peru. That morning a delegation from Lima, including the president of the Peruvian Chamber of Deputies (Cámara de Diputados) and other high dignitaries, was to arrive by plane at the Juliaca airport. The visitors were to be met by local officials at the airport and escorted forty kilometers to Puno for the celebrations and the dedication of a number of public works recently completed in that city.

However, the mass of *juliaqueños* was determined to prevent this. In the space of a few hours, they blockaded all the main roads into Juliaca, captured the airfield, cut telephone and telegraph communications between the two towns, and prepared to derail any trains passing to Puno through Juliaca. Local police (*guardia civil*) and a detachment of assault guards (*guardia republicana*) tried without success to clear the roads and permit the official cars from Puno to pass. Two of the vehicles were overturned and burned, while the others were stoned, their drivers beaten, and their tires slashed.

Although military reinforcements were sent into the area and constitutional guarantees suspended, the rioting and violence continued for over a week, leaving a toll of at least five dead, twenty-seven demonstrators and twenty-two *guardia* and other officials wounded, twenty-nine others arrested, and over twenty reported missing.

On the face of it, the rioting might be attributed to no more than a geopolitical rivalry between two cities of equal size over a limited number of improvements financially feasible in the area. However, the striking differences between the two cities make it possible to speculate about the conflict having a deeper significance.

The Lima newspaper *La Prensa* stated the differences between the cities as follows:

The department of Puno is overpopulated and extremely poor; and Juliaca, by being a communications hub, . . . escapes this poverty. Puno, the departmental capital, is languishing and defends herself. Juliaca grows uncontrolledly and rejects submission.

In Puno reside the landowners. In Juliaca are the businessmen. In Puno there are feudalist traces. In Juliaca . . . a *bourgeoisie* surges forth with a clear social conscience. Puno has tradition and culture. Juliaca is young and lacks solid traditions . . . Puno is afraid of dying and is on the defensive. Juliaca is growing, wants to grow more, and permits no interference. In this turbulent river of passions, the politicians are thriving.[1]

As the special product of economic and social collaboration between mestizos and Indians, the city of Juliaca and its leaders symbolized the forces of change in the department. The thesis sustained in this study is that the Puno-Juliaca geopolitical cleavage, rather than crosscutting the underlying socioeconomic cleavages in the department, closely coincided with them. Were it not for the altiplano area being part of the wider Peruvian system, the events of this period would have triggered a rapid revolutionary chain of events transforming the region socially, economically, and politically. The injection of financial and coercive resources from the national level temporarily contained the use of violence as a means of political change. But the processes of change continue, safeguarded and given a legitimate expressive channel by the continuing geopolitical rivalry in the department.

The origins of Puno's socioeconomic transformation and the various political ramifications of this change process—both leading up to and following its violent phase—should be of relevance to students of development problems in the "third world." This particular study was

[1] *La Prensa* (Lima), magazine supplement, November 7, 1965, p. 7, my translation.

prompted by the obvious importance of political change in the backward areas of the Andes, which Fidel Castro has said will be Sierra Maestra, or seeding place, for a revolution to sweep across all of South America.[2] The department of Puno was selected because of its extreme poverty and the reported organization of its peasants into political unions by several competing groups.

Field research, consisting of a survey of newspaper files and local documents and studies, and of interviews with local congressmen, officials, and leaders, was carried out in the cities of Puno, Juliaca, Cuzco, and Lima in the spring of 1965. Subsequent research was conducted in Peru between July and December of 1966.

[2] Fidel Castro, speech of July 26, 1960, reported in the *Hispanic American Report*, 13 (September, 1960): 449.

POLITICS IN THE ALTIPLANO
The Dynamics of Change in Rural Peru

POLITICAL CHANGE IN A PLURAL
SOCIETY: *A Framework for Analysis*

POLITICS IN ANY SOCIAL SYSTEM involves the moderated conflict of system members over the different resources in which they have an interest. Political change thus involves any change in the relative allocation of resources among the members of a social system that is achieved through conflict.

"Resources" have been defined to include not only material goods, but also less tangible qualities and capacities for exercising one's will over another, such as education, skills of violence, communication, and organization.[1] The accurate measurement of these qualities, in order to assess any system member's resource base, or power, is clearly impossible. Nevertheless, man's political (i.e., conflict-oriented) behavior may best be analyzed in terms of his unceasing expenditure of his existing resources (constructively or destructively, efficiently or inefficient-

[1] Harold Lasswell classifies the objects of, and bases for, power as "goods, symbols, violence and practices" (*Politics: Who Gets What, When, How*, pp. 31–94).

ly) with the object of obtaining more, or different, resources. Hence, the concept of resources must remain at the heart of political analysis, regardless of the difficulties of measurement.

Conflicts are moderated to some extent in every political system. This process of moderation may take a number of forms. It may occur as a result of the monopolization of resources by a member group in the system that utilizes its resources to suppress the expression of conflict by or among the subordinate groups. In a system in which resources are more randomly or equitably distributed, conflict moderation may be the function of individuals or groups who are cross-pressured by loyalties and common interests with the parties to a dispute. In such a system, conflict resolution might also be the function of groups from outside the system injecting resources to satisfy or suppress the interests of the conflicting groups. As this alternative implies, political systems are part of wider systems with which some interaction is inevitable. In any political system (whether resources are distributed randomly or monopolistically) the injection or removal of resources by forces outside the local system level will tend to support or upset the local system's stability, depending upon the resultant distribution of these new resources among the groups in the system. For this reason, conflict moderation may also be a function of voluntary cooperation and self-denial by all members of the system to defend or increase the system's existing resource level in its conflicts with the outside world.

The Socioeconomic Roots of Political Change

The political system is not static in terms of its resources. Resources are generated or depleted, not only redistributed, through conflicts. The change in resource capacity of a social system or of its members that occurs apart from conflict may be included within a wider category that should be labeled socioeconomic change. Nevertheless, any kind of socioeconomic change, because of its impact upon the the relative resource capacities of system members, has a high political significance.

Neil Smelser analyzes socioeconomic change in terms of the concept of "structural differentiation" of role patterns in the progressive movement from preindustrial to industrial society.[2] As formally defined by Smelser, structural differentiation is a process whereby

one social role or organization . . . differentiates into *two* or *more* roles or organizations which function more effectively [to generate socioeconomic resources] in the new historical circumstances. The new social units are structurally distinct from each other, but taken together are functionally equivalent to the original unit.[3]

While socioeconomic differentiation makes possible the generation of more resources than existed in the undifferentiated system, it also creates rivalries among differentiated groups over the relative value of the products or services of each and their proper distribution in the system. Clearly, however, this rivalry is mitigated by the interdependency that the groups have upon each other. Emile Durkheim has called such a differentiated society an "organic society," and has contrasted it to the undifferentiated society, which he called a "segmental society." The latter "carries with it no other solidarity than that derived from likenesses, since the society is formed of similar segments and these in their turn enclose only homogeneous elements."[4] For this analysis, the most relevant characteristic of the so-called segment, be it an extended family, clan, or village community, is probably its socioeconomic self-sufficiency relative to the total society of which it is a part.

M. G. Smith has elaborated this contrast between social groups as part of his analysis of plural social systems.[5] By virtue of sharing common cultural institutions (such as uniform practices regarding kinship, marriage, language, and religion), a "segmental society" becomes a distinguishable collectivity, even in the absence of any common political organization.[6] According to Smith, the crucial character-

---

[2] Neil J. Smelser, *The Sociology of Economic Life*; see especially Chapter 5, "Sociological Aspects of Economic Development."

[3] Neil J. Smelser, *Social Change in the Industrial Revolution*, p. 2; quoted in Smelser, *Sociology of Economic Life*, p. 106.

[4] Emile Durkheim, *The Division of Labor in Society*, pp. 176–177.

[5] M. G. Smith, "Institutional and Political Conditions of Pluralism."

[6] *Ibid.*

istics of all societies, whether approximating the segmental or organic variety, are their perpetuity, closure, determinate identity, form, and membership.[7] In addition to these features, the organic society possesses an inclusive organization, a set of distinctive affairs common to all members, and the procedures and autonomy necessary for regulating these affairs.[8] A society that is unified organically possesses common political institutions and regulative organs. The functional integration derived from organically shared cultural institutions is thus enhanced by the specialization of a single collective structure authorized to administer certain common internal affairs and to represent the unit externally.[9]

A society in the midst of industrialization will undoubtedly contain approximations to both the segmental and the organic group types. As socioeconomic differentiation occurs, old institutions of both the organic and segmental variety break down, and individuals find themselves forced to adapt to the new values and institutions of the industrial order. As mobility out of the old and into the new institutions cannot be automatic, frustration and conflict may be expected to accompany these changes.

The range and extent of new conflicts that follow upon such socioeconomic differentiation are influenced by the following factors, according to Smelser:

1. The scope and intensity of the social dislocation created by structural changes . . .

2. The structural complexity of the society at the time when development begins. In the least developed societies, where "the language of politics is at the same time the language of religion," protest movements more or less immediately take on a religious cast . . . The secularization of protest increases as development and differentiation proceed.

3. The access of disturbed groups to channels of influencing social policy. If dislocated groups have access to those responsible for introducing reforms, agitation tends to be relatively peaceful and orderly. . . .

[7] *Ibid.*
[8] *Ibid.*
[9] *Ibid.*

4. The overlap of interests and lines of cleavage. . . . Those societies in which economic, political or ethnic cleavages coincide are likely to produce more diffuse kinds of conflicts and social movements than societies in which these cleavages crisscross.

5. The kind and extent of foreign infiltration and intervention on behalf of protest groups.[10]

CONFLICT IN A PLURAL SOCIETY

More important than the *fact* of conflict, which is inevitable in any political system, is its mode of moderation in the system: (1) forceful suppression by one side of the other, (2) restraint or self-suppression by both sides, or (3) brokerage through cross-pressured individuals or groups who enjoy the confidence of and access to the parties in a conflict. The type of moderation likely to occur most frequently in a given system will, as Smelser indicates, depend upon the social structure of that system. Several structural models or ideal types relevant to this problem have been proposed in the social sciences, deriving in part from distinct historical experiences and in part from divergent social philosophies. They tend to cluster around two basic conceptions, which Leo Kuper calls the "equilibrium" and "conflict" schools.[11]

Both schools view society as a plural entity, but their definitions of "plural" differ considerably. The equilibrium model views society as composed of different social, occupational, ethnic, geographic, and other groupings intermediate between the individual and the state, to which individuals belong in such a way that their multiple loyalties make political extremism by any group or combination of groups unlikely. E. E. Schattschneider describes American politics in these terms:

In view of the fact . . . (1) that there are many interests, including a great body of common interests, (2) that the government pursues a multiplicity of policies and creates and destroys interests in the process, (3) that each individual is capable of having many interests, (4) that interests cannot be mobilized perfectly, and (5) that conflicts among interests are not

---

[10] Smelser, *Sociology of Economic Life*, pp. 114–115.
[11] Leo Kuper, "Plural Societies—Perspectives and Problems."

cumulative, it seems reasonable to suppose that the government is not cap-
tive of blind forces from which there is no escape. There is nothing hope-
lessly wrong about the raw materials of politics.[12]

In such a system, it is profitable for some members to specialize in the
skills of political brokerage—that is, knowledge of the laws, practices,
and the differentiated interests that make up the political system. The
ability to gain the trust of both parties to a dispute, and the capacity
for negotiating effective agreements between them, are profitable attri-
butes for an individual in a society in which the threat of violence is
not a reliable device for obtaining one's political objectives.

However, where the variables in Schattschneider's description do not
hold true, his reasoning contains sobering implications. For example,
in a political system where political interests are few but well mobilized, or where a cumulative cleavage exists, the political broker's maintenance of a neutral or authoritative position will be either difficult
(because of the pressure for him to take sides) or futile (because of
the absence of an interest in the system for his services).

It is just such a situation that provides the conflict model for M. G.
Smith's theory of the plural society. The plurality in this model is not
of loose compatible groupings with overlapping memberships, but of
tightly knit incompatible cultural groups, of either the segmental or
organic type, with little or no overlapping memberships. Such societies, according to Smith, depend for their survival on the regulation of
intergroup relations by one or another of the component cultural
groups. When the dominant group is also a minority, "the structural
implications of cultural pluralism have their most extreme expression,
and the dependence on regulation by force is greatest."[13]

The differences between the equilibrium and conflict views are not
insurmountable. Although the characteristics contributing to stability
in the Schattschneider equilibrium model may be equally useful in
explaining the dynamics of Smith's conflict model, it is likely that most
societies will be found midway between automatic equilibrium and
predictable violence or suppression.

[12] E. E. Schattschneider, *Party Government*, p. 34.

[13] M. G. Smith, "Social and Cultural Pluralism," *Annals of the New York
Academy of Sciences*, 83 (1960): 773–774.

Differences in degree, Kuper argues, need not imply differences in kind.[14] Thus, to properly study the feasibility of evolutionary change in a culturally plural society, comparisons should be made over time, with attention given to changes toward common cultural institutions or toward increasing cleavage and cultural estrangement.[15]

DOMINANCE AND CHANGE IN A CULTURALLY PLURAL SOCIETY

A political system is bound to be unstable if its cultural institutions are not integrated or mutually shared to some extent.[16] One of the regulatory means by which the plural society may be kept stable is through the fragmentation of the subordinate population under the direct supervision and intervention of individuals among the dominant group. Forms of personal servitude, such as serfdom, slavery, peonage, and indenture, are identified with this method of political subordination. The other method discussed by Smith is the territorial segmentation of the dominated group.[17] According to Smith, these two alternative modes of instituting dominance establish patterns of intergroup relations that differ considerably in their immediacy, intensity, and continuity, as well as in the opportunities for cultural and social assimilation they provide. In Europe and Japan, for example, serfs were generally subjected to rigorous, personal supervision and lacked sufficient incentives and opportunities for revolt. But where the collective organization of the dominated group is better maintained, by its location on reserves or in isolated communities, some sense of cultural distinctness and solidarity may be fostered. According to Smith, communally segregated Spartan helots, like the Russian serfs, maintained a spirited collective life apart from their masters and repeatedly revolted.[18]

It may be that socioeconomic and political change is better fostered by the more feudal type of domination, where personal contact between culturally distinct groups may foster greater varieties of socioeconomic role differentiation. For example, William Carter shows that after the

14 Kuper, "Plural Societies."
15 *Ibid.*
16 Smith, "Social and Cultural Pluralism," p. 776.
17 Smith, "Institutional and Political Conditions of Pluralism "
18 *Ibid.*

sweeping redistribution of lands following the Bolivian revolution of
1952, the agrarian reform authorities found a greater receptivity and
organizational capacity among former hacienda workers than among
freeholding peasant families, whose habitual autonomy and self-sufficiency made them resistant to new ideas or practices in farming.[19] But
the greater likelihood of anomic outburst in the second type of system
does not necessarily make it less stable. Although revolts by segmented
collectivities may be exceedingly violent, they are easy to suppress because of the poor resource position of any given segment or group of
segments relative to the dominant group, and because of the segment's
lack of access to all other segments of the same cultural group. Unsuccessful conflict with the dominant cultural group results in attrition
of the subordinated group's resources, leaving it subject to greater control and potential abuse, and capable of no further significant political
activity except at its most basic level of organization: within the extended family and other local units of its cultural institutions.

There appear to be three major long-run political alternatives for
the plural society of either the feudal or the segmented types. One
alternative is continued coercive control by the dominant group. The
second alternative is a "status reversal,"[20] through which the subordinated group seizes control from the dominant group, usually through
violence, and thereafter applies the same coercive methods against the
former elite. The third alternative is social, economic, and political
evolution, with groupings becoming more integrated, resources more
evenly distributed, and methods of control less coercive or culturally
biased.

In societies where cultural cleavages are compounded by social, economic, and political cleavages, the relationship of individuals of different cultural backgrounds will be subject to a number of serious
constraints. Nevertheless, as the volume and intensity of such relationships increase (e.g., in the field of commerce), the individuals involved will become increasingly cross-pressured by their ties with each

[19] William E. Carter, *Aymara Communities and the Bolivian Agrarian Reform*, pp. 57–64.
[20] This concept is used by Michael Lofchie in "The Plural Society in Zanzibar."

other and by their roots with their own racial and cultural groups. The number and depth of such cross-pressuring relationships can have important consequences in the moderation of conflict in a plural society, for their presence may reduce the number of instances in which sheer force must be used to exert one group's will on another.

But if natural processes of democratization or equalization between divergent cultural groups are too slow, can a subordinated cultural group be mobilized to challenge the domination of the cultural minority? The dominant group may make natural investments in the subordinate group in the fields of education, welfare, or technical assistance, for reasons of humanitarianism or even for encouraging eventual assimilation. Such investments may have a "multiplier effect" in the generation of new resources among the subordinated group. But if new access to power is not the product of these new resources, the gradual mobilization of the subordinated group may intensify the expression of conflict between the cultural groups. Kuper argues that widespread sentiments of hostility and prejudice, engendered by the conflict between cultural groups, offer a constant invitation to dissident elements among the political elite of the dominant cultural group to exploit these conditions for their own personal advantage.[21]

The political relationship of such dissidents to other members of the dominant group and to the subordinate group they seek to manipulate is rather complex and delicate. Smith writes that "clientage," the institutionalized association of men of different status or cultural background in contexts of political competition, has sometimes served to integrate members of the differing cultural groups in a plural society.[22] This is, basically, the feudal type of domination, mentioned above, viewed from the perspective of political competition within the dominant group itself. But clientage can only erode these cultural divisions if it is a widespread phenomenon, and if the cleavages within the dominant group are deep, or if the system as a whole is insecure with regard to its external environment.[23]

Clientage relationships such as Smith describes may often be identi-

[21] Kuper, "Plural Societies."
[22] Smith, "Institutional and Political Conditions of Pluralism."
[23] Ibid.

fied on a larger scale with geopolitical subdivisions of the political system. In Latin America, for example, this phenomenon has appeared under the name of *caudillismo*, and has been widespread for reasons, principally, of the topographical separation of peoples in many of the countries there. But, examined more closely at the regional rather than the national level, the relationship between *caudillo* and "client" may be far from reciprocal. The latter's usefulness may be in suppressing his fellows (through the role of local policeman or hacienda foreman) and, hence, perpetuating cultural pluralism, or it may be in strengthening the local *caudillo's* hand against personal enemies at the national level. As Smith points out, clientage is unlikely to erode the boundaries between culturally distinct groups where these differences are prominent.

In a situation where the culturally subordinate group is both quiescent and denied effective access to decision-making arenas, a form of pluralist democracy might even be expected to exist *within the dominant group itself*, with various issues producing various kinds of limited, and usually crosscutting, cleavages among the (limited) body politic. Political brokers—the specialized individuals or groups able and expected to contrive or negotiate solutions to such conflicts—will thrive. And their rivalry for obtaining political office, in order to institutionalize their brokerage services, will, in turn, guarantee the generation of still other issues, cleavages, and opportunities for brokerage.

A "crisis of brokerage," however, can be predicted where the culturally subordinate group, by virtue of its own increased resources or help from the outside, demands participation in the political system. In such a case, its demands constitute a series of cumulative cleavages within the overall system, sharply reducing the significance of the crosscutting cleavages within the dominant group itself. In such a situation, the following propositions may be of relevance:

1. Political brokers either will be captured by one or the other conflicting sides, losing any former access to the other side, or their neutrality between groups will cause them to be isolated and suspect.

2. Under conditions of sustained hostility, when political brokers become unable to convey accurate information from one side

to the other, there will be a tendency for each side to miscalculate the intentions of the other and an increased probability of incidents of violence.

3. Unbrokered conflict either will be total, ending with domination by one group over the other, or will be resolved with the injection of resources from an outside system level to meet or suppress the demands made by one or both of the conflicting sides.

4. However, unless the resources thus injected are permanently available, and unless they serve to foster the crosscutting of cultural institutions and the growth of an intermediate group capable of providing effective political brokerage, then the earlier cleavages will continue to be cumulative, and violence will be predictable upon the withdrawal of the external resources.

Within the Peruvian political system, such a theoretical model might be expected to apply to rural departments of the Andes, where cultural cleavages between Indians and mestizos (people of Western orientation) may be kept from becoming explosive by the strategic injection of resources from the national level. The material in this study deals with one such department, the altiplano department of Puno in southern Peru.

METHODOLOGICAL NOTE

In the American literature of community power studies there have emerged two schools of analysis that resemble the equilibrium and conflict models discussed above. It is worth noting this because of the methodological implications in each school.

In the approach we have identified with the conflict school, a community was analyzed in terms of the social and economic conditions prevailing there, with special attention devoted to the reported influence and attitudes of the principal members of the social and economic elite.[24] The problem with this approach, as Nelson Polsby argues, is that it "encourages research designs which generate self-fulfilling prophecies [and] that it leads to the systematic misreporting of facts and to the formulation of vague, ambiguous, unrealistic, and un-

[24] Nelson W. Polsby, *Community Power and Political Theory*, pp. 14–68, 112–121.

provable assertions about community power."[25] Invariably, the communities thus studied are found to have a tightly knit ruling elite dominating political life.

The alternative method of studying communities, which we have identified with the equilibrium approach, involves an examination of the "outcomes of actual decisions within the community."[26] As the ruling-elite students have "the habit of never specifying issues,"[27] this alternative method pursues a strategy of examining several important decisions in order to determine the patterns of participation and opposition. "More than a single issue-area is always chosen," writes Polsby, "because of the presumption among pluralist researchers that the same pattern of decision-making is highly unlikely to reproduce itself in more than one issue-area."[28] However, this leaves the pluralist method open to the criticism that it, too, biases its results with its expectations of findings. In particular, the definition of current, visible issues as the proper subject for research begs the question of underlying class, ethnic, or other hostilities that do not often have a channel for expression in day-to-day political issues. Polsby's response to this criticism is that the stipulation by the observer of certain "non-events" as worthy of study (i.e., issues that may have been kept from the surface by political manipulations) is likely to prejudice the outcome of the research.[29]

The conclusion to draw from this instructive debate between the two schools is that the study of a political system should integrate both methodological approaches. The integration or divergence of distinct social and economic groups should be analyzed along with the type of political activity that reaches the surface in terms of such guides as newspaper coverage, administrative decision-making, and public discussion. It may be that two antithetical views of the same system will emerge, with deep latent conflicts underlying a pluralist array of cross-cutting political groups, whose leaders all participate in various extents in the production of relatively important political decisions, none of

---

[25] *Ibid.*, p. 112.
[26] *Ibid.*, p. 121.
[27] *Ibid.*, p. 68.
[28] *Ibid.*, p. 113.
[29] *Ibid.*, p. 97.

which basically affects the underlying *status quo*. Such a conclusion would help in the prediction of levels of violence possible in the event that a given issue, or series of issues, coincided with the underlying cleavages. The moderation and stability achieved in resolving other issues in such a system might then be replaced by anomic or even revolutionary violence.

A HISTORICAL SKETCH: *Pre-Incaic Period to 1955*

THE PRE-CONQUEST PERIOD

ARCHEOLOGICAL INVESTIGATION of the Titicaca basin is still in its formative stage, and our knowledge of cultural developments in the area is fragmentary at best. Edward Lanning, who has pieced together many strands of data regarding pre-Incaic cultures of Peru, reports that farming villages in the altiplano were in evidence as early as 1000 B.C.[1] Two fairly large cities, Tiahuanaco, in the southern Titicaca basin, and Pucará, in the northern Titicaca basin, appeared sometime before the time of Christ. "Each was the focal point of a synchoritic system which also included rural and urban towns and numerous villages. [Either or both of the] major cities may have had populations in excess of ten thousand persons."[2]

Although the Pucará site was evidently abandoned after no more than two hundred years or so,[3] the Tiahuanaco people, beginning about A.D. 600, embarked upon a military conquest of the surrounding peo-

[1] Edward P. Lanning, *Peru before the Incas*, pp. 27, 104.
[2] *Ibid.*, p. 115.
[3] *Ibid.*, p. 116.

ples, leading quickly to the establishment of an empire encompassing the Titicaca basin, all of Peru south of Arequipa, and the coast and highlands of northern Chile.[4]

The Tiahuanaco Empire, combined with the Huari Empire (established in the same period in central Peru), had a striking effect on the cultural development of the Andean area. According to Lanning:

> Neither empire lasted more than a century or two but, during this brief span, there was an interchange of goods and ideas across the Central Andes such as had never been seen before. Though regional styles and cultures would again emerge, the Huari and Tiahuanaco conquests put an end to the old regional isolation. Never again would the ancient Peruvians live in ignorance of the country beyond the nearest valley or two.[5]

The causes for the decline of the Tiahuanaco Empire are not known. Nor do we have much evidence regarding subsequent developments in the Titicaca basin in the years preceding the Incan conquest. From the accounts of Indian informants interviewed by the Spanish chroniclers, however, it has been possible to reconstruct a picture of the Incan experience in the altiplano.

According to the legend cited by Garcilaso de la Vega, the Incan civilization began on Titicaca Island, near the center of Lake Titicaca, when the Sun God created Manco Cápac, the first Inca, and his sister-wife, Mama Ocllo Huaco, sometime after A.D. 1000.[6] Although this legend, and its geographical placement of the Incan tribe's origin, are generally discredited by the other chroniclers and modern authorities,[7] the first Inca's voyage by *balsa* across the lake from Titicaca Island is re-enacted every year in Puno, and the area is popularly honored as the birthplace of the first Inca.

After the Incas finally became established in the fertile Cuzco Valley, one hundred miles northwest of the altiplano, they were continually forced to defend themselves against neighboring tribes. Developing

[4] *Ibid.*, pp. 127, 132.

[5] *Ibid.*, p. 127.

[6] Garcilaso de la Vega, *Royal Commentaries of the Incas*, trans. Harold V. Livermore, pp. 42, 46.

[7] For an evaluation of various accounts of the Incan prehistory, see J. Alden Mason, *The Ancient Civilizations of Peru*, pp. 110, 269–270.

skills in the art of warfare, they gradually widened and secured their domains. Finally, in the fifteenth century, the Incas began a systematic conquest of all the tribes of the Andes. The other principal peoples that engaged in the power struggle of the early part of the fifteenth century included the Chancas and Quechuas, in the Apurímac basin to the west, and the Lupacas and Collas, in the Titicaca basin to the south.[8]

The rapid succession of military victories by the Incas did not include a definitive pacification of the nearby Aymará peoples inhabiting the altiplano. Romero writes:

Not only did the brave Collas [of the northern altiplano] defend themselves against the attacks of the Inca imperialism, but they also dared to make frequent incursions as far as the Valley of Vilcamayo [just beyond the pass that now divides the departments of Puno and Cuzco], at which point it is said that the Inca ordered a wall constructed in order to contain the advances of the brave inhabitants of the Collao [altiplano].[9]

Although they were unable to pacify the area thoroughly, the Incas, possibly with help from the more conciliatory Lupaca tribe of the Chucuito area,[10] were able to contain and suppress the Collas' rebelliousness. In addition, the Incas resorted to the practice of forced dispersion and resettlement of conquered peoples. The intermingling of culturally dissimilar peoples, obliged to maintain distinctive modes of dress, served to inhibit local revolt. La Barre writes that Inca Cápac Yupanqui settled the representatives of no less than forty-two peoples on the Copacabana peninsula of Lake Titicaca and on the nearby islands of Titicaca and Coati.[11]

By such political and administrative stratagems, Incan power was finally sufficient to enable the systematic extraction of tribute from the

[8] Lanning, *Peru before the Incas*, p. 157.
[9] Emilio Romero, *Monografía del Departamento de Puno*, p. 6, my translation.
[10] John Murra, "Una Apreciación Etnológica de la Visita," in *Visita Hecha a la Provincia de Chucuito por Garci Diez de San Miguel en el Año 1567*, by Garci Diez de San Miguel, p. 425.
[11] Weston La Barre, "The Aymara Indians of the Lake Titicaca Plateau, Bolivia," *American Anthropologist*, 50 (January, 1948): 28.

altiplano's inhabitants and the establishment of a hierarchically organized system of supervision and control.[12] Although it may be assumed that efforts were undertaken by the Incas in the altiplano, as elsewhere in their domains, to impose the Quechua language on the conquered population, their ultimate failure in this region attests to the durability of the regional and cultural identities that had developed over the centuries. In fact, the arrival of a rival imperial power in Peru not only cut short the Incan experiment in cultural imperialism, it also appears to have precipitated a short-lived conflict between Colla and Lupaca peoples for political pre-eminence in the altiplano.[13]

THE COLONIAL PERIOD

In 1531 the Spanish, under the leadership of Francisco Pizarro and Diego de Almagro, began their conquest of Peru. In 1533 they captured Cuzco, and by January, 1534, the first Spaniards had arrived in the altiplano. These first visitors came in search of "a very wide river in which there is an island where there are certain houses, among which is a very large one covered with gold."[14] Although the Spaniards did not find the gold building, this first visit met with no resistance and was followed by countless others. The altiplano became a major thoroughfare for Spanish troops passing to the fabulous silver mines of Bolivia, and a base for explorations of the high selva in search of vast gold deposits that were reported by the Indians. Along with the adventurers came the missionaries—first the Dominicans and later the Jesuits—who established several missions around the lake.

With the arrival of the Spaniards in the altiplano, changes in the political structure affecting local affairs were at first relatively mild. While Spanish churchmen and officials replaced their Incan counterparts at the higher levels of the imperial hierarchy, native, hereditary *caciques* (regional and provincial officials) continued to supervise the

[12] For a description of some of the Incan organizational practices in the altiplano, see Diez de San Miguel, *Visita Hecha,* pp. 23, 34, 39, 42 and *passim.*

[13] Murra, "Una Apreciación Etnológica," p. 425 n. 21.

[14] Francisco de Xeres, quoted by Romero, *Monografía,* p. 12, no citation, my translation.

administration of local affairs, including the ongoing collection and allocation of tribute.[15] Although the Spanish colonists, and especially the local priests, increased the levels of tribute and diverted much of it to nonproductive ends (personal service, church construction),[16] the early years of Spanish rule did little to upset the traditional patterns of community affairs in the altiplano.[17]

One of the reasons for delegating continued authority to the *caciques* may have been Spanish recognition of their skills in managing the peculiar agricultural institutions of the altiplano. John Murra has pointed out, for example, that "since the pre-Incaic era the alpacas and llamas had been used as a kind of 'bank' or reserve for periods of drought, frosts, and other calamities," and that the Aymará peoples were particularly gifted in the field of livestock management for these contingencies.[18] Nevertheless, as Spanish exactions increased—both in terms of taxation and drafted labor for the mines—local autonomy was more and more undermined.

After the arrival of Viceroy Francisco de Toledo in 1569, a quixotic attempt was made to safeguard the Indian populations by gathering them together in urban centers called *reducciones*, where they could be Christianized and civilized under the supervision of enlightened over-seers called *corregidores*, who were administrative officials of the Crown. There were 614 such *reducciones* established during the Toledo regime.[19]

Toledo's plan, however well intentioned, was easily abused, as the Indians' idle lands were seized by members of the Spanish clergy, mil-itary, and colonial bureaucracy, as well as by the *corregidores,* them-selves. Because of continued persecution within the *reducciones*, many Indians fled to the jungle or to the remote highlands, while others re-turned to their lands seeking protection from the new landowners under varying kinds of informal contractual agreements. The resultant

[15] Diez de San Miguel, *Visita Hecha.*

[16] *Ibid.*, pp. 15–16, 109–110, 112.

[17] See William E. Carter, *Aymara Communities and the Bolivian Agrarian Reform*, pp. 34–35; Murra, "Una Apreciación Etnológica," p. 422.

[18] Murra, "Una Apreciación Etnológica," p. 423, my translation.

[19] Thomas R. Ford, *Man and Land in Peru*, pp. 33–34.

system might be called "manorial" (rather than the more general term "feudal"), because of the autonomy from any semblance of central control enjoyed by the new Spanish *hacendados* (landowners).[20] In fact, it appears that the geographical and political autonomy of the *hacendados*, rather than special privileges, made it possible for them to offer the Indians protection from the *mita* (forced labor) service in the mines.[21]

La Barre writes that "the Spanish domination of the Aymara . . . was a long, bloody, incredibly cruel and savage oppression."[22] A seventh of the population of each *reducción* had to work in the silver mines of Potosí at any given time, where the miner's life span was short and the conditions brutal. Eight million natives, most of them Aymará, are estimated to have disappeared in the *mita* service during the colonial period.[23] Kubler writes that "in Chucuito Province, whence one of the great *mitas* was levied for the mines of Potosí, the Indian population shrank by two-thirds between 1628 and 1754."[24] But besides oppressive conditions, per se, the Indian was vulnerable, along with his Spanish overlord, to frequent and widespread epidemics of smallpox, measles, plague, influenza, diphtheria, and typhus.[25] The decimation of the Indian population must also, at least partially, be attributed to this source.

The Jesuits, who gained the most in lands of any single group, probably also did the most in return for the Indians, dealing with them

[20] Manorial organization is discussed in Henri Pirenne, *Economic and Social History of Medieval Europe*, pp. 57–85.

[21] Emilio Romero, *Historia Económica del Perú*, p. 216; for detailed accounts of the establishment of the colonial system of domination, see George Kubler, "The Quechua in the Colonial World," in *Handbook of South American Indians*, ed. Julian H. Steward, 2: 340–354, 364–379; Frederick B. Pike, *The Modern History of Peru*, pp. 13–20, 24–33; and Florencio Díaz Bedregal, *Apuntes Para Una Reforma Agraria en el Departamento de Puno*, pp. 27–38.

[22] La Barre, "Aymara Indians," p. 30.

[23] *Ibid.*, p. 31. Many, of course, may have "disappeared" only to have begun the process of assimilation to the emergent Bolivian and Peruvian nationalities. See Murra, "Una Apreciación Etnológica," pp. 423–424.

[24] Kubler, "Quechua in the Colonial World," p. 339.

[25] See Henry F. Dobyns, "An Outline of Andean Epidemic History to 1720," *Bulletin of the History of Medicine*, 37 (November–December, 1963): 493–515.

in their own language in an honest but often unsuccessful way to improve their condition and to shake them from their traditional beliefs. Because of the vast wealth the Jesuits had accumulated, they had made jealous enemies of the Crown, the other religious orders, and the landowning elite. It was not surprising, then, that these three conspired to have the Jesuits expelled from the Americas in 1767. "With them," writes Owens, "went the last of the protectors of the Indian."[26]

In 1780 the Indians rose up in a massive revolt throughout the south of Peru, under the leadership of José Gabriel Condorcanki, a descendant of the Incas, who called himself Túpac Amaru II, after the last of the Inca warriors, executed in 1571 by Toledo. Educated by the Jesuits, Túpac Amaru II sought to use his influence with the Crown to better the Indian's position. Unsuccessful, and discouraged by the expulsion of the Jesuits and the increased cruelties that followed, he organized an Indian army and within months controlled much of the highlands of southern Peru and northern Bolivia.

Supported by vast Indian hordes [writes Pike], by many of the *mestizos* of the sierra, and in the beginning by a considerable number of creoles, the Túpac Amaru uprising has been described by some as a genuine bid for Peruvian independence and by others as a more limited endeavour to achieve the Indian's social redemption within the colonial framework. Túpac Amaru II proved a vacillating commander and his movement soon got out of hand, turning into a race war in which Indians indiscriminately slaughtered whites and mestizos. As a result many early supporters were alienated and Spanish forces were able to suppress the uprising in 1781, punishing its leaders with barbaric cruelty.[27]

With the death of Túpac Amaru II, however, violence became widespread throughout the Andes. One Indian army, in particular, continued to operate with excessive brutality in the altiplano. La Barre estimates that over forty thousand Spaniards were killed there before the area was finally pacified.[28]

Soon after Spanish troops from Buenos Aires had converged with

[26] R. J. Owens, *Peru*, p. 321.
[27] Pike, *Modern History of Peru*, pp. 33–34.
[28] La Barre, "Aymara Indians," p. 31; also, Romero, *Monografía*, pp. 32–35, gives a detailed account of this action.

others from Lima to put down the Túpac Amaru revolt, the entire altiplano region was transferred from the viceroyalty of Lima to that of
the recently created viceroyalty of La Plata (Buenos Aires), where it
remained until 1796.[29] This brief interlude of control by Buenos Aires
may have helped to precipitate another rebellion. The La Plata region
had declared itself independent in 1810, at the same time as liberation
movements were launched in Mexico and the northern Andes. Although Peru was the most valued possession of the Spaniards, and its
population was the most loyal and conservative, the air was filled with
talk of reform and even revolution. The most promising and massive
revolt was initiated in 1814 by the mestizo president of the *audiencia*
of Cuzco, Mateo García Pumacahua.

Protesting the threatened reinstitution of Indian tribute (suspended
as a gesture of conciliation after the Túpac Amaru revolt), Pumacahua
and others easily rallied a force of Indians, mestizos, and creoles in an
effort that carefully avoided the racism of the earlier revolt. Crudely
armed but enthusiastic armies proceeded south across the altiplano to
sieze La Paz, north along the intermontane valleys of the Andes to
occupy the vital communications center of Huamanga (Ayacucho),
and west to capture the large city of Arequipa, where the independence of Peru was first declared on December 4, 1814.[30]

Although the rebels were quickly defeated on all fronts and Pumacahua executed, sporadic guerrilla warfare continued in southern Peru
and the highlands of Bolivia throughout the ensuing Wars of Independence. Although largely directed against the Spanish Crown, guerrilla activity was also directed at the liberation armies of Buenos Aires,
which tried unsuccessfully to capture the highland Bolivian area
(called Upper Peru) as a springboard for an invasion of the viceroyalty of Lima.[31]

THE REPUBLICAN PERIOD

The altiplano's revolutionary traditions and remoteness from both
centers of colonial administration created a number of problems for

[29] Jorge Basadre, *Historia de la República del Perú*, 1: 105.
[30] Pike, *Modern History of Peru*, pp. 45–46.
[31] For a detailed account of the complex and fascinating events of this peri-

the leaders of the independence movements, once they began to set the boundaries for their new republics.[32] Even after the Peruvian stronghold of Spanish resistance had been overcome (with Sucre's defeat of the royalists at Ayacucho in 1824), the disposition of Upper Peru was still unclear, "a vague afterthought of the wars of liberation," as Herring puts it.[33]

After the battle of Ayacucho, Bolívar commissioned Antonio José de Sucre to proceed to Upper Peru for the purpose of creating a "Republic of Bolivar."[34] Sucre arrived at Puno, February 1, 1825, and there appointed one of his officers, General Miller (a British mercenary), as the first prefect of the new department of Puno. Miller apparently accepted without question the pre-existing colonial boundaries that had divided the altiplano into two parts, administered by Puno and La Paz, respectively.[35]

Sucre proceeded unopposed into La Paz, where he issued a decree on February 9, 1825, assuring the peoples of Upper Peru that the Bolivarian army would not intervene in their domestic affairs. This decree, according to Arnade, and its provision for an assembly to decide the fate of Upper Peru, provided "the very cornerstone of Bolivia's independence."[36] Had Peru's capital been Cuzco or Arequipa, the separation of the "Bolivians" might have been prevented. As it turned out, representatives from Puno were not invited to the assembly of Chuquisaca, and only two of the forty-eight delegates (both representing La Paz) voted for incorporation into Peru. The majority prevailed, and Bolivia was declared independent on August 6, 1825. Since it was

---

od in Upper Peru, see Charles W. Arnade, *The Emergence of the Republic of Bolivia.*

[32] Basadre, *Historia,* 1: 98.

[33] Hubert Herring, *A History of Latin America,* p. 524.

[34] Arnade, *Republic of Bolivia,* p. 150.

[35] Romero, *Monografía,* p. 45. In the colonial period the basic political and economic divisions of Peru were the *corregimientos* (about the size of Peruvian provinces today). A number of these *corregimientos* together constituted a religious diocese. In 1784 these dioceses became political units as well, called *intendencias.* With the coming of independence, the *intendencias* became departments.

[36] Arnade, *Republic of Bolivia,* p. 165.

agreed to share the capital between Chuquisaca (later called Sucre) and La Paz, the delegates from La Paz acquiesced in the decision to keep the southern altiplano area in Bolivia.[37] As a result, a national boundary dropped across Lake Titicaca, where before only a minor jurisdictional line had existed. The Aymará Indians of the Titicaca basin, already outnumbered by Quechua Indians to the north and south, were now divided from each other. Through the next fifteen years, as several attempts were made to link Peru and Bolivia in a federation, the only accomplishment of lasting effect was the reiterated agreement upon this boundary.[38]

The Federalist Movements

Throughout most of Republican Peru's history, the established form of government was a centralized, unitary state, divided into departments, whose administration was delegated to prefects, appointed by the President. The centralization of this administrative system seemed as oppressive in the more remote areas of Peru as the colonial system had before it. Though wielding little influence in the numerous constitutional conventions that experimented with these and other aspects of the new Peruvian state, the *puneños* had a strong interest in federalism, and in the beginning they frequently championed the creation of a federal state that would include Bolivia.[39]

Soon after the independence of Bolivia, Basadre reports, the prefect of Puno attempted to persuade the prefects of his neighboring departments of Arequipa and Cuzco to join him in seceding to Bolivia.[40] Almost continuous warfare plagued the altiplano and southern Peru in the following years, as various schemes and revolutionary movements in Bolivia and Peru were tried in attempts to resolve the geopolitical tangle of interests between the two countries.[41] The separatist tendencies in the department of Puno seem to have ended in 1840, after fail-

[37] For an account of these decisions, see *ibid.*, pp. 183–205.
[38] See Romero's chronology of boundary treaties, *Monografía*, pp. 266–274.
[39] *Ibid.*, pp. 47–57.
[40] Basadre, *Historia*, 1: 110.
[41] For a brief account of the rivalries and military actions involving the *caudillos* of Peru and Bolivia in this era, see Pike, *Modern History of Peru*, pp. 58–60, 69–75, 79–87.

ure of the last attempt by the Bolivian military dictator Santa Cruz to forcefully create a federation of North, South, and Upper Peru. Guerrilla bands in the Puno area in 1842 were credited with sufficiently diverting a new Bolivian army so that it never reached Cuzco.[42]

Economic Development and Public Works

Following the independence of Peru and the opening of its ports to free trade, British firms were established in Arequipa to purchase alpaca and llama wool for the British woolen mills. The link between Arequipa and the altiplano, where these animals were abundant, became more important, although communications between the two were still extremely primitive.[43] Until this time, Puno's tenuous link with the outside world was through Cuzco and along the old Incan road that joined the central Andean towns of Ayacucho and Huancayo before dropping to the coast at Lima.[44]

Beginning in the 1840's, a much larger economic development was experienced on the coast, and on the off-shore islands of Peru, with the exploitation of guano and its sale to the depleted lands of Europe. Financed by the revenues of its exports, the Peruvian government undertook an extensive program of public works, which included the construction of most of the railroads in existence today. Of particular concern for the altiplano was the Matarani-Arequipa-Juliaca-Puno railroad, constructed in 1870–1874, toward the end of this boom period. Work on a connector line from Juliaca to Cuzco was begun soon thereafter, but was suspended during Peru's disastrous war with Chile, 1879–1883. This war, greatly increasing Peru's foreign debt and costing her some valuable nitrate fields as well, put an end to the public works projects.

Nevertheless, the new railroad from Arequipa to Puno facilitated the growth of Arequipa as a supplier for both the altiplano *and* Bolivia, as well as encouraging the development of wool-raising in the altiplano. Sheep, which had been introduced to Peru by the Spanish, but never raised extensively, now became the subject of intensive invest-

[42] Basadre, *Historia*, 2: 497–499.
[43] Romero, *Historia Económica*, pp. 355–356.
[44] Romero, *Monografía*, p. 466.

ment because of their higher rate of production.[45] The number of stock-raising haciendas in Puno increased from 705 in 1876 to 3,219 in 1915.[46]

Further Land Alienation of the Peasantry and Revolts

The creation of the latifundian estates in the nineteenth century was accompanied by a sharp increase in the Indian population for the first time since the Conquest. This combination of events was potentially explosive and certainly significant for its political implications. Kubler relates the increase in Indian population "in part to the cessation of Colonial mining enterprises, and to the reversion of the Indian populations to an agropecuarian [cropping and animal-raising] economy."[47] But, legally and politically, the creation of the Republic did not change the status of the Indian. Tribute continued to be levied, as the Republican government, like its predecessor, "depended for at least one-sixth of its income on Indian assessment."[48]

In 1854 the *caudillo* Ramón Castilla, as part of his attempt to regain power in Peru, abolished slavery and ended the collection of Indian tribute.[49] The effects of this action were mixed. On the one hand, the new regulations were poorly enforced.[50] But where they were enforced, they had the effect of further weakening regional autonomy.

Previously [writes Pike], Peruvian departmental governments, especially in the sierra where the large concentrations of native population were found, had relied upon Indian tribute, only a portion of which went to the national treasury, for the revenue with which to meet necessary annual expenditures. These governments now found themselves dependent upon the largesse of the central bureaucracy in Lima. Most frequently money was doled out from Lima not to aid the development of the provinces, but to entrench in power supporters of the political machine that was at the moment in control of the capital. The reduction of the provinces to mendicancy produced a type of centralism that actually still further separated the

[45] Romero, *Historia Económica*, p. 356.
[46] Romero, *Monografía*, p. 426.
[47] Kubler, "Quechua in the Colonial World," p. 353.
[48] *Ibid.*
[49] Pike, *Modern History of Peru*, p. 105.
[50] Kubler, "Quechua in the Colonial World," p. 353.

various parts of the country rather than binding them together. The longer this centralism, which was based on the exploitation of the many parts of Peru, especially the sierra, by the capital, remained in effect, the more intense became the regional animosities that it generated.[51]

The development of the great haciendas, with a large class of *colonos* (contractually bound Indian residents) enjoying the use of land only in return for labor, followed the pattern of the earlier land-alienation process of the sixteenth century in Peru.[52] Again, the process was made possible by laws that seemed to favor the Indian but in fact left him defenseless.

The 1852 Civil Code, which defined the status of the Indian as a Peruvian citizen with the same legal rights and obligations as other Peruvians,[53] assumed that the Indians could act in their own interest. But, as Romero points out, "it was immediately following the promulgation of this Code that the latifundian oligarchies began to be formed in Peru . . ."[54]

In 1886 a widespread Indian revolt took place in the altiplano against the aggressive *hacendados* and local authorities. After several months of fighting and great bloodshed, the Indians were finally subdued.[55] Other uprisings took place in the 1870's and at the end of the century.[56] Between 1903 and 1928, still other revolts took place in the districts of Asillo, Huancho, Chucuito, Huancané, Samás, Platería, Ilave, and Lampa.[57]

Those of Huancané and Huancho [writes Escobar] were the most severe. In the latter site . . . the Indians tried to revive the Incan Empire and to separate themselves from the country. (Even today, the Indians call Huancho "Lima Huancho," referring to the capital of their would-be empire).[58]

[51] Pike, *Modern History of Peru*, pp. 112–113.
[52] Kubler, "Quechua in the Colonial World," pp. 353–354.
[53] Ford, *Man and Land*, p. 46.
[54] Romero, *Historia Económica*, p. 282, my translation.
[55] Basadre, *Historia*, 4: 1700–1703.
[56] Romero, *Historia Económica*, p. 282.
[57] Gabriel M. Escobar, *Organización Social y Cultural del Sur del Perú*, p. 10.
[58] *Ibid.*, pp. 10–11, my translation.

As Indian unrest was becoming general throughout the Peruvian sierra, the government of Augusto Leguía, assuming office in 1919, set up a Bureau of Indian Affairs in the Ministry of Development. In addition, Leguía appointed a commission of prominent and sympathetic students of Indian affairs to investigate the sources of this unrest. This commission, writes Pike,

established its headquarters in Puno and began an extensive investigation of land ownership titles. It also prepared and submitted for congressional approval a comprehensive legislative code, intended to implement Article 58 of the constitution which provided for the protection and education of the natives. Greatly alarmed by these developments, the landowners of the sierra expressed their dissatisfaction to Leguía and the President promptly dissolved the . . . commission. Its legislative proposals were never so much as considered in congress. . . .

Not able to hope for redress of grievances from the government, the Indians between Puno and Azángaro resorted increasingly to violence. The army was therefore ordered into the sierra and, after a number of Indian massacres, succeeded by the end of 1923 in making the area safe once again for the white and *cholo* landowners.[59]

Those who were able to escape the ensuing repression fled to the selva, where some found employment with American rubber companies, which for a brief period after 1910 were in operation there.[60] Again, in 1945, as prosperity and a new liberal government came to Peru, peasant uprisings and land seizures were reported in the provinces of Azángaro[61] and Chucuito.[62]

The Constitution of 1920 had seemed to make a new gesture to the Indians by offering corporate recognition to communities (as *comunidades indígenas*), if they so desired, thus securing their communal lands from the claims of the *hacendados*, and offering other benefits. This recognition was reaffirmed in the Constitution of 1933 and the Civil Code of 1936.[63] But, as later authors have pointed out, recogni-

[59] Pike, *Modern History of Peru*, p. 222.
[60] Héctor Martínez, *Las Migraciones Altiplánicas y la Colonización del Tambopata*, pp. 81, 91.
[61] *The Peruvian Times* (Lima), December 14, 1945, p. 2.
[62] Pedro Ortiz V., *Hacienda y Colonato en Villurcuni*, pp. 24–37.
[63] Ford, *Man and Land*, p. 50.

tion as a *comunidad indígena* required a long and laborious process of legal settlements, as well as surveying, which left the community vulnerable to any fraudulent claims that its neighboring *hacendados* might choose to bring.[64] This may explain why, among the hundreds of Indian communities in the department of Puno, only thirty-nine were officially recognized as *comunidades indígenas* by 1960. Of this number, more than half were not in the altiplano at all, but were located in the mountains or the upper reaches of the selva.[65]

Later Economic and Political Development

Although the public works projects carried out during the guano boom were the most spectacular of the Republican period, several other experiments and break-throughs in the economic development of the altiplano are worth mentioning. One such experiment was the fiscal decentralization of the *caudillo* President Andrés Cáceres, which established separate sources of departmental income in the hands of popularly chosen departmental councils, presided over by the prefects.[66] Although provision still exists in the Peruvian Constitution of 1933 for these departmental councils [Articles 188–202], the system was ultimately abolished because of local corruption and lack of planning. According to Romero, this had not been the case in Puno.[67] He contends that the law failed because it did not provide enough resources

[64] François Bourricaud, *Changements à Puno: Étude de Sociologie Andine,* p. 90; see also Richard W. Patch, "How Communal Are the Communities?" *American Universities Field Staff Newsletters, West Coast South America Series,* 6, no. 5 (Lima, June 12, 1959): 16–17. Patch argues that the registration of Indian communities "means a reaffirmation of the system which has bound them to these communities and to the earth for no other reason than to provide labor for the *latifundios*" (p. 17). It would be more correct to say that communal organization is generally pointless in those communities that have lost much of their communal lands to neighboring landowners. The inability to sell one's lands, once a part of a *comunidad indígena*, does create the effect of "locking in" the members to their impoverished way of life—the only escape being part-time labor on the neighboring estate.

[65] República del Perú, Comisión Ejecutiva Interministerial de Cooperación Popular, *Datos Distritales para Fines de Desarrollo* (hereinafter cited as *Datos Distritales*).

[66] Romero, *Monografía,* pp. 516–525.

[67] *Ibid.,* p. 524.

to the departments, while at the same time burdening them with expenses previously covered by the national government.[68] A partial resumption of local autonomy in regards to public works and development decisions in Puno came about in 1962, but only after a series of climactic events (which shall be the subject of Chapters 5 and 6).

An impressive series of improvements was carried out during the dictatorship of Augusto Leguía (1919–1930). Leguía ushered Peru into the automotive age with a massive road-building program, carried out by forced peasant labor.[69] Most of the roads in the altiplano were built at this time.[70] Although this work often involved only the widening of horse trails across the flat altiplano, several critical road links out of the altiplano were begun, including the highway to Cuzco, and the more challenging highways from Puno and Juliaca to Arequipa and from Puno to Moquegua. The former was completed during Leguía's dictatorship. The roads to Arequipa, starting separately from the two altiplano towns and merging into one road near the border between the two departments, were finished under the regime of General Oscar Benavides (1933–1939), while the link with Moquegua is still little more than the pack trail that it was in the pre-Conquest period.

The Emergence of Juliaca

One of the most important results of both the railroad and the later road-building programs was the establishment of Juliaca as a commercial center. Until that time, Puno was the dominant center of commercial activity in the altiplano—most of it being carried on by boat between Puno and the many towns around the lake in Peru *and* in Bolivia. When the railroad was built, this at first enhanced Puno's dominance because of the increased volume of goods that could be delivered dockside in Puno for transshipment to Bolivia and elsewhere.

---

[68] *Ibid.*, p. 525.

[69] This was the Law of Road Conscription, establishing obligatory road work for all male residents of the country between the ages of eighteen and sixty, or requiring that they pay a fine equivalent to the worth of the work assigned to them (*Ley 4113*, May 10, 1920, cited in Romero, *Monografía*, pp. 472–473).

[70] *Ibid.*, p. 473; also *Los Andes* (Puno), March 20, 1965, p. 2.

But the junction of the rail line from Arequipa to Cuzco was at Juliaca rather than Puno. This meant that some of the altiplano's produce could be stored and loaded aboard the Arequipa-Cuzco trains at Juliaca rather than Puno. Thus, some impetus was also given to Juliaca's development in the late nineteenth century.[71] According to Romero, writing in 1928, "the 'Old Town' [of Juliaca] is today almost deserted, there being a new area of settlement next to the railroad, to such an extent that one can speak of it as a new Juliaca."[72]

Because of Juliaca's more centrally located and accessible position in the altiplano, the construction of roads and the arrival of motorized transport spurred this development even further. Already by the 1930's the competition of truck transport had forced the closure of boat service from Puno to many of the lakeside communities.[73]

In 1929 the Peruvian Congress made Juliaca the capital of a separate province, called San Román. Romero's description at that time of the town's future economic importance is instructive:

Juliaca is becoming like a port of active commercial movement on the vast sea of the pampas [flat-lands] in the altiplano. Built at the end of a string of hills, the settlement has a dominating postion for many leagues . . . This makes it a center of concentration for the clusters of Indians of the haciendas and *ayllus* [villages] in the region. The Indians are those who support *juliaqueño* commerce, which consists especially of the wool trade. There are two wool-washing establishments and offices of packing and shipment of all manner of livestock.[74]

As Table I reveals, the growth rate of Juliaca has been over twice that of the city of Puno in the period after 1940.

Legal and Administrative Framework

As pointed out above, Peru is administered as a unitary republic, divided into twenty-three departments, whose prefects, or governors,

---

[71] Because of the war with Chile in the 1870's, the projected rail line from Arequipa to Cuzco was completed only as far as Sicuani in the department of Cuzco. The railroad was finally extended to Cuzco during the regime of José Pardo, 1904–1908 (Pike, *Modern History of Peru*, pp. 193–194).

[72] Romero, *Monografía*, p. 318, my translation.

[73] Raúl Galdo Pagaza, *El Indígena y el Mestizo de Vilquechico*, p. 9.

[74] Romero, *Monografía*, p. 319, my translation.

TABLE I
Populations of Puno and Juliaca, 1940 and 1961

City	1940	1961
Puno	15,999	24,459
Juliaca	7,002	20,351

Sources: República del Perú, Ministerio de Hacienda y Comercio, Dirección Nacional de Estadística, *Censo Nacional de Población de 1940*, 8:4; and República del Perú, Instituto Nacional de Planificación, Dirección Nacional de Estadística y Censos, *VI Censo Nacional de Población* (1961), 1:15.

are appointed by the President. The prefect, in turn, appoints his "subprefects," each of whom governs a province within the department. At the district and subdistrict levels, public administration is delegated by the subprefect to "governors" and "lieutenant governors," respectively. Although some degree of local patronage has been possible in the selection of the last three groups of offices, the creation of autonomous local political machines is handicapped by the centralization of the administrative structure and the ultimate loyalty of all appointees to the national executive and his local agents, the prefects.[75]

The centralization of government functions extends also to the specialized services of each of the ministries—health, agriculture, education, police, labor and Indian affairs, and roads. As Schaedel argues,

The members of the community don't possess any mechanism for influencing the course of operations or controlling the labor of the public services. In order to make their needs known, the members of the community resort to petitions to the central government through the hierarchy of appointed administrative functionaries [ranging from lieutenant governor to the President]; or through direct petition to Congressional representatives.

In either case, the system functions effectively only in the periods near to elections. Since elections are carried out every six years, the process of presenting petitions and getting help from the government functionaries generally depends on the power of personal contacts, favors, and influence.[76]

[75] A detailed description of the pathologies of local government and administration in Puno may be found in Escobar, *Organización*, pp. 12–50.

[76] Richard P. Schaedel, *La Demografía y los Recursos Humanos del Sur del Perú*, p. 58, my translation.

The government services offered to the interior regions of Peru in this century have been limited or half-hearted, like the abortive investigation in Puno of the Bureau of Indian Affairs during the Leguía administration. Programs in health and education, for example, have been poorly equipped, understaffed, and mostly oriented to residents of the urban areas.

After the creation of the Ministry of Agriculture in 1943 and the establishment of an Inter-American Cooperative Service for Food Production (SCIPA) by the Peruvian and United States governments, a few agricultural extension services were supplied in the department, consisting of demonstrations and the sale of improved quality seeds and fertilizer. Credits were made available to *hacendados* and some Indians by the creation of an Agropecuarian Development Bank during the Second World War, but its capital was limited.[77]

In 1952 the International Labor Organization, in conjunction with other specialized agencies of the United Nations (including UNESCO and the Food and Agricultural Organization), organized an Andean Program of studies and aid to the Indian peoples of Colombia, Ecuador, Peru, and Bolivia.[78] One of the areas chosen for the Andean Program's operations was the Peruvian altiplano, where several technical schools have been sponsored along with a pilot colonization project in the selvatic region near Tambopata (in the province of Sandia).[79]

While these programs have undoubtedly had some impact upon the economic and social development of the altiplano, the conditions of life in this region, as will be shown in the following chapters, are still very backward. Programs, such as those mentioned here, when combined with continued social and economic exploitation of a large mass of people, may have served only to intensify the tensions and frustrations of the altiplano's political system.

[77] Owens, *Peru*, pp. 112–113; also interview, David Brown, Iowa State Agricultural Mission, Puno, March 8, 1965.
[78] República del Perú, Ministerio de Trabajo y Asuntos Indígenas, *Informe del Plan Nacional de Integración de la Población Aborigen*, pp. 57–59.
[79] *Ibid.*, pp. 98–113.

THE PHYSICAL AND DEMOGRAPHIC SETTING

Physical Features

Area

THE DEPARTMENT OF PUNO is the fourth largest of Peru's twenty-three departments, with a total area of 27,940 square miles (including almost 2,000 square miles of the Peruvian portion of Lake Titicaca). This is roughly equivalent in size to the state of Ohio. Unlike Ohio, however, the altitude of the department of Puno varies from around 1,000 feet above sea level to over 19,000 feet, with ecological zones that range from tropical and subtropical in the far north to alpine and nival in the two Andean ranges that enclose Puno's altiplano on the northeast and southwest (see Map 1). In the department, 23,020 square miles are classified as sierra (mountainous) and 4,920 square miles as selva (tropical forest).[1] Of this area, only 144,116 hectares, or about 2 percent of the total area of the department, is under cultivation, the remainder constituting natural pastures and unsettled or unproductive land.[2]

[1] República del Perú, Ministerio de Agricultura, Universidad Agraria, *Estadística Agraria 1963*, p. 8 (hereinafter cited as *Estadística Agraria 1963*).
[2] *Ibid.*, p. 6.

Of the department's total area, 40 percent can be classified as altiplano,[3] with an elevation that ranges slightly from the level of Lake Titicaca at 12,468 feet to 13,014 feet at Santa Rosa, eighty-five miles to the north, near the border of the department of Cuzco. The altiplano extends an even greater distance beyond Lake Titicaca southward into Bolivia.

The department of Puno is divided into nine provinces: Chucuito, Puno, and Huancané (bordering Lake Titicaca on the south, west, and north, respectively); San Román, Lampa, Melgar, and Azángaro (comprising the rest of the altiplano area in a half circle moving clockwise from southwest to north); and Carabaya and Sandia (in the far northwest and northeast, respectively, in the selva region of the department). (See Map 2.)

The altiplano is watered by a number of rivers that flow into Lake Titicaca, the most important of which are the Ramis River in the north, flowing through the flat pampas (plains) of Azángaro and Huancané provinces, and the Ilave River in Chucuito Province in the south. The lake itself is drained by the Desaguadero River, which for a short distance forms the Peru-Bolivia boundary to the south, thence veering into Bolivia, where it empties into Lake Poopó. In the selvatic north, there are a number of rivers, the principal ones being the San Gabán, Inambari, and Tambopata Rivers, all of which eventually join tributaries of the Amazon.

Weather

The variation of the climate in the altiplano has been exceedingly important economically and politically, although the range of variation to the outsider would appear somewhat limited. A play on the word *estación* (which in Spanish means both "station" and "season") provides a popular saying that "in Puno there are only two *estaciones* —those of winter and of the railroad company."[4] Because of the altitude, temperatures, which are usually between 50° and 75° Fahrenheit

[3] Interview, David Brown, Iowa State Agricultural Mission, Puno, March 8, 1965.

[4] François Bourricaud, *Changements à Puno: Étude de Sociologie Andine,* p. 36.

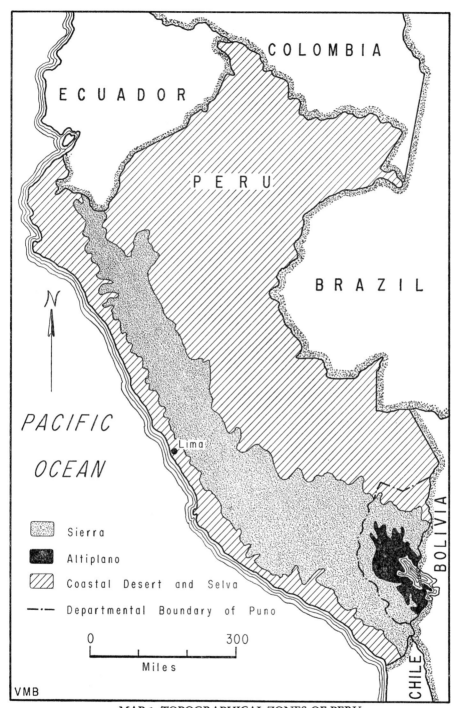

ECUADOR

P E R U

BRAZIL

N

PACIFIC

OCEAN

Lima

BOLIVIA

CHILE

Sierra

Altiplano

Coastal Desert and Selva

Departmental Boundary of Puno

0   300

Miles

VMB

MAP 1. TOPOGRAPHICAL ZONES OF PERU

MAP 2. PROVINCES AND RIVERS IN THE DEPARTMENT OF PUNO

in the daytime, drop to between 20° and 35° at night.[5] The chief variation in temperature comes not so much with altitude or season as with distance from the lakeshore. As Preston James writes:

> Around the shores of Lake Titicaca extremes of temperature are moderated by the presence of the open water. Because the lake is very deep—about 700 feet at the maximum depth—the temperature of Lake Titicaca remains nearly constant throughout the year, at about 51°. As a result, the air temperatures around the margins of the lake do not drop so low at night or in winter as they do at similar altitudes farther from the water.[6]

Seasonal variations, which are slight with regard to temperature, are very pronounced with regard to rainfall. Although the pattern is always unpredictable, heavy rainfalls are expected between January and March, and a dry period is common from May through August. Total annual rainfall may vary from a disastrously low 200 mm. to as high as 1,000 mm.[7] The absence of rain in the periods immediately before January or after March, and/or the incidence of heavy frosts in these periods, can have serious effects on agriculture. Equally dangerous, in the heavy rainfall period, is the possibility of flooding, facilitated by the shallowness of the Titicaca basin and poor conditions for rapid drainage.

During the agricultural season, which extends from September to May, it is likely that at least one of these "disasters" will affect crops in portions of the altiplano. Combinations of these disasters caused serious economic, social, and political crises in six of the ten years from 1956 through 1965. In 1956, 1957, and 1964 there were serious droughts; in 1962 there was a serious flood; and in 1960 and 1963 there were February floods followed by severe frosts and a premature end to the rainy season. In 1965 part of the pampa of Taraco (province of Huancané) was covered by several feet of water from the Ramis River, stranding hundreds of the Indians' conical huts, while flooding others; in the pampa of Ilave a bridge was closed because of

[5] República del Perú, Ministerio de Hacienda y Comercio, Dirección Nacional de Estadística y Censos, *Anuario Estadístico del Perú 1955*, p. 32 (hereinafter cited as *Anuario Estadístico 1955*).

[6] Preston E. James, *Latin America*, p. 211.

[7] *Anuario Estadístico 1955*, p. 32.

the high water. In both cases, however, it was explained that these conditions were by no means as serious as those during the 1962 and 1963 floods.

It might be hypothesized that the Aymará Indians' traditional threefold reliance on (1) lakeside agriculture, (2) animal-grazing at the higher altitudes,[8] and (3) colonization of the coastal valleys of Ilo and Moquegua,[9] may have constituted a socioeconomic adjustment to the ecological uncertainties of the area. If this is so, the Conquest's disruption of Aymará control over the three zones—in particular the gradual displacement of traditional authority in the coastal valleys and altiplano grazing lands—complicated the making of adjustments to the periodic crises of lakeside agriculture. As the events of 1956–1961 will reveal, the costs of adjustment to such crises were borne by the national government in Lima with little foresight, skill, or dispatch.

Flora and Fauna

In the altiplano the predominant natural growth is a bunch grass known as ichu (or *jichu*), which serves as fodder for livestock as well as being used for making rope, matting, thatching, and fuel, and for binding adobes. Around the lake is an abundance of totora reeds and thick algae called *llachu*, both of which are used to feed cattle, the reeds also being used in the weaving of baskets and the construction

[8] See "The Colonial Period" in Chapter 2; John Murra, "Una Apreciación Etnológica de la Visita," in *Visita Hecha a la Provincia de Chucuito por Garci Diez de San Miguel en el Año 1567*, by Garci Diez de San Miguel, p. 423.

[9] In the *Visita* document of Garci Diez de San Miguel (Note 8) there is reference throughout to a traditional tie between the *caciques* and other Indians of the Chucuito area and "their cornfields in Moquegua and in Sama" (p. 17 and *passim*), implying a colonial or semicolonial relationship between the two areas. Whether this relationship was first achieved under the Tiahuanaco Empire of A.D. 600, the Lupaca tribe of the 1400's, or the later Incan conquests, the economic interdependence of the areas was made very clear to Garci Diez in 1567. The traditional migratory orientation of the Aymará Indians to the Moquegua and Tacna Valleys, as opposed to the Arequipa area (to which the Quechua Indians of the Southern sierra are drawn) was noted by Héctor Martínez as recently as 1961 (*Las Migraciones Altiplánicas y la Colonización del Tambopata*, p. 63). The emotional value these traditional links may have, over and above the more objective economic or geopolitical arguments for the Puno-Moquegua road, is impossible to determine.

of boats. Trees are almost wholly absent, except where men have planted them, and these are rare.

Descending the Andes in the north of the department, one encounters a dense growth of smaller trees at about 11,000 feet. This high selva is called the *ceja de la montaña* (or "eyebrow of the forest") by the Peruvians. Where topographical conditions are favorable, the *ceja* is valued for colonization purposes because of the general fertility of the soil and the temperateness of the climate. Closer to sea level, however, the selva's soils are less fertile and the climate more oppressive.

Animals native to the altiplano include the famous *auquénido* (or American camel) family, which comprises the llama, alpaca, vicuña, and guanaco. Foxes, deer, and chinchillas are also found. Cattle, sheep, and pigs constitute the most important animals that have been introduced into the area. The fish found in Lake Titicaca and the other, smaller lakes of the Andes, as well as the rivers of the Titicaca basin, include several native varieties as well as recently introduced trout, all of which are an important resource for the area. There is some hunting of birds, mostly around Lake Titicaca.

DEMOGRAPHY

Population figures for the altiplano are highly contradictory, as well as controversial. Partly, this may derive from the difficulties of properly canvassing the population in the country's infrequent censuses. It may also be a result of the relatively mobile character of the population, moving between the coast, the mines, the selva, and the altiplano, according to the dictates of the climate or economic opportunities. Table II illustrates the fluctuations and leaps of the estimated population of the altiplano from 1793 to the present. Because of the difference between the 1955, 1958, and 1961 figures, there is widespread skepticism about the 1961 figures' reliability. Most of the informants for this study estimated the real population of the department to be between 1,000,000 and 1,500,000.[10] However, based upon the 1961

[10] Róger E. Cáceres Velásquez, *Puno: Universidad y Corporación*, p. 123; also interviews with Father Robert Kearns (Maryknoll Mission), March 9, 1965, Oscar Espinoza (manager of Corpuno), April 7, 1965, and Juan Sotomayor (Communist lawyer), Puno, April 13, 1965. The 1961 Census itself

TABLE II
*Estimated Population of the Department
of Puno, 1793–1961*

1793*	186,682
1854	230,797
1862	224,678
1876	259,449
1896	537,345
1921	567,265
1940	646,385
1955	731,150
1958	863,950
1961	686,260

* The figure is for the *intendencia* of Puno.

Sources: Emilio Romero, *Monografía del Departamento de Puno*, pp. 225–228; Sociedad de Propaganda del Sur del Perú, *Guía General del Sur del Perú*, p. 187; *1940 Census*, 8:3; *Anuario Estadístico 1955*, p. 43; República del Perú, Plan Regional Para el Desarrollo del Sur del Perú, *Informes*, 5:11 (hereinafter cited as PRPDSP, *Informes*); and *1961 Census*, 1:1.

Census figures, Table III indicates the population of the nine provinces of the department of Puno and the density of their populations. The average density for the department as a whole is 23.75 inhabitants per square mile. However, some districts and settlements, especially those near the shores of Lake Titicaca and in the pampas of Taraco and Ilave, have a density that exceeds 250 inhabitants per square mile.[11] (See Map 3.)

The density of population around the lake and along the major rivers feeding the lake presents a serious problem if one is interested in estimating rural and urban percentages of the population.[12] A dense

---

calculates that 41,049 inhabitants were not included in the census, bringing the total to an estimated 727,309. However, the legally effective number remains 686,260 (República del Perú, Instituto Nacional de Planificación, Dirección Nacional de Estadística y Censos, *VI Censo Nacional de Población* [1961], 1:13; hereinafter cited as *1961 Census*).

11 Corpuno, *Boletín de Divulgación* (Puno, 1964), p.3.

12 The well-known requirement of 2,500 inhabitants to differentiate an urban from a rural community in the United States need not be the best criterion, writes Harold Kaufman. Other criteria could include population density, social differentiation, social and/or spatial mobility, rates of social change,

TABLE III
Provincial Population, Area, and Population
Density, Department of Puno, 1961

Province (and Capital)	Population	Area (sq. m.)	Density
Puno (Puno)	124,823	1,973.4	63.4
Azángaro (Azángaro)	111,468	2,486.9	44.9
Carabaya (Macusani)	28,179	5,907.3	4.7
Chucuito (Juli)	147,385	4,428.9	33.2
Huancané (Huancané)	107,170	1,578.7	68.1
Lampa (Lampa)	34,655	2.370.9	14.5
Melgar (Ayaviri)	48,201	1,654.7	30.1
Sandia (Sandia)	38,550	4,822.4	8.0
San Román (Juliaca)	45,829	787.8	58.5

Source: *1961 Census*, 1:6.

but unclustered settlement pattern in an agricultural area may permit considerable urbanlike intercommunication and division of labor without visually meriting the label "urban." The district of Acora (in the province of Puno), for example, has a population that is classified as 941 urban and 25,076 rural. Yet it has a post office and telegraph, a limited power supply, a church, the third highest number of schools of any district in the department (43), and a relatively large number of teachers (69) and students (2,587).[13] Furthermore, it is difficult to fix the urban boundaries around the principal towns in the department because of the cultural difference between the Indian and mestizo populations. A peasant's hut on the fringe of a provincial town does not do much to urbanize him if his cultural behavior prevents his access to alternative social and economic activities, or if his days are spent in traditional labor in his fields. But neither is a peasant family altogether unaffected if the location of the home permits a daily visit to a nearby market place for the wife and a half day in school for the children without sacrificing their duties at home.

Since these qualifications would hold true for other sierra areas, it is noteworthy that the department of Puno has a population estimated in

and agriculture as a major occupation (Julius Gould and William L. Kolb [eds.], *A Dictionary of the Social Sciences*, p. 612).

[13] *Datos Distritales.*

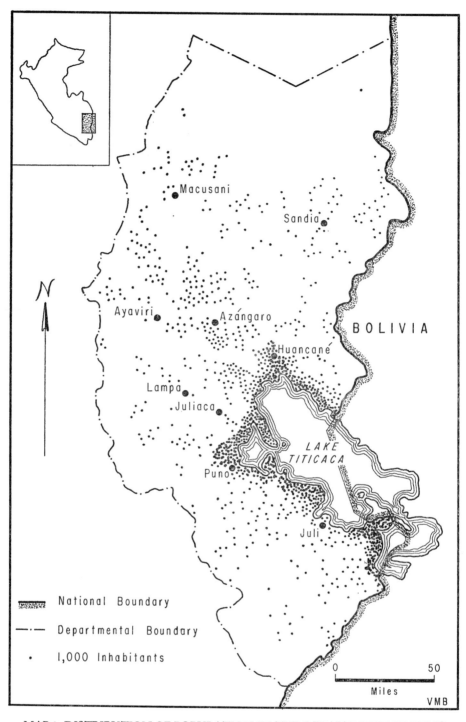

MAP 3. DISTRIBUTION OF POPULATION IN THE DEPARTMENT OF PUNO

the 1961 Census to be 81.9 percent rural, a figure surpassed only by the northern sierra department of Cajamarca (85.1% rural).[14]

ECONOMIC PRODUCTION

Economic activity in an underdeveloped region of a country often involves the extraction of natural resources, while their elaboration in terms of processing and manufacturing is often assumed by more developed regions of the country (or by more developed countries). The problems of establishing subsidiary processing and manufacturing industries in the altiplano—at or near the area's resources—has provided a major focus of political concern in recent years. The argument at the base of this concern is the alleged victimization of Puno in the terms of trade of manufactured goods for raw materials imposed by the coastal industrial sector of the country on the more remote regions.[15]

Agricultural Production

Economic production in Puno is, as the department's rural character might imply, largely oriented to agriculture and cattle-raising. In 1940 the number of economically active population in these fields was 212,206 (or 78% of the total economically active population).[16] The number in 1961, utilizing a different criterion of measurement, was 161,530 (or 71%).[17]

Among the most important agricultural crops in Puno are potatoes, barley, quinoa (*quinua*, an indigenous type of food grain), coffee, and corn. The hectares sown and the crop yields in 1955 and 1963, as well as their values, are shown in Table IV. The most impressive changes seen on this table are the increase in coffee production and the decline in potatoes and other tuber crops. The increased production of coffee and, to a lesser extent, corn (along with the development of banana and

[14] *1961 Census*, 1:10.

[15] *El Comercio* (Lima), April 30, 1957, p. 13; "Senate Debates," April 1, 1959, p. 4; September 30, 1959, p. 15; September 7, 1960, p. 9.

[16] República del Perú, Ministerio de Hacienda y Comercio, Dirección Nacional de Estadística, *Censo Nacional de Población de 1940*, 8:45–46 (hereinafter cited as *1940 Census*).

[17] *1961 Census*, 4:63.

TABLE IV
Major Agricultural Crops, Department of Puno, 1955 and 1963

Crop	Hectares in Production		Production (Metric Tons)		Value in Sols*	
	1955	1963	1955	1963	1955**	1963
Coffee	5,300	7,770	975	2,830	S/14,167,500	S/41,122,000
Barley	33,410	33,000	39,431	30,330	45,212,500	34,778,400
Coca***	354	490	184	90	3,685,500	1,802,700
Frijol***	150	130	120	110	525,200	481,470
Corn	4,242	5,790	5,434	7,230	11,849,400	15,765,600
Oca-Olluco-Mashua***	3,790	1,720	22,740	4,800	30,016,800	6,336,000
Potatoes	54,320	46,520	298,770	89,580	430,228,800	128,995,200
Quinoa	17,255	18,500	22,759	15,530	52,118,100	35,563,700
Wheat	1,167	1,350	1,396	1,150	2,589,900	2,073,550
Total	119,988	115,280	391,809	151,650	S/590,393,700	S/266,918,620

*The sol is roughly equal to $.04.

**Estimated in terms of 1963 prices.

***Coca is a shrub from which cocaine is obtained; Frijol is a variety of bean; Oca, Olluco, and Mashua are varieties of tuber, consumed indigenously.

Source: Estadística Agraria 1963, p. 75; Anuario Estadístico 1955, pp. 123–128.

TABLE V
Livestock Population, Department of Puno, 1941, 1955, and 1963

Year	Cattle	Sheep	Horses	Auquénidos	Poultry	Pigs
1941	307,392	6,579,424	62,125	(*)	(*)	(*)
1955	489,300	8,258,000	140,800	1,676,600	456,000	116,300
1963	433,000	7,269,000	122,000	1,678,000	482,000	129,000

(*) Not available.

Sources: 1940 Census 8:9; Anuario Estadístico 1955, p. 15; Estadística Agraria 1963, pp. 81–87.

citrus fruit production) is a result of the opening of access routes into the northern selva. The declines in potato, quinoa, barley, *oca*, and other tuber production, are a result, partly of the reduction in hectares seeded, but also of a severe flood followed by a frost that struck much of the altiplano in 1963.[18]

In livestock and allied production, Puno enjoys its greatest reputation, possessing well over half the sheep and *auquénidos* (llamas, alpacas, guanacos, and vicuñas) in Peru, as well as the largest beef cattle stock of any department except Cajamarca (in northern Peru). Table V shows the comparative stocks in the altiplano in 1941, 1955, and 1963.

The chief products of the livestock industry are wool and meat, although skins, milk, cheese, and fat are produced to some extent. The value of the total livestock production is about equal to that of the agricultural crop production. In 1963 the value of meat production was roughly S/84,000,000 (beef) and S/120,000,000 (lamb), while wool was valued roughly at S/19,000,000 (from *auquénidos*) and S/100,000,000 (from sheep).[19]

Other Production

Mineral production, while it is only a fraction (2 percent or less) of the total mineral production of Peru, provides about a tenth of the total economic product of the department of Puno. The principal minerals and their 1954 and 1955 values in Peruvian sols are summarized in Table VI. Swings in the production of the various minerals may be a reflection both of price swings in the world prices of the minerals and of the marginal character of many mining operations. Layoffs have periodically taken place at several mines for these reasons.[20] Oil explorations were conducted in the provinces of Huancané and Azángaro during the Second World War,[21] but further exploratory drilling was suspended until recently (1963).[22]

[18] *El Comercio* (Lima), February 3, 1963, p. 1; April 20, 1963, p. 1.
[19] Author's estimates from *Estadística Agraria 1963*, pp. 81–103.
[20] *El Comercio* (Lima), June 7, 1958, p. 11; *Los Andes* (Puno), August 29, 1963, p. 1; *El Tiempo* (Puno), February 3, 1965, p. 3.
[21] *El Comercio* (Lima), December 14, 1957, p. 15.
[22] *Ibid.*, February 19, 1963, p. 9.

TABLE VI

Mineral Production, Department of Puno, 1954 and 1955

Mineral	1954	1955
Antimony	S/2,245,706	S/1,080,027
Copper	9,968,400	16,009,850
Manganese	779,624	30,030
Gold	2,076,574	2,235,450
Silver	11,123,458	13,898,977
Lead	27,699,066	30,318,304
Salt	431,762	288,499
Tungsten	1,444,152	588,706
Zinc	9,795,226	11,427,943
Total	S/65,571,942	S/75,877,786

Source: *Anuario Estadístico 1955*, p. 194.

Among the altiplano's artisan and cottage-industry products are spun wool, hand- and loom-woven goods, ceramics and pottery, and leather goods. The number of individuals involved in any one enterprise is usually small, although a few larger weaving operations exist in the vicinity of Juliaca.

Infrastructure in the Altiplano

Although there are no paved roads in the department outside Juliaca and Puno, there were 1,245 kilometers of improved roads and 1,476 kilometers of unimproved (seasonably passable) roads in 1955.[23] Compared to the rest of the Peruvian sierra, this is a relatively high proportion of road development. It is due, of course, to the level altiplano, whose challenge to road construction comes mainly with periodic flooding, which necessitates the lifting of main arteries above the vulnerable pampas. While the roads to Cuzco and La Paz are fairly well maintained and more heavily traveled, the roads leading out of the altiplano to the coast and to the selva are typical of roads elsewhere in the Peruvian sierra. Where they exist, they are narrow, exceedingly vulnerable to slides, and poorly maintained. Yet it is asserted

[23] *Anuario Estadístico 1955*, p. 231.

to be of major importance for the department's economic growth that these access roads be better developed.[24]

The railroad connecting Puno with Arequipa, one of a series of spectacular engineering feats by the famous American soldier of fortune, Henry Meiggs, was completed in 1874. Its operation was taken over by the Peruvian Corporation, a British holding company, incorporated in 1890 to take over the external debt of Peru. The Peruvian, as it is called, owns a number of other enterprises and lands in Peru. In Puno it also operates a steamship line, providing twice-weekly service across Lake Titicaca from Puno to the Bolivian port of Guaqui, where another rail line extends to La Paz. The Peruvian also used to provide regular shipping service to a number of other lakeside ports on both the Peruvian and Bolivian sides of Lake Titicaca. But with the construction of roads and the increased costs of maintaining this service, The Peruvian discontinued it.[25]

The most important transportation development in recent years has been the opening of an airfield in Juliaca. There had been service to Puno by Lufthansa until the outbreak of the Second World War in 1939.[26] But, as we shall see below, the resumption of air transport into the altiplano favored Juliaca over Puno, with political implications of some importance in the growing rivalry between the two cities.

It was mentioned above that several rivers flowed into Lake Titicaca, and that others in the northern selva were among the tributaries of the Amazon. Attempts to harness these rivers for hydroelectric power have generally been discounted because of the inadequate topography of the altiplano for damming, as well as the reportedly weak thrust of the altiplano rivers,[27] while the selvatic rivers are too far from the altiplano (and over too rugged a terrain) to make delivery economical. Proposals have been made to divert waters from Lake Titicaca in order to irrigate the coastal departments of Arequipa, Tacna, and Moquegua, while at the same time providing energy for Puno's industrial develop-

[24] *El Comercio* (Lima), June 17, 1956, p. 2; *Los Andes* (Puno), March 20, 1965, p. 2.
[25] Raúl Galdo Pagaza, *El Indígena y el Mestizo de Vilquechico*, p. 9.
[26] *El Comercio* (Lima), October 26, 1957, p. 15.
[27] Martínez, *Migraciones*, p. 6.

ment.[28] Similar proposals have been made for the diversion of waters
from the glacial lakes Lagunillas and Saracocha, near the Puno-Are-
quipa border.[29] Cost estimates on these projects have been heatedly
debated, and their priority in the overall development plan of Puno
has been a subject of political conflict, especially after the creation of
the autonomous departmental development corporation (Corpuno), as
we shall see below.

In 1921 there were seven electric plants reported in the department.[30] Five were small hydroelectric generators for use in mining
operations and two were gas-driven plants for public use, located in
Puno and Juliaca.[31] By 1963 power was available in over thirty district
capitals in the department.[32] However, most of this power came from
small, diesel-driven motors, serving a limited number of families and
enterprises, and operating for limited periods each day. The per capita
production of electricity in the department in 1958 was 11.6 kilowatt
hours.[33] This contrasts with the national Peruvian average of 290 kilowatt hours per capita, and over 5,000 kilowatt hours per capita in the
United States.[34]

CONCLUSIONS

In terms of ecological, demographic, productive, and infrastructural
endowments, the department of Puno is clearly one of the more backward areas of the world—densely populated, limited in its range of
possible economic activities, beset by climatic uncertainties, and cut off
by encircling mountain ranges from the outside world. As we shall see
in the next chapter, the convergence of these physical properties, combined with social and economic practices in the altiplano, produced a

[28] Some of these proposals are summarized in "Plan del Perú," *El Comercio*
(Lima), March 4 and 5, 1958, p. 3.

[29] *Los Andes* (Puno), June 10, 1964, p. 1; March 5, 1965, p. 4.

[30] Sociedad de Propaganda del Sur del Perú, *Guía General del Sur del Perú*,
pp. 227–231.

[31] *Ibid.*

[32] *Datos Distritales.*

[33] PRPDSP, *Informes*, 5:11.

[34] University of California, Latin American Center, *Statistical Abstract of
Latin America, 1964*, pp. 9, 89.

plural society in which the local system's scant resources were firmly controlled by minority groups within (and outside) the area. To some extent, the infrastructural developments of the last eighty years, limited as they have been, aided the socioeconomic differentiation of roles—both within the Indian majority and the dominant white minority, complicating the resultant political dynamics of the system.

THE SOCIAL AND ECONOMIC SYSTEM
OF THE ALTIPLANO

M. G. SMITH HAS GIVEN CRITERIA for distinguishing a plural society from what he terms heterogeneous and homogeneous societies. The criteria are as follows:

Pluralism . . . consists in the coexistence of incompatible institutional systems. . . . A society whose members all share a single system of institutions is culturally and socially homogeneous. A society having one basic institutional system in a number of styles or one basic system and a number of institutional alternatives and specialties is culturally and socially heterogeneous.[1]

To illustrate this distinction, he contrasts the Canadian and South African nations. In the former case, some divergent cultural institutions are made compatible by the existence of a number of other institutions held in common, such as agreement on the federal principle, Western values, and economic *laissez faire*.[2] In the latter case, the absence even of common institutions like these necessitates an autocratic regulation of the

[1] M. G. Smith, "Social and Cultural Pluralism," *Annals of the New York Academy of Sciences*, 83 (1960): 774.

[2] *Ibid.*, p. 773.

subordinate majority by the culturally distinct but dominant minority.[3] Determining the type to which a given society corresponds will enable a better analytic understanding of the likelihood and kind of conflicts that might occur within it.

The material in this chapter describes the different cultural groups in the altiplano, first from a broad cultural and economic perspective, and then from a closer inspection of life styles and attitudes of the members of these groups toward each other and toward themselves. Finally, the phenomenon called "cholification" will be examined, along with the role played by a prominent Juliaca family in exploiting this phenomenon.

THE PROBLEMS OF LANGUAGE AND LITERACY

The altiplano has a predominantly Indian population composed of two linguistic groups, Aymará and Quechua. According to the 1961 Census, those with Spanish as their mother language were outnumbered

TABLE VII

Provincial Population (Aged Five and Over) by Mother Language, Department of Puno, 1961

Province	Total	Aymará	Spanish	Quechua	Other
Puno	105,003	48,296	9,327	46,521	859
Azángaro	92,702	216	2,343	89,476	667
Carabaya	23,651	57	1,199	22,236	159
Chucuito	122,332	116,339	4,265	952	776
Huancané	89,474	71,812	1,680	15,240	742
Lampa	28,890	110	1,034	27,406	440
Melgar	40,125	100	2,075	37,709	241
Sandia	32,992	5,339	1,593	25,825	235
San Román	38,273	1,065	5,584	31,433	191
Total	573,442	243,334	29,100	296,798	4,210

Source: *1961 Census*, 3:40.

almost twenty to one by residents whose mother language was Aymará or Quechua. As Table VII reveals, the ratio by which native Spanish-speakers are outnumbered varied from seven to one in Juliaca to over fifty to one in Huancané.

[3] *Ibid.*

TABLE VIII

Provincial Population over Five Years of Age, According to Language and Sex, Department of Puno, 1940

Province	Spanish	Quechua	Aymará	Spanish and Quechua	Spanish and Aymará	Spanish and other
Puno						
Men	1,467	13,189	15,874	6,200	5,586	119
Women	1,300	17,034	21,270	3,031	1,755	61
Azángaro						
Men	235	31,314	42	6,473	14	24
Women	167	40,762	47	2,096	11	6
Carabaya						
Men	163	8,004	4	1,349	6	34
Women	61	7,950	0	706	2	9
Chucuito						
Men	209	195	33,946	115	10,288	35
Women	192	219	44,792	96	2,600	18
Huancané						
Men	232	4,299	24,451	1,533	7,256	21
Women	133	5,854	35,253	435	1,624	3
Lampa						
Men	113	7,850	1	3,119	0	11
Women	83	11,489	4	999	3	1
Melgar						
Men	277	12,106	6	4,107	18	37
Women	224	16,186	1	1,897	18	9
Sandia						
Men	166	8,437	286	2,811	101	29
Women	37	8,464	113	824	23	0
San Román						
Men	497	7,090	26	3,367	134	53
Women	434	9,794	13	1,578	48	25
Departmental Total						
Men	3,359	92,484	74,636	29,074	23,403	363
Women	2,631	117,752	101,493	11,662	6,084	132

The Aymará language is identified now with all the lakeside settlements on both the southern shore (province of Chucuito) and northern shore (province of Huancané). In the province of Puno, encompassing most of the western shore of the lake, settlements to the north of the city of Puno are Quechua-speaking, and those to the south are Aymará. It is popularly said that the dividing line between both groups is the main street in downtown Puno. Most settlements away from the lake are Quechua-speaking, except for a few Aymará colonies established in the Tambopata region of Sandia.

As a general rule, communication between the language groups takes place in Spanish. As Table VIII reveals, the number of residents bilingual in Spanish and a native language was not very great in 1940. The province of San Román had the highest proportion of bilingual residents (approximately one out of every four). The 1961 Census shows a fourfold increase in the number of Spanish speakers. Those bilingual in Spanish and either Quechua or Aymará jumped from 52,477 in 1940 to 190,385, in 1961.[4] Nevertheless, over 60 percent of the Indian population was still listed as monolingual.

In 1940 adult literacy was estimated at 14 percent (44,946 of an adult [17 years or older] population of 316,013).[5] In 1961 the percentage of literacy had increased to 34 percent (124,717 of an adult population of 366,691).[6] The 1961 figures, broken down according to urban-rural and male-female patterns, are given in Table IX. An obstacle to literacy, of course, is the language problem. Although Quechua and Aymará have been reduced to writing, little has been published in these languages, especially in the area of literacy training. Thus, to learn to read, a peasant has first to learn to speak Spanish. Traditionally, education in the Peruvian sierra has been conducted in Spanish only, with the effect that beginning students are greatly discouraged.[7] Besides the hurdle of Spanish, Héctor Martínez cites a number of other causes for peasant illiteracy:

[4] *1961 Census*, 3:46–47. Province-by-province figures for bilingualness had not been released by the end of 1966.
[5] *1940 Census*, 1:34.
[6] *1961 Census*, 3:146–147.
[7] "Plan del Perú," *El Comercio* (Lima), February 20, 1958, p. 3; also inter-

TABLE IX
Provincial Literacy among Adults, by Sex and Urban-Rural Categories,
Department of Puno, 1961

| | | LITERATES | | | | |
| Province | ALL ADULTS* | Urban | | Rural | | Total Literates |
		Men	Women	Men	Women	
Puno	67,273	6,671	3,929	12,218	3,355	26,173
Azángaro	58,168	2,270	941	10,086	2,627	15,924
Carabaya	15,980	1,180	352	2,722	374	4,628
Chucuito	77,550	3,169	1,610	16,682	4,310	25,771
Huancané	56,777	1,940	938	11,271	4,096	18,245
Lampa	18,457	1,256	609	3,838	1,293	6,996
Melgar	25,174	2,331	1,106	3,296	749	7,482
Sandia	23,271	1,945	467	5,291	822	8,525
San Román	24,041	5,058	2,531	2,580	804	10,973
Department Total	366,691	25,820	12,483	67,984	18,430	124,717

		ILLITERATES				Total Illiterates
Puno	67,273	1,466	3,885	11,048	24,701	41,100
Azángaro	58,168	1,556	3,267	11,064	26,357	42,244
Carabaya	15,980	748	1,410	3,373	5,821	11,352
Chucuito	77,550	727	2,101	15,316	33,635	51,779
Huancané	56,777	509	1,358	10,496	26,169	38,532
Lampa	18,457	512	1,410	2,765	6,774	11,461
Melgar	25,174	1,235	3,063	4,441	8,953	17,692
Sandia	23,271	1,082	1,220	5,145	7,299	14,746
San Román	24,041	1,149	3,224	2,706	5,989	13,068
Department Total	366,691	8,984	20,938	66,354	145,698	241,974

* Seventeen years of age and above.

Source: *1961 Census*, 3:146–147.

(a) the scarcity of schools and teachers; (b) the lack of interest by the government in the education of the Indian masses; (c) the slight utility of literacy; (d) the imperious rule of the *haciendas*; (e) the utilization of youths in agricultural and grazing activities; (f) the almost exclusive presence of masculine teachers which evokes a certain suspiciousness in parents about

---

view with Dr. Nathan Kravetz, former head of the American Educational Mission in Peru, Los Angeles, July 13, 1963.

sending their daughters to school; and (g) the fact that the teachers have not tried to go beyond the four walls of the schools where they function.[8]

In 1860, Emilio Romero reports, there were 15 schools in the department, with a total of 741 students.[9] In 1926, he says, the number had increased to 131 schools with 7,960 students and 184 teachers.[10] By 1955 the total number of schools had risen to 827, while the number of students enrolled was 63,077, with 1,577 teachers.[11] Many of these schools, however, were small one-room buildings with poor lighting, no blackboards or desks, and poor attendance on behalf of both students and teachers.[12]

The role of language and literacy as institutions dividing the altiplano society will be further discussed later in the chapter.

Differences in Man-Land Relationships

The most interesting and politically significant aspect of economic production in the altiplano is the man-land configuration. An unpublished survey by the National Agrarian Reform Office (ONRA) estimates an average land parcel size of 0.22 hectares per family in the area close to Lake Titicaca, while the average parcel for the altiplano area away from the lake is 1.97 hectares, and in the foothills and mountains it varies from 6.61 to 8.97 hectares per family.[13] Although the lands near the rivers and lake are the most intensively cultivated in the department, their productivity is not entirely dependable, because of the climatic disasters mentioned in the previous chapter. Agricultural production in this area is devoted to potatoes, quinoa, barley, tuberous vegetables, and aquatic products (reeds and algae) for cattle fattening. The higher and drier portion of the altiplano is devoted largely to sheep- and cattle-raising, with limited cultivation of quinoa, barley, and fodder, mostly on haciendas. As the *auquénido* thrives at a still

[8] Héctor Martínez, *Las Migraciones Altiplánicas y la Colonización del Tambopata,* p. 47, my translation.

[9] Emilio Romero, *Monografía del Departamento de Puno,* p. 379.

[10] *Ibid.,* p. 538.

[11] *Anuario Estadística 1955,* pp. 742–803.

[12] "Plan del Perú," *El Comercio* (Lima), February 20, 1958, p. 3.

[13] Figures provided by David Brown, Iowa State Agricultural Mission, Puno, March 8, 1965.

higher elevation, where only bunch grass (ichu or *jichu*) will grow, communities and haciendas that are devoted almost exclusively to the raising of *auquénidos* can be found in the mountains up to the snow level.

The recent ONRA figures show that of 112,486 farm units in the department with a total of 3,565,019 hectares, 33,167 units (or 28%) farmed a mere 7,801 hectares (or 0.2%), while 270 units (0.2%) operated a total of 2,137,868 hectares (60%).[14] But, because the productivity and utilization of the soil varies in each of the three agropecuarian zones (lakeside, altiplano, and mountains), figures such as these, showing the extremes in landholdings between large and small proprietors, must be handled with some caution. *Hacendados*, for example, argue that the remote lands of the higher altiplano and mountainsides are fit only for grazing, and that, because of the barren condition of these areas, sheep and *auquénidos* need as much as 3 hectares grazing land per animal.[15]

Also complicating the analysis of landholding extremes is an intensive kind of land use for cattle-fattening, developed by the peasants around the lakeshore and along the rivers. Most cattle, after being bred and raised on large haciendas in drier regions of the altiplano, are sold at the age of three or four to *engordadores* (cattle-fatteners) in the cattle markets of Huancané and Ilave (Chucuito). It is estimated that 6,500 peasant families are engaged in cattle-fattening in the department.[16] The *engordador*, usually buying no more than one or two head of cattle at a time, drives them to his lake- or riverside plot of land, where he fattens them with the *llachu* algae that floats near the shore, or that the *engordador* "harvests" by *balsa*. The fattening process lasts about six months, whereupon the cattle are resold to meat dealers from the coast in the same market places.

[14] *Ibid.*

[15] Interview, Angel Reyes, *hacendado*, Huancané, April 4, 1965; also *Comunicado de las Asociaciones Agropecuarias de Puno*, April 11, 1964; and José Luís Lescano, "La Pequeña y Mediana Propiedad Sentenciada a Desaparecer?" *Los Andes* (Puno), October 13, 1965, p. 2.

[16] República del Perú, Oficina Nacional de Reforma Agraria, "Informe Técnico de la Zona de Puno para los Fines de la Reforma Agraria," by C. Bambi Díaz, p. 5.

Despite the economic rationale behind the extremes in landholdings between the *hacendados*, on the one hand, and the Indian peasants, on the other, the relationship between the two groups is politically complicated by the former's reputation for taking the latter's lands, and by the population pressures, which have caused the increasing fragmentation of the latter's remaining lands.

Indian peasants in the altiplano may be classified as *comuneros* (communal landholders and freeholders) and *colonos* (resident hacienda laborers). Estimates of the number in either category are difficult to make because of the dependence of some *comuneros* for seasonal or part-time employment on neighboring haciendas. As Thomas Ford points out, "many persons who were the possessors of diminutive plots may have listed themselves [in the Census] as owners or landlords, even though their principal source of livelihood was employment as farm laborers on the holdings of others."[17] In 1958 a government-sponsored study of southern Peru estimated the number of *comuneros* in the department of Puno to be 511,500, while the estimated number of *colonos* was 137,800.[18] However, in the same year, the Lima newspaper, *El Comercio*, estimated the number of *colonos* to be closer to 420,000.[19] This latter figure included 200,000 free-holding peasants who were working, at least part time, for a hacienda.

The economic condition of the *colono* is not uniform or unambiguously inferior to that of the *comunero*, as can be gauged from the following description by Héctor Martínez of three distinct forms of *colonato* that he discovered in Puno:

(a) the *hacendado* proportions lands to the *colono* and, in payment of that usufruct, the *colono* works for the *hacendado*, with his own tools in some cases and with those provided by the *hacendado* in others; in some cases he is given money for the days he works and in any case he is given coca and the *merienda* or mid-day meal; (b) the *hacendado* proportions not only lands but also grazing rights, especially on the livestock-raising haciendas, the *colono* having as much of his own *huacchas* or personal stock as he wishes, as well as growing whatever quantities and types of vegetables he

[17] Thomas R. Ford, *Man and Land in Peru*, p. 74.
[18] PRPDSP, *Informes*, 5:11.
[19] "Plan del Perú," *El Comercio* (Lima), February 2, 1958, p. 5.

chooses; in this case, the *colono* works on the days that the *patrón* orders
him to, receiving money in some cases, but always the coca and *merienda*
for agricultural labor; in the case of the *colono* dedicating himself exclusively to grazing activities, he receives food for the whole year; (c) in the haciendas in the process of capitalization . . . the *patrón* is limiting the number
of *huacchas* that each *colono* can have and is paying him a salary that varies
between 150 and 400 sols [$6.00–$15.00] monthly according to the
quantity of livestock that the *colono* possesses . . .; in these, they proportion
lands to the *colonos* besides, but not the annual foodstocks that the others
are accustomed to.[20]

The average hacienda (in 1940) had under ten families (approximately 50 people) on it, but the range was from countless single-fam-
ily operations to nine haciendas involving one hundred families or
more.[21]

One other factor of importance in understanding the man-land relationship in Puno is the fragmentation of parcels that make up the
average small freeholder's agricultural unit. In 1961 the average agricultural unit in the altiplano was composed of 4.7 parcels (*predios*).[22]
But on the lake- and riverside lands, the average number of parcels is
much higher. Galdo estimates that the number is closer to 20.[23] This
dispersion is a result, he says, of centuries of division among children
of their paternal and maternal inheritances. The traditional endogamy
of the Indian communities has tended to keep the parcels within walk-
ing distance of each other, but the size of each parcel, quite obviously,
becomes smaller with each generation. Although considerable time and
possibilities for economies of scale are lost by this phenomenon, Galdo
writes, "the Indians consider that the dispersion of properties is a
means of defense from the frost and hail, since these attack the land
not along continuous and uniform areas, but, on the contrary, in dis-
continuous patches . . ."[24] The same argument can be made for own-

[20] Martínez, *Migraciones*, p. 20, my translation.
[21] *1940 Census*, 8 (Part Two): 88–186.
[22] República del Perú, Instituto Nacional de Planificación, Dirección Nacional de Estadística y Censos, *Primer Censo Nacional Agropecuario, 2 Julio
de 1961: Principales Resultados Obtenidos por Muestreo*, p. 16.
[23] Raúl Galdo Pagaza, *Economía de las Colectividades Indígenas Colindantes con el Lago Titicaca*, p. 222.
[24] *Ibid.*, my translation.

ing parcels at the lake level (to take advantage of the greater availability of water and fertile soil) and above it as well (to insure against
flood loss). Short of a program that would attack the problem of the
weather itself, any attempt to consolidate land parcels (as part of an
agrarian reform) is bound to meet with considerable resistance for
these reasons.

The wages paid for agricultural labor are exceedingly low in the
altiplano. Near Accopata (in the Azángaro area), they reportedly
range from two to four sols daily ($0.07–$0.15).[25] *El Comercio* reported a departmental average of between three and four sols daily.[26]
These figures should be contrasted with those reported by Martínez on
the capitalized haciendas, which average from five to over thirteen sols
daily. Clearly, the *comunero's* economic position is by no means better
than that of the *colono*. Job opportunities on coastal sugar plantations
or on the new coca and coffee plantations in the selva exert a constant
pull on the altiplano peasant. The reduced size of his parcels both permits and necessitates this seasonal migration.

OCCUPATIONAL, LIFE-STYLE, AND ATTITUDINAL DIFFERENCES

Two major cultural types are found in the altiplano, the mestizos
(or Westernized elite) and the *indios* (culturally subdivided into Aymará and Quechua linguistic groups). Between these two groups are
interposed two subtypes, the *forasteros* (mestizo "outsiders" from another region or abroad) and the *cholos* (Indians who have in some
measure acquired traits identified with the mestizo culture).[27] Table X,

---

[25] Hernán Castillo, *et al., Accopata: The Reluctant Recipient of Technological Change*, p. 10.

[26] *El Comercio* (Lima), May 3, 1960, p. 15.

[27] The term "mestizo" is used very liberally in the altiplano to apply to anyone who is fully Westernized, culturally. The original meaning of mestizo
implied "of racially mixed origins." Ralph Beals uses the term in both its
racial and cultural senses in "Social Stratification in Latin America" (in *Contemporary Cultures and Societies of Latin America*, ed. Dwight B. Heath and
Richard N. Adams, pp. 342–360). Culturally, Beals finds that mestizo may
convey "a host of specific and readily identifiable meanings in different countries . . ." (p. 350). In no place, however, does he find it used generally to
indicate any person of fully Western orientation or behavior. Nevertheless,

adapted from the 1958 government-sponsored study of southern Peru, estimates the population of the altiplano according to the occupation of the principal breadwinner in the family. The estimates were then roughly subdivided along economic-class and cultural lines. The neatness by which occupational groupings fall within, and do not crosscut, cultural or class lines is undoubtedly oversimplified. Yet, from personal observation, it is clear that downward mobility is generally possible only within, not between, the cultural groupings implied in this table. Also, it is clear that movement into the middle or upper classes is possible only for someone of racially Indian origins who has culturally undergone a total Westernization. This process appears to take at least several generations. Even then, the Indian features of the individual tend to provoke continual defensiveness and insecurity, expressed in some cases by extensive intellectual activity, and in others by haughty disdain for the traditions and behavior of the Indians and *cholos.*

The Mestizo Cultural Group

The typical "upper-class" mestizo (or *misti,* as he is sometimes called) is a landowner with a home on his land, possibly one in Puno or a provincial capital, and, much less frequently, one in Arequipa or Lima.[28] His average income is estimated to be equivalent to the upper middle class in Lima or Arequipa.[29] To the extent that he can afford it, he will aspire to educate his children in Lima or Arequipa, if not overseas, and to eventually reside permanently away from the altiplano.[30]

---

this was the usage found by the author in the altiplano. Similarly, the term *cholo* has traditionally meant "of racially mixed origins"—specifically of Indian and Spanish parentage (Ozzie Simmons, "The *Criollo* Outlook in the Mestizo Culture of Coastal Peru," in *Contemporary Cultures and Societies,* ed. Heath and Adams, p. 520). Nevertheless, the term has come now to have a cultural meaning, applying to individuals of racially Indian origins "who are rapidly acculturating to the mestizo culture group but have not yet 'arrived' " (*ibid.*).

[28] François Bourricaud, *Changements à Puno: Étude de Sociologie Andine,* p. 60.

[29] PRPDSP, *Informes,* 5:7.

[30] *Ibid.,* p. 8.

TABLE X

Estimated Population of the Department of Puno by Cultural Group, Class, and Occupation, September, 1958

Cultural Identification	Class and Occupation	Number (Including Dependents)	Percent of Total
Mestizo	UPPER		
	Hacendados	4,000	
	Public officials	2,000	
	Private administrators	2,400	
	Independent (*rentistas*)	400	
		8,800	(1%)
	MIDDLE		
	Smaller landowners	6,000	
	Merchants	2,000	
	Public employees	12,000	
	Private employees	6,000	
	Other	500	
		26,500	(3%)
Cholo	LOWER		
	Small merchants	32,000	
	Independent	8,450	
	Skilled workers	5,500	
	Artisans	9,000	
	Peons	10,000	
	Apprentices	5,000	
	Miners	5,000	
	Domestics	12,000	
		86,950	(10%)
Indio	LOWEST		
	Minifundistas	511,500	
	Colonos	137,800	
	Agricultural workers	25,000	
	Miners	15,000	
		689,300	(80%)
	Subtotal	811,550	
	Emigrants (outside the department)	50,000	(6%)
	Total Population	861,550	

Source: **PRPDSP,** *Informes,* 5:11.

This aspiration is shared by members of the mestizo "middle class," as well.

Wealth is relatively minor in determining upper-class status in the altiplano.[31] Of equal or greater importance are criteria of birth, education, landholdings, profession, and consumption patterns. In Puno, birth is fairly critical within the range of a few generations. But few of the "good families" can trace their names to colonial or independence-movement figures.[32] Men are expected to have a university education. Secondary school and university educations for both men and women of the upper class are expected to be received in Arequipa or Lima.

Ideally, the upper-class mestizo is a leisured intellectual with sufficient income from his lands to make additional work unnecessary. However, within the traditionally large families of the upper class, some children decide upon (or are pressed into entering) professional careers. Among the professions most respected, and which may provide some mobility into the upper class, are medicine and law.[33] Because of the relative leisure of these occupations, at least as practiced in the Peruvian sierra, they permit a high degree of intellectual and political activity on the side.

Most upper-class *puneños* pride themselves as being men of letters, writing poems or essays for the local newspaper, *Los Andes*, or for the sporadic publications of local cultural groups. Because of this high value placed upon leisure, the upper class is slow to concede admission into its ranks to merchants or engineers, that is, men whose work is more time consuming or manual. This rule does not hold true in Juliaca, however, where the city's livelihood and position as a rival to Puno depend upon commerce and industry.[34] The result, as we shall see, is a far more fluid society, but one that is greatly disdained by the Puno elite.[35]

In Puno, style rather than expense of consumption provides a means of discouraging outsiders or *nouveau riche* from attempting entrance

[31] Bourricaud, *Changements*, p. 70.
[32] *Ibid.*, pp. 71–72.
[33] *Ibid.*, pp. 52–57.
[34] *Ibid.*, pp. 64–65.
[35] *Ibid.*

into the upper class. With capital generally tied up in landholdings, there is often little aside from the produce of the land that can be expended on social entertainment. Upper-class homes, although large, are not particularly well maintained, at least on the outside. Automobiles or pickup trucks are purchased for utility rather than display. Liquid assets, where they do exist, are not allowed to be hoarded. As Bourricaud puts it, "wealth is clearly regarded as an occasion, a pretext, or even perhaps as an obligation, for expenditures in making and keeping friends."[36] The test of generosity and of *savoir faire* is entertaining one's friends in Puno's exclusive Club de la Unión or at the expensive Hotel Turista.[37] It is interesting to compare the upper-class and peasant communities for their conspicuous sharing of limited resources in a nonproductive fashion. It appears that social sanctions play a far greater restraining role in these groups than in any others in the society.

While the upper class tries to bar the door to very rapid mobility from below, it feels similarly discriminated against by those above it— the wealthy landowners or mining operators, who permanently live away from the department and who are felt to be exploiting the region's resources without contributing to its cultural development or welfare.[38] This feeling, one might even call it a persecution complex, that wealthy and powerful interests on the coast are manipulating the affairs of the department while draining it of its resources, has produced a curious kind of political radicalism among the upper and middle classes. Despite the very restricted electorate, local Communists have been elected to Congress periodically since the 1930's (1939–1945 and 1956 to the present). Yet their appeal is basically intellectual, and their legislative activity is limited to cultural and educational projects. Schaedel points out that, although the members of the upper and middle classes

prefer radical ideologies that help them express their frustrations and hopes, they are in practice conservatives and disinterested in direct participation ... They especially value stability, order and work as an obligation. Their

[36] *Ibid.*, p. 71, my translation.
[37] Bourricaud describes these tests in some detail, *ibid.*, pp. 70–74.
[38] *Ibid.*, pp. 60–61.

basic attitudes . . . are dependence, fatalism, and pessimism. And they show ambivalence toward cooperation, emulation, individualism, or efficiency.[39]

Nevertheless, in the political ambivalence of some of the upper and middle class can be seen a sort of pragmatic opportunism that belies both their vocal radicalism and their orientation to the *status quo*. Lawyers, who are among the most vocal of the radicals, are reported by many informants to be among the worst exploiters of the Indians. After attracting Indians with legal difficulties to them by virtue of their radical views, they reportedly charge such high fees that, in lieu of cash payments, they often take over their clients' lands, subjecting them to a kind of "debt servitude." As Bourricaud reported, "they purposefully complicate the cases and draw their advantage from this confusion."[40] Though not particularly productive, the redistribution of resources implied in this example shows the upper class to be not entirely devoid of the entrepreneurial qualities they so disdain.

The rigid social barriers to mobility in the altiplano combined with the availability of a more fluid social system on the coast (with greater economic opportunities and material comforts), have traditionally acted to drain the department of its best-trained people among the population. Recently, however, although emigration continues, the ranks of the middle class have increased through the immigration of technically trained or commercially oriented mestizos from the coast and urban areas of other departments. A kind of accommodation by the upper class with this new group (the *forasteros*, or outsiders),[41] has taken place in the service clubs of the department—especially the Lions Club. Here, aspirants for either political or social influence are taken in as members and encouraged to take part in the occasional service activities that the clubs undertake in the community. Presumably, an energetic and capable contribution may be rewarded with election to one of the many club offices.[42] Finally, after one has won acceptance by the club's elite, and possibly an elective or appointive

[39] Richard P. Schaedel, *La Demografía y los Recursos Humanos del Sur del Perú*, pp. 41–42, my translation.
[40] Bourricaud, *Changements*, p. 53, my translation.
[41] This group is discussed in greater detail below.
[42] Bourricaud, *Changements*, pp. 73–74.

public office as well, one might be invited to join the more exclusive Club de la Unión. To succeed in this climb of the social ladder, leisure time and material resources are of great importance. But to proceed too rapidly is to guarantee social resistance. As Escobar points out: ". . . when the individual shows more pronounced tendencies to use his talent for his own benefit, in the form of prestige or economic advantage and when he displays originality in his dress, speech, or actions, the resulting ambivalence is one of blocking him, accompanied by secret admiration."[43]

Included under the heading of "middle class" in the occupational breakdown of Table X were white-collar employees, shopkeepers, medium-scale farmers, and farm administrators. However, some of the doctors and lawyers in the department, and all the teachers, would also fall into this category, as well as such professionals as engineers, agronomists, and journalists.

The number of white-collar employees has grown in recent years with the national government's extension of services to the department, and by the generation of new jobs, especially within the department's development corporation (Corpuno). The second group, that of shopkeepers, includes the large and medium-size store owners in Puno and Juliaca, as well as one or two storekeepers in the smaller towns. The smaller shopkeepers and vendors in the open markets tend to belong to the *cholo* class. The medium-scale farmers are individuals who are employed or self-employed in the cities, having acquired some rural holdings for purposes of social prestige and as a kind of insurance for the future. The chief of the National Agrarian Reform Office, Pompeyo Díaz, told the author that most urban residents in Puno, when they have saved enough money, try to buy a little hacienda for security. Never do they try to improve it, he says. Their only thought is hedging against old age and inflation.[44]

Farm administrators are seldom found living in the cities and do not constitute a very visible sector of the middle class. For political purposes, however, they have disproportionate influence because of their

[43] Gabriel Escobar M., *Organización Social y Cultural del Sur del Perú*, p. 138, my translation.
[44] Interview, Pompeyo Díaz, Puno, April 20, 1965.

vocal and intelligent opposition to the land reform expressed through the medium of the landholders' associations.

In spite of the differences in origins and occupations in the middle class, a few characteristics are important in defining the lower edges of the class. These include fluent Spanish, urban residence (except for the farm administrators), and Western clothing for both husband *and* wife. While these traits may not be highly consequential in terms of economic mobility, they do serve as a means of socially differentiating the middle class from the *cholos* immediately below it.

To some extent, the mestizo middle class collaborates with and provides a mobility channel to the youth of the urban *cholo* group in *barrio* (or neighborhood) sporting and cultural associations. As children of the middle-class mestizos and of the *cholos* often go to school together in the urban centers, they also collaborate in sports clubs that sponsor soccer and basketball teams in the *barrios*, which compete in a number of leagues in the larger urban centers. The *barrio* cultural associations sponsor dancing groups and small *conjuntos* (bands) for the various holiday fiestas throughout the year.[45] The feeling of competition among the *barrios* in Puno appears to be as strong as that reported by Richard Adams in Muquiyauyo, Peru.[46] The result, at the time of Carnaval in February, is a striking series of dances through the streets of Puno by groups from all the social levels and cultural traditions (Spanish, Quechua, and Aymará) represented in the city.

A mestizo group that merits special classification apart from the upper- and middle-class categories used for the urban altiplano society is the provincial elite. With an income that makes residence in the cities of Puno or Juliaca as inconvenient as for the urban upper class to live in Lima, the provincial elite is privileged only in contrast to the peasantry. Called *mistis* or *vecinos* by the rural populations, members of this group are mostly dependent on agriculture, although they may also run small stores and hold appointive public office. "Socially and economically they exploit the Indians and the *cholada*," writes Martí-

[45] Bourricaud, *Changements*, p. 74.
[46] Richard N. Adams, *A Community in the Andes: Problems and Progress in Miquiyauyo*, pp. 66–68.

nez, "by taking advantage of the ties of *compadrazgo* [godfather-hood] and their offices of public authority."[47]

Their prestige, again, is not strictly of birth, as many can date their stay in the department only from the great "landgrab" of the late nineteenth and early twentieth centuries.[48]

Their skills, wealth, education, and Western consumption patterns may be below the levels achieved in Puno or Juliaca, but they are conscious of those standards and use them to maintain strict barriers to social mobility from below. Their active disdain of the *cholos* and Indians appears to be the strongest of any mestizo group thus mentioned.[49] Because they are less able to prevent the economic mobility of the *cholos* and Indians, this social disdain is obviously combined with envy and fear. As a result of tensions provoked by the economic aggressiveness of the *cholos*, some of these provincial *mistis* reportedly have made the costly move to Puno.[50] Thus, in the future, the *cholos* may increasingly provide the upper strata of the provincial urban society, rather than the more Westernized *mistis*.

The Indian Cultural Group

There are problems in giving a general description of life style and attitudinal characteristics of the Indian cultural group, because of its division into Aymará and Quechua subgroups, and because this division is, to some extent, crosscut by the socioeconomic distinction between *colonos* and *comuneros*.

For purposes of a political analysis, the differences between the Quechua and Aymará traditions may be disregarded as fairly irrelevant. Several informants for this study remarked upon the greater autonomy and industriousness of the Aymará peasants. The southern Peru study found that conditions in the Quechua zone in the north of the department, away from the lake, were more stable, and that attitudes were

[47] Héctor Martínez, *El Indígena y el Mestizo de Taraco*, p. 95, my translation.

[48] Raúl Galdo Pagaza, *El Indígena y el Mestizo de Vilquechico*, p. 28.

[49] *Ibid.*, pp. 42–43.

[50] PRPDSP, *Informes*, 5:8.

more conservative.[51] Peasant uprisings in the last century have occurred in both zones. But Escobar concludes that:

as a consequence of the rebellions, those that have evolved most are the Aymará, especially those who live on the shores of the lake. They are the ones who have lost more land. And their participation in commercial activity has re-enforced their individualistic tendencies . . .[52]

However, efforts by local political groups to organize the peasants into syndicates have been successfully undertaken among both peoples. In addition, both groups share roughly similar living conditions, work systems and technology, and patterns of folk custom and belief.

Standards of prestige in the peasant community, according to Bourricaud, include wealth, education, familiarity with the mestizo world, and familarity with the forces of nature.[53]

An Indian's wealth is judged by the number, size, and location of parcels of land he owns, as well as the number and condition of his livestock. He also gains prestige from the way he is able to contribute to the short-run prosperity of the community. As with the mestizo upper classes, liquid assets among the peasants generally are not put to any productive ends. Social sanctions and personal insecurity combine in such a way that an individual prefers to go into debt to sponsor a lively local fiesta than to advance his economic output. As the southern Peru study argues, the "Indians of the highlands do not hoard their profits from years of plenty but spend them at once on festivals, drinks, and attractive articles of minor importance."[54]

A world view characterized by fatalism is reportedly common among the Indian cultural groups.[55] An extensive body of beliefs regarding the relationship of dreams to agricultural events exists in the communities around Lake Titicaca. Magicians and seers are found throughout the area making a living from their interpretations of these

[51] *Ibid.*, p. 33.
[52] Escobar, *Organización*, p. 49, my translation.
[53] Bourricaud, *Changements*, p. 121.
[54] PRPDSP, *Informes*, 5:35, my translation.
[55] A recent survey revealed that in Cuzco, 77 percent of the peasants on haciendas believed it was impossible for any man to change his destiny (*Caretas*, no. 328 [March 15, 1966]: 18).

dreams in addition to their other personal services for the peasants in diagnosing and curing sicknesses.[56] As an illustration of the influence of these magico-religious institutions, Galdo describes a situation in which a peasant leader of a settlement in the pampa of Ilave (province of Chucuito) was advised by an agricultural agent to use disinfectants to combat a worm disease. Before deciding what to do, the peasant

first consulted with a *colliri* [a curer or seer] who was famous in the zone. The *colliri* took several worms and "questioned" them about what they would do in the future. They "responded" that the following year they would go to another *estancia* [or settlement], whereupon the peasants decided not to use the disinfectants.[57]

Distrust of the mestizos is general everywhere, but in the remote communities of both the Quechua and Aymará peoples there is a widespread belief in a light-skinned "Jack the Ripper," who is identified with the mestizo community.[58] Called *ñacaj* by the Aymará and *pishtaku* by the Quechua, this creature allegedly catches and kills his Indian victims in order to extract their fat for use in the lubrication of the mestizos' machinery. The belief has affected research and work projects in various parts of the Andes, including the altiplano, where, after the disappearance of a local villager, members of a Cornell University research team were accused of being *pishtakus* and were forcibly driven out of the village of Accopata in 1963.[59]

Table XI, from the 1961 Agropecuarian Census, reveals the state of agricultural technology in the altiplano. Although for the most part the level of energy use is not much advanced over pre-Conquest times,

TABLE XI

Number of Agropecuarian Units According to Energy Use, 1961

Total Units	Animal	Machine	Both	Human Only
105,691	67,420	458	368	37,445

Source: *Primer Censo Nacional Agropecuario, 2 Julio de 1961*, p. 54.

[56] Galdo, *Economía*, pp. 64–65, 74–86.
[57] *Ibid.*, p. 65, my translation.
[58] Galdo, *Vilquechico*, pp. 53–54.
[59] Castillo, *Accopata*, pp. 81–88.

there are some haciendas that are highly advanced in the use of modern machinery and techniques, such as artificial insemination, barbed wire enclosures, and sheep dips. The animal power used by the altiplano peasant is largely that of the team of oxen for plowing.[60] The technology involved in the final category (human energy only) is similar throughout the Andes, and involves pre-Columbian tools, such as the handmade footplow (*chaquitaclla*).[61]

Although the traditional forms of labor exchange are still practiced in the altiplano, they seem to be on the decline. The most widely known forms include the *ayni*, involving the exchange of labor or tools, usually among the extended family,[62] and the *minka* (or work bee), involving voluntary communal labor for the benefit of either an individual or the community. Among the projects involving *minka* work are road repairs, canal-clearing, raising the beams of a new house, school construction, and plaza improvement.[63] The tradition of *minka* labor was used by former President Fernando Belaúnde Terry to carry out a number of rural development works under the organizational supervision of his Executive Interministerial Commission of Popular Cooperation.[64]

In recent years, the *ayni* system, with its strong sanctions for fairly prompt reciprocity, has generally produced acrimonious dispute over the conditions of "fair" repayment, leading to increased reliance on cash payment for labor.[65] The institution of *ayni* has also suffered from the combination of *minifundia*, the tiny and ever smaller total landholdings per family, and the growing population density in the department. The pulverization of landholdings near the lake and rivers has

---

[60] Galdo, *Economía*, pp. 37–46.

[61] For a detailed discussion of these implements and their uses, see Galdo, *Economía*, p. 608; for comparisons with other sierra regions of Peru, see Richard Adams, *Community in the Andes*, pp. 118–120, and William W. Stein, *Hualcán: Life in the Highlands of Peru*, pp. 90–91.

[62] Martínez, *Migraciones*, p. 23.

[63] Galdo, *Economía*, p. 54; see also Ford, *Man and Land*, pp. 97–98, and Bourricaud, *Changements*, pp. 110–113.

[64] *República del Perú*, Comisión Ejecutiva Interministerial de Cooperación Popular, *El Pueblo Lo Hizo*.

[65] Bourricaud, *Changements*, p. 113, and Castillo, *Accopata*, p. 10.

diminished the need of a peasant for outside assistance.[66] One continuing form of *ayni* is related to the *minka* system itself—that is, the substitution of individuals for one another when called upon for the *minka* work projects. If an individual should seek seasonal work away from his land and be called upon by lot, during this time, to contribute to a community project, a relative or friend may volunteer, or be urged, to take his place in return for a later favor.[67]

These traditions have evolved from pre-Columbian times to provide security to individual families in the event of personal hardships. But, as hardships become general, afflicting *all* members of a community, such arrangements lose part of their value. Especially in recent years, these rudimentary community bonds have been strained by continued economic disaster and the increasing tendency of peasants to seek economic opportunities away from the community. But, as Mangin has pointed out, these ties to the old community sometimes provide invaluable material and moral support to the peasants as they attempt to enter the urban mestizo world.[68]

A. The Comuneros. Although their economic position may be no greater than that of the *colonos*, the *comuneros* enjoy a social advantage over them by virtue of their independence and slightly improved condition of acculturation.[69] Stein has noted this attitude in another section of the sierra, in Hualcán, a community that is divided into two sections, Monus (with a population of *colonos*) and Huanté (with a population of *comuneros*):

Monus and Huanté are ranked with regard to each other, Huanté being considered superior. Huanté people look down on those from Monus as being poor and dependent on their *patrones* [landlords]. Monus people feel that those from Huanté put on airs because they have a few more things. Actually, of course, there are individuals of high status in Monus

---

[66] Martínez, *Migraciones*, p. 23, and Castillo, *Accopata*, pp. 11, 25–26.

[67] Martínez, *Migraciones*, p. 23.

[68] William P. Mangin, "The Role of Regional Associations in the Adaptation of Rural Population in Peru," *Sociologus*, 9 (1959): 23–26.

[69] Martínez, *Migraciones*, p. 26; Pedro Ortiz V. and Raúl Galdo P., *El Indígena de la Isla de Amantaní*, pp. 39–40.

and individuals of low status in Huanté. Still, the poorest Huanté man resents being taken for a resident of Monus.[70]

The *comuneros*, as pointed out earlier in the chapter, are small land-holders, especially numerous in the areas near the lake and rivers of the department. They produce mostly for their own family consumption, although they increasingly market part of their produce. In the case of artisans and the fatteners of cattle, they may use part of their income to purchase foodstuffs.

It was mentioned above that Indians traditionally fail to save their profits from years of plenty, spending them instead on fiestas, and in other nonproductive ways.[71] Nevertheless, the Maryknoll fathers of the Catholic Church have had considerable success among the *comuneros* in setting up savings cooperatives.[72] This is a recent phenomenon, the first such cooperative being founded in Puno in late 1955.[73] Also, limited credit has been made available by the Agropecuarian Development Bank to peasants, with a *cholo* or mestizo as guarantor. Finally, it should be pointed out that many *comunero* parents have encouraged their children to seek an elementary education and have made obvious sacrifices to dress them properly and to forego their assistance in chores at home or in the fields.

The relationship of *comuneros* to the *cholo* and mestizo groups is worthy of discussion. One aspect of this relationship is *compadrazgo*— the practice of naming a friend or relative as the godfather of one's child, at the time of his baptism, first haircutting, marriage, house completion, and other special events. Martínez points out that, in the past, *compadrazgo* was an important means for keeping the extended family's bonds strong. However, in recent years the *comunero* peasant has sometimes invited a mestizo or *cholo* to act as godfather. This, says Martínez, is a "phenomenon encouraged by the search for new signs of emotional and economic security, as well as protection from the external authorities with regard to the incessant struggle for the pos-

[70] Stein, *Hualcán*, p. 220.
[71] PRPDSP, *Informes*, 5:35.
[72] *Ibid.*, p. 28.
[73] *Peruvian Times*, October 12, 1956, p. 13.

session of land . . ."[74] This tendency is not evident on the haciendas, however.[75] Presumably, on the hacienda, contacts with outsiders are rare, and relationships of the peasants with their mestizo landlord and supervisors are fairly inalterable.

Aside from individual cases of *compadrazgo* with the mestizo class, the *comunero* peasant's attitude toward the *cholos* and mestizos remains basically one of fear and distrust. Galdo found in Vilquechico that:

the peasants view those among the *cholada* and *mistis* negatively. Between them there are a series of tensions. They look upon the *cholada* somewhat as traitors to their race. They hate the *mistis*, even though they feign submission and respect in their presence.[76]

Personal frustration, possibly with regard to the linguistic barriers between peasants and mestizos, results in a remarkably aggressive self-assertion among peasants when under the influence of alcohol.[77] Galdo notes that the *mistis* of Vilquechico, when confronted with normally "obedient" Indians who have gotten drunk and become aggressive, call them "hypocrites."[78]

The Cornell University research team reported a local *hacendado's* description of the *comuneros* in Accopata as follows:

There are three classes of Indians: Indians "huacachadores," Indians "humildes" and Indians "Cholos." The Indians "huacachadores" are those who talk all of the time when with Mestizos. They talk unnecessarily, shout, and cry to obtain something for themselves. They are "like thieving dogs." The Indians "humildes" do not talk and they show humility, but they are even greater thieves. In front of a Mestizo, an Indian "humilde" talks in a low voice with his head bowed and appears to be obedient although he may not carry out the wishes of the Mestizo. The Indians "Cholos" who are more acculturated because they have had contact with customs outside of their region—they are the most insubordinate and disobedient to the Mestizos.[79]

[74] Martínez, *Migraciones*, p. 56, my translation.
[75] Abner Montalvo V. and Raúl Galdo P., *Análisis Estadigráfico en Seis Localidades Seleccionadas en la Zona Circundante al Lago Titicaca*, p. 26.
[76] Galdo, *Vilquechico*, pp. 49–50, my translation.
[77] PRPDSP, *Informes*, 5:26, and personal observation.
[78] Galdo, *Vilquechico*, p. 55.
[79] Quoted in Castillo, *Accopata*, pp. 33–34.

This is a striking manifestation of the chasm of distrust and prejudice separating the two groups.

Another manifestation is the Indians' use of their native languages in the presence of representatives of the mestizos, even when they could use Spanish. Clearly, the superior knowledge of and literacy in Spanish among the mestizos has permitted considerable exploitation of the Indians. Yet the Indians' "non-Spanish" has also been a useful weapon, at least for defensive purposes. Bourricaud reports that his own research in Ichu (a peasant community near Puno) was frustrated by this phenomenon. Only toward the end of his stay in the community, as his presence had ceased to be threatening, did he find it possible to interview some of the inhabitants in Spanish.[80]

B. The *Colonos*. Because their distance from urban centers tends to be greater, and because their subordination to individual mestizos tends to be more direct, the *colonos* occupy the lowest grade in the social hierarchy in the sierra, with the least hope of moving out of it. Martínez writes that:

among the *colonos* one notes a lower grade of acculturation. They have few possibilities to emigrate, in some cases for lack of money and in others for lack of clothing. Among them one also notes the highest index of illiteracy for the reason that schools don't exist on the haciendas.[81]

But the combination of outward subservience to, and conscious resentment against, the landowner (or his staff) does not make the *colono* utterly powerless or socially subhuman. Bourricaud writes that, although the *colono* has no control in the hacienda's operations, he is very aware of his interests and will act together with his fellow *colonos* to defend them if threatened by the *hacendado*.[82]

What is very remarkable—if not very surprising—is that the two parties have the sentiment of being exploited. The Indian complains that the lands he has received are of mediocre yield, that their [*colono*] neighbors have been treated better, and that the *patrón* has excessively reserved the best lands for his own use. In short, he has the sentiment that his work is worth

[80] Bourricaud, *Changements*, p. 14.
[81] Martínez, *Migraciones*, p. 26, my translation.
[82] Bourricaud, *Changements*, pp. 127–128.

more than the remuneration he receives. The *patrón* stresses the poor quality of the Indian labor, the negligence of the shepherds who let the sheep die, and the spirit of theft by which he alleges the Indian profitably substitutes the animals of his own flock for those of the hacienda. Distrust is certainly the tone in which the owner's relations are developed with his *colonos*. This distrust gives rise to endless discussions when the question arises of evaluating the payment of services furnished in return for the advantages granted by the *hacendado*.[83]

The services that the *colono* renders the landlord for use of part of his land have been described earlier in this chapter. In addition, there have been personal services, consisting of cooking and housekeeping by the *colono*'s wife or children in the house of the landowner. While these services are supposed to be voluntary and remunerated,[84] they are often forced and gratuitous.[85] The *comuneros* on occasion have also been obliged to render such illegal services to public officials and priests, to pay off fines or debts, or under other more contrived and questionable circumstances.[86] A *colono* is usually protected from these additional abuses by his mestizo landlord, who is in a position to intervene in his behalf. Thus, the *colono*'s lack of freedom is at least accompanied by a certain degree of security, while the *comunero*'s freedom is not only economically uncertain but also politically vulnerable.

Of course, the conditions of *colonos* vary from one hacienda to the next. A recent survey of forty-five haciendas reported conditions for their *colonos* (in terms of housing, wage rates, medical care, school facilities, social benefits, and human relations) poor in 41 percent of the cases, fair in 39 percent, and good in 20 percent.[87] Another study, several years earlier, reported that a few larger haciendas had instituted profit-sharing, joint livestock improvements, and cooperative market-

[83] *Ibid.*, p. 135, my translation.

[84] *Peruvian Constitution* (1933), Article 55.

[85] Ortiz and Galdo, *El Indígena*, p. 35; and Florencio Díaz Bedregal, *Apuntes Para una Reforma Agraria en el Departamento de Puno*, pp. 67–68.

[86] Interviews, Father Robert Kearns, Puno, March 9, 1965; Congressional Deputies Róger Cáceres and Fernando Manrique, Lima, March 27 and May 7, 1965, respectively. See also Escobar, *Organización*, pp. 13–24.

[87] David Brown, "Monthly Report," Iowa State Agricultural Mission, Puno, January, 1965.

ing operations, with very positive results.[88] The head of the landowners' association in Puno has said that many *colonos* lend money to their
landlords, and that their economic position is often the subject of envy
to the *comuneros*.[89] Thus, for example, it is not surprising to find that
the *colonos* in the Taraco area (province of Huancané) could enjoy a
higher level of living than the more numerous free Indians, since the
former enjoyed the use of more land under conditions of greater
security.[90] In addition, "the *colono* may have a larger average livestock
herd than the *minifundista*, if the hacienda administration is indifferent
or generous."[91]

This curious ambiguity between *colonos* and *comuneros* in their economic and social status is significant politically because of the potential
for conflict between the two groups over the subject of agrarian reform.
By offering his *colonos* incremental benefits, a *hacendado* can probably
keep them opposed to the demands by neighboring *comuneros* for expropriation. And if it can be made to appear as if the peasantry is
divided among itself on such a crucial matter, then support for agrarian reform from elsewhere in the political system may be less likely to
materialize.

CONFLICT VERSUS ASSIMILATION: THE *Cholo* AND *Forastero* PHENOMENA

Judging by what has already been stated, tensions seem to exist both
between and *within* the principal cultural groups of the altiplano. Barriers to mobility, such as inequalities in landholding and acculturation,
tend to engender resentments between socioeconomic strata. But the
limited opportunities for social mobility or merely economic better-
ment give rise to competitive behavior within the same socioeconomic
strata (even within the extended family itself).

Bourricaud's conclusion about the predominant type of conflict is
summed up in two hypotheses:

1. The conflicts between *misti* and Indians are much more intense within

[88] PRPDSP, *Informes*, 5:22.
[89] Interview, José Luís Lescano, Puno, April 13, 1965.
[90] Martínez, *Taraco*, p. 30.
[91] Schaedel, *La Demografía*, p. 29, my translation.

the heart of the community or on the hacienda than in a town like Puno. . . .
2. In Puno, the tension is the strongest, not between the Indian group and
the *misti*, but rather within each group, and most of all, within the *misti*
group.[92]

However, the situation in the altiplano is not as simple as the fore-
going would indicate. Although the system bears a striking resemblance
to the plural society model that M. G. Smith describes, there are two
additional subgroupings somewhere in between the mestizo elite and
the Indian mass. These are the *forasteros* (mestizo outsiders) and the
cholos (partly Westernized Indians). The roles they play in the altiplano's social, economic, and political systems must be examined if a
predictive understanding is to be achieved of the feasibility and direction of political change between the two principal groups in the altiplano.

The Cholos

The *cholos* (or *cholada*) are considered by the mestizos to be a
mixture of the worst of two cultures—the Western and the Indian.[93]
They are clearly a culturally mixed group, but the cause for mestizo
concern is more likely the group's rapid growth and challenge to the
old order in economic and political, rather than cultural, terms.

The *cholo*, as the term is used in the southern Peruvian sierra, is
best defined as a bilingual, urban-oriented Indian in search of upward
economic and/or social mobility. The process of becoming a *cholo*, according to Schaedel, is initiated among four types of groups:

The two categories that receive the greatest influx of Indians in the
process of converting themselves into *cholos* are the unskilled workers and
the servants. Both undergo the process of urbanization when they enter
this group, abandoning their rural families and accommodating themselves
to the urban patterns of the lower class.

A third group, which frequently makes the transition from Indian to

[92] Bourricaud, *Changements*, pp. 69–70, my translation.
[93] See the discussion by Frederick B. Pike (*The Modern History of Peru*,
pp. 20–23), concerning the ideological heritages in regard to questions of racial
and cultural mixing.

cholo is that of migratory workers [especially those remaining for more than a year in their new places of work] . . .

The fourth group is formed by Indian conscripts from the armed forces. Although this process is generally imposed on the Indians, . . . in Puno, the Indians have shown much interest in receiving such training.[94]

The lateral mobility of the *cholos* is as marked as their search for upward economic and social mobility. Increasingly freed from ties of village or extended family, *cholo* men wander the sierra seeking opportunities for trade or labor. While some shuttle between the villages and the large market places of the altiplano selling wool or other products on commission for the peasantry,[95] others move between the towns of the sierra and the cities of the coast, handling more specialized goods.

The *cholada* in Puno became a growing and thriving group with the opening of roads and railroads to the coast, and the increased economic opportunities that followed therefrom. This process of cholification was facilitated in some areas by the evangelistic activity of the Seventh Day Adventists, who established a number of missions around Lake Titicaca, beginning at the turn of the century. These missions provided education to many peasant communities for the first time and encouraged economic individualism by their religious strictures against alcoholism, coca-chewing, and the magico-religious practices that constituted a drain upon the community's resources.[96]

Another major factor that prepared part of the peasantry for cholification was the tradition of temporary migration in times of drought or flood to the coast, to the selva, or to the mines of Puno or Cuzco. While the majority of these journeys took many days and were not often repeated, most adult male Indians had made such a trip at least once in their lives, and were at least somewhat familiar with the broad and alien world beyond their own village.[97] These migratory experi-

---

[94] Schaedel, *La Demografía*, pp. 37–38, my translation.

[95] Galdo, *Vilquechico*, p. 45.

[96] *Ibid.*, p. 46; also, interview with Harold Burden, Adventist Mission, Puno, April 21, 1965.

[97] Pedro Ortiz V., *Hacienda y Colonato en Villurcuni*, p. 15; Galdo, *Vilquechico*, p. 48; Martínez, *Taraco*, p. 65.

ences became more widespread and recurrent with the opening of better means of transportation to these outside areas.

Passage from the category of Indian to *cholo* depends upon one's performance of several functions: (1) acquisition of a nonagricultural skill (e.g., salesmanship, auto mechanics, driving a vehicle, construction); (2) knowledge of Spanish, and, for men, some literacy in it; (3) change in apparel from Indian to Western styles for a man, and, for a woman, improved quality of Indian apparel and the use of shoes;[98] and (4), where possible, the acquisition of some liquid capital assets (e.g., cash, a savings account, a vending stall or cart, a bicycle or, ultimately, a motorized vehicle). Other noted characteristics of the *cholos* have been their commercial orientation, their neglect of hygiene and personal cleanliness (carried over from Indian habits), their garish tastes, and the matriarchal tendency of their family life (the mother, as a servant or vendor, often being the principal breadwinner).[99]

In the context of economic development, the *cholada* is the group best predisposed to accept and initiate changes. According to Schaedel, "they represent the element that is the most dynamic and adaptable to rapid changes. They are very energetic and ambitious, being generally free of the social prejudices that tend to inhibit the initiative of both the mestizos and the Indians."[100] The failure to harness this growing social force, Schaedel argues, would cost Peru not only economically, but also politically. If they are frustrated in their search for social and economic opportunities of advancement, "it is probable that the *cholos* would be the base of protest movements and uprisings."[101]

Another description of the *cholada* concludes with the following remarks: "They have an uneasily suppressed desire to develop a species of regional ethnocentrism and to take the initiative politically, as

98 The men clearly abandon the Indian styles of dress (ponchos, knee breeches, sandals, coca bag, and knitted cap) for Western-style work clothes, sport coat, felt hat, and shoes. The women continue to wear multiple skirts, peasant blouse, shawl, and bowler derby, merely improving the quality of the materials used (especially of the outer skirts, shawl, and shawl pin) and wearing shoes.
99 PRPDSP, *Informes*, 5:10.
100 Schaedel, *La Demografía*, p. 48, my translation.
101 *Ibid.*, my translation.

representatives of the native masses, in overthrowing the domination
of the higher classes."[102] This attitude toward the mestizos above and
Indians below them is not uniform everywhere. Martínez argues that
"one notes tensions and conflicts among them [the *cholos*] and especially with the Indians as a result of the struggle for the possession of
the land and of the break from their traditional patterns and values
. . ."[103] Galdo, in his study of Vilquechico, notes that the *cholada* is
divided in its attitude toward the *mistis*. One group emulates the *mistis*,
and another group acts with open contempt for them. The latter,
writes Galdo, "are at odds constantly with the *mistis*, for whom they
have a series of conscious insults, which gives them a certain satisfaction and horrifies the *mistis* who, with great dismay, see this strata
growing day by day and, which is worse, to their eyes, acquiring more
and more economic power."[104]

Cholo nonconformity, according to Escobar, has both its positive
and negative sides. In certain popular art forms—the *huayno* (a kind
of folk song and dance), folk tales, and verbal imagery—the *cholos*
exhibit great creative potential. "Other forms of expression," he writes,
"such as alcoholism and exaggerated sexuality, are manifestly noxious
and probably self-destructive."[105]

Bourricaud is particularly intrigued with the emergence of the *cholada* and the cholification of Puno's culture.[106] The *cholo*, he says, is a
peasant who aggressively used mestizo ties of *compadrazgo* to better
his social or economic position, thence proceeding into the urban society. Here he uses new ties of a less stable or solidary character to
further advance his fortunes. Bourricaud concludes that the *cholo* is
"better armed" for making the transition to mestizo life than might
appear to be the case.[107]

There are some *cholos*, however, that reveal the risks involved in
this transition away from the land. These are the *cargadores* (or bun-

[102] PRPDSP, *Informes*, 5:11.
[103] Martínez, *Migraciones*, p. 18, my translation.
[104] Galdo, *Vilquechico*, 6. 47, my translation.
[105] Escobar, *Organización*, p. 134.
[106] Bourricaud, *Changements*, pp. 215–228.
[107] *Ibid.*, pp. 227–228.

dle carriers), who occupy the lowest social and economic position in the entire society (apart from beggars). Undoubtedly, the possibility of ending up as a *cargador* serves to deter some peasants from leaving the security of their land to try their luck in the cities.[108]

Since literacy is a prerequisite to voting, the *cholada* are important politically because of their partial acculturation. Although their Spanish is not as fluent as that of the middle class, and while many *chola* women are illiterate, many voters come from this group. In 1956 the number of registered voters was 43,312.[109] In 1962 the number had increased to 69,132.[110] This was well below the 1961 literacy estimate of 124,717 (see Table IX), but above the 1959 estimate of upper- and middle-class population of 36,500, including dependents (see Table X). Thus, it appears that the *cholo* class may now hold the largest share of votes in the department.

The Forasteros

One mestizo group that has extensively interacted with the *cholos*, primarily on a commercial basis—but with interesting social and political implications—is the *forasteros*. In the department of Puno in 1961, there were 12,263 residents who had been born in other departments, and 1,013 who had been born abroad.[111] Over half of these "outsiders" were residents in the provinces of Puno or San Román, the administrative and commercial centers, respectively, of the department.[112] Although these numbers undoubtedly include members of the mestizo elite who were born in Lima or Arequipa, they also include many individuals who have come to the altiplano in search of an economic livelihood. They are not integrated rapidly into the social system, because their roots and affiliations belong to some other area. The *forasteros* appear most frequently to be engaged in commercial, government, or missionary activities, although this group would also in-

---

[108] *Ibid.*, p. 45.

[109] *El Comercio* (Lima), June 16, 1956, p. 6.

[110] Hermogenes Vera Salazar, *El Proceso Electoral de 1962 en el Departamento de Puno*, p. 10.

[111] *1961 Census*, 2:8–9.

[112] *Ibid.*

clude such individuals as farm administrators, school teachers, and wives of local residents.

It seems possible that the relatively high number of *forastero* merchants in the department is related to the economic opportunities for trade that exist, but which are not filled by the economically capable families because of the social sanctions that befall the entrepreneur in a society oriented to landholding. Ortiz reports that a number of Italians came to Yunguyo (near the Bolivian border in the province of Chucuito) after World War I to capitalize on the trade between Bolivia and Peru. However, they left as commercial opportunities deteriorated after the fall of the Bolivian currency during the Chaco War (1932–1935). As the Bolivian economy recovered, new traders came to Yunguyo, but, once again, few local residents took advantage of the opportunities. Ortiz says that three of the four store owners in Yunguyo were non-*yungueños*. Five of the eight truck owners, three of the five *restaurateurs*, and all three hotel owners were also outsiders.[113]

An interesting illustration of the *forastero* phenomenon that is also of background importance for understanding recent political developments in the altiplano is the rise of the Enrique B. Cáceres family in Juliaca.[114] Enrique Cáceres, the son of an impoverished former captain in the Peruvian military, was forced to assume the responsibility for nine brothers and sisters at the age of fourteen, when his elder brother died in prison. He began to travel from his hometown of Arequipa to fairs in Juliaca on the newly constructed railroad, peddling such varied products as ironwork, books, paper, medicinal drugs, and glassware, for a German import-export firm. He brought back leather and wool purchased at the fairs from peasants. In 1898 he opened a small store in Juliaca and continued to deal with the German company. As he accumulated more money, he began to speculate in land, buying haciendas in both the altiplano and the department of Arequipa. Because of the shortage of strategic materials during World War II, he enjoyed a great windfall from his large stock of metal goods (plating,

---

113 Ortiz, *Villurcuni*, pp. 83–85.

114 The following material about the Cáceres family is from a series of interviews with Pedro Cáceres Velásquez, Puno, April 2, 6, and 19, 1965.

pots, pans). After the war he abandoned land speculation and gradually expanded his merchandise to include manufactured clothing and denim cloth, corrugated metal roofing, transistorized radios, Japanese bicycles, and even automobiles. For one son, who had become an engineer, he established a construction company, and went into the business of manufacturing piping. For another, who had studied economics, he financed a consulting firm. Both enterprises are located in the Cáceres office building, the tallest and most modern structure in the department.

Enrique Cáceres' children, six sons and one daughter, were born after the father was in his fifties. The oldest son, Róger, ran for and was elected to Congress immediately after his graduation from law school in 1956. He was re-elected in both the elections of 1962 and 1963. The next son, Luís, who managed the store following his father's death in 1964, was elected mayor of Juliaca in 1963. A third son, Néstor, who studied economics and operated the consulting firm, also organized the department's extensive peasant union movement (Frente Sindical de Campesinos) and was elected to Congress in 1963. Two other sons, Oscar, the engineer, and Pedro, a journalist, in their own ways contributed to the others' political planning and success. The youngest son, Jesús, was studying social science at the Universidad Católica in Lima at the time this study was written. The daughter, Aída, was married to an engineer, who administered the concrete tubing factory.

All the brothers were despised by the mestizos of Puno. Even in Juliaca, although Bourricaud reported conditions there differently, the Cáceres family was somewhat isolated socially. It is interesting that the family would thus invest in a political alliance with the peasant clientele from which it derived much of its wealth. The organization of the peasantry, as we shall see later, was initiated in 1961 by Néstor Cáceres with the help of a *cholo* employed by the Cáceres firm, who was fluent in all three languages of the area—Spanish, Quechua, and Aymará. In 1962 the Cáceres brothers inaugurated their own radio station in Juliaca, and in 1963 they started a newspaper in Puno. These combined activities produced striking electoral results. But they also increased the bitterness between the Cáceres family and the mestizo elite of Puno.

Conclusions

Clearly, the political problem for the altiplano, deriving from the traditional castelike separation of mestizo and Indian cultural groups, is the feasibility of *cholo* assimilation into the mestizo cultural and social institutions, although this would lead, as Bourricaud puts it, to the cholification of these institutions.[115] Where this assimilation is blunted (i.e., where *cholos* are allowed economic mobility but not political and social assimilation), the regulative institutions of the political system may be forced into continually arbitrating conflicts between *cholos* and mestizos. If any local political institutions are captured by the *cholos* in a future election, the mestizo minority may be subjected to a process of systematic persecution and resource expropriation that would greatly diminish its remaining power.

To examine the possibilities for revolutionary or evolutionary change in the altiplano, a study in detail of the political events of the period 1956–1966 will be presented in the following chapters. Surface political cleavages are found in many cases to crosscut the deeper socioeconomic and cultural cleavages described here. But events throughout the period, and especially in 1965, revealed that the underlying cleavages could no longer be ignored.

[115] Bourricaud, *Changements*, pp. 216–228.

5

THE GREAT DROUGHT AND ITS
AFTERMATH, 1956–1961

IN 1956, TWO EVENTS TOOK PLACE in the altiplano that had great importance for later developments there. A democratic Presidential election was held for the first time since 1945, and a major drought began, which was to last for two years, seriously upsetting the area's economic and social structure. Emergency relief supplies from the United States alleviated some of the suffering, but the administrators were accused of extensive irregularities in their management of the supplies. Many successful efforts were made by local congressmen and other altiplano groups to acquire development projects for the area. In short, the domestic crisis encouraged a degree of political collaboration and unification in the altiplano that to a large extent cut across party, class, and regional lines. Before new elections were to occur six years later, this collaborative effort was to meet with some success in obtaining a partial redistribution of national resources for the department's benefit.

THE 1956 ELECTIONS

The national elections in June, 1956, followed eight years of dictatorship by General Manuel Odría.[1] The 1956 Presidential elec-

[1] A national election had been held in 1950 in which General Odría was

tion was contested by three parties: the Movimiento Democrático Pradista (MDP), a personalist party organized around the candidacy of former President Manuel Prado (1939–1945); the Movimiento Nacional de Unificación (MNU), a party organized by General Odría and his followers, offering the candidacy of one of his cronies, Hernán Lavalle; and the Partido de Acción Popular (AP), a radical personalist party formed by a young Lima architect, Fernando Belaúnde Terry, to support his own candidacy for President. Besides these largely *ad hoc* parties, there were three fairly well-organized, programmatic parties, the Partido Aprista Peruano (PAP),[2] the Partido Comunista Peruano (PCP), and the newly formed Partido Demócrata Cristiano (PDC). All three ran candidates for Congress, independently, or on the tickets of the other parties—the first two because they were outlawed, and the third because of its weakness in areas other than the south. The *apristas,* a predominantly labor party, with strong support on the northern coastal plantations and in Lima, threw their support to Prado at the last minute, assuring the former President of a narrow victory over Belaúnde, who finished a surprisingly strong second. Communists reportedly divided their support between Lavalle and Belaúnde,[3] although in Puno a Communist ran and was elected to the Chamber of Deputies on the *pradista* ticket as well. The Christian Democrats, supporting Belaúnde for President, got several of their members in Congress, including a senator and a deputy from Puno. Nevertheless, the showing of the joint Acción Popular-Demócrata Cristiano ticket was not as strong as Belaúnde's own showing, and the joint *pradista-aprista* forces won control of a majority of seats in Congress, assuring President Prado of six years of unchallenged Presidential rule.[4]

"elected," unopposed, to the Presidency, which he had seized in a *coup d' état,* two years before. A largely hand-picked Congress was elected with him.

[2] The term *aprista* derives from the letters APRA (Alianza Popular Revolucionaria Americana or Popular American Revolutionary Movement). Originally established as an inter-American political movement, Aprisimo had to acquire a strictly Peruvian name to avoid the constitutional prohibition (Art. 53) against international political parties.

[3] Robert J. Alexander, *Communism in Latin America*, p. 233.

[4] Rosendo A. Gomez, "Peru: The Politics of Military Guardianship," in *Political Systems of Latin America,* ed. Martin C. Needler, p. 311. The Peruvian Congress, by tradition, has been weak and overshadowed by the Presi-

In Puno, Belaúnde got 13,743 votes to Prado's 12,159 and Lavalle's 5,705.[5] The relatively strong showing for the Belaúnde ticket apparently revealed the resentment of *puneños* against both the former administration of Prado and the more recent Odría regime. Among the congressmen elected from Puno, two of the three senators were *pradistas* (Enrique Torres Belón and Juan Manuel Peña Prado, a nephew of the President-elect).[6] The third senator was a Christian Democrat, running on the *belaundista* ticket (Juan Chávez Molina). Three *belaundistas* were elected to the Chamber of Deputies (Teófilo Monroy, Róger Cáceres—a Christian Democrat—and Fernando Manrique—a Communist) along with three *odriístas* (Emilio Frisancho, Julio Jesús Arguedas, and Julian Rivera), and five *pradistas* (José Alemán, Guillermo Briceño, Humberto Eduardo, Ernesto Calmet, and Ernesto More—the last named, a Communist).[7]

THE GREAT DROUGHT: ECONOMIC CRISIS AND FOREIGN AID

In the midst of the elections and the activity preceding them, *puneños* were suffering from the worst drought in many years. First reports in March and April, 1956, estimated crop losses of 80 percent[8] and a threatened 30 percent loss of cattle herds.[9] On May 8, 1956, it was announced that the United States, under the International Cooperation Administration's Point Four Program, would immediately send $3,600,000 worth of foodstuffs to the distressed areas. The Peruvian

---

dent. Nevertheless, the right of Congressional interpellation (*Peruvian Constitution* [1933], Articles 169–171) and censure of ministers (Articles 172–174) gave the Peruvian Congress strong potential powers in the event a President with only minority support in Congress should be elected. Such a reversal of the traditional pattern occurred under the subsequent Belaúnde regime (1963–1968).

[5] *El Comercio* (Lima), July 2, 1956, p. 11 (hereinafter cited in this chapter as *EC*).

[6] Peña Prado's election came by virtue of the electoral board's contrived ruling that the frontrunning senatorial candidate (Daniel Castillo) was really a Communist and not a *belaundista*. Peña Prado had run fourth behind the two *belaundista* candidates and Torres Belón (*ibid.*, July 21, 1956, p. 4).

[7] *Ibid.*, July 2, 1956, p. 11.

[8] *Ibid.*, March 30, 1956, p. 9.

[9] *Ibid.*, April 18, 1956, p. 15.

government, which would oversee the distribution of these foodstuffs, could choose from three methods of distribution: (1) outright donation, (2) donation in payment for work on public works projects, or (3) sale, the income from which would finance such work projects providing employment to the peasantry.[10] On June 14, 1956, three days before the national elections, the first shipment of foodstuffs arrived in the harbor of Mollendo, where it was transferred to a waiting train for shipment to Arequipa, Puno, and Cuzco.[11] The same day it was reported that the Ministry of Public Works would resume operations on a number of roads in the department.[12]

Much of this activity may have been timed by the Odría regime to strengthen the candidacy of its favorite, Lavalle. With Lavalle's defeat, the government's interest in these programs seemed to wane. A month after the elections, El Comercio complained that the government had cynically decided to sell the foodstuffs rather than give them away, and that nothing had been done yet in regard to the road-building program.[13] In the meantime, a massive migration of Indians from the department of Puno was reported in Arequipa, Mollendo, Lima, and other cities along the coast.[14] Also, contraband was reported to be increasing across the Bolivian border.[15]

As a culmination of its earlier requests for aid, the outgoing government of General Odría signed an agreement with the United States on June 30, 1956, to create and develop a program "for the maximum utilization for economic ends of the human and material resources of the Departments of Southern Peru."[16] The United States would contribute $466,750 to this program, which would be called the Plan Regional Para el Desarrollo del Sur del Perú (Regional Plan for the Development of Southern Peru, PRPDSP). The Peruvian government

[10] United States, Department of State, "Press Release 350" (May 26, 1961), The Department of State Bulletin, 44 (June 12, 1961):923.

[11] EC, June 14, 1956, afternoon edition, p. 3.

[12] Ibid., p. 17.

[13] Ibid., July 11, 1956, p. 2; July 15, 1956, p. 19.

[14] Ibid., July 21, 1956, p. 13; November 26, 1956, p. 3; January 3, 1957, p. 11.

[15] Ibid., March 16, 1956, p. 2; June 12, 1956, p. 13.

[16] Ibid., April 9, 1959, p. 13; Peruvian Times, July 6, 1956, p. 2.

would finance the rest in annual allocations in accordance with the program's needs, as decided after preliminary studies.[17] In November, 1956, it was decided that the Peruvian share of the expenses would come from the sale of the emergency foodstuffs, and not from additional allocations from the national budget.[18]

The Fondo Nacional de Desarrollo Económico

At the same time, another development project (this one of national scope) was being created. In September, 1956, two months after the new President and Congress were installed, a bill was proposed in the Senate to create a National Economic Development Fund (Fondo Nacional de Desarrollo Económico, FNDE).[19] After considerable debate and revision, the bill was passed by both houses on December 6, 1956, and promulgated by President Prado on January 10, 1957. As passed by the Congress, the FNDE's object was "to systematically invest the required funds for study and development of public works of a reproductive nature and social need in the various Departments of the Republic."[20] Resources for the FNDE were to come from previous sources of revenue for public works, plus small shares of several other national taxes. The investment plans for each department were to be prepared by each department's Council of Public Works (Junta de Obras Públicas), subject to the approval of the Superior Council of the FNDE, which was to be constituted by the Ministers of Development, Public Health, and Agriculture, along with four delegates, one from each part of the country (north, central, south, and selva). Resources, estimated to reach S/550,000,000 (or $30,000,000) annually, were to be divided among the departments roughly in proportion to population, although no department (i.e., Lima) would be considered as having more than double the average departmental population.[21] In the 1957 budget, however, only S/275,000,000 were allocated to the FNDE.[22] As we shall see in the next chapter, the debates and contro-

[17] Ibid.
[18] EC, April 9, 1959, p. 13.
[19] "Senate Debates," ibid., September 22, 1956, p. 4.
[20] Peruvian Times, December 14, 1956, p. 1.
[21] Ibid., pp. 1–2.
[22] Ibid., January 4, 1957, p. 2.

versy that accompanied the FNDE's first two years of operation were of significance in the development of decentralized institutions in Puno, and several other departments as well.

Other Development Proposals

From the altiplano itself came other proposals and demands for projects, prompted by the economic crisis. The most frequently heard of these was the long-standing request for road work, especially the opening of new roads to the selvatic provinces of the north, and to the departments of Moquegua and Tacna on the coast.[23] Demands were also voiced for the lifting of export duties on Peruvian wool, whose production costs were rising precipitously, largely as a result of the drought.[24] Government financing for the construction of a slaughter-house and refrigerator plant was asked, so that through local processing and storage the fluctuating prices of meat in Lima would not be so harmful locally.[25] As shipments of food by train were running far behind schedule, a great demand arose for construction of an airport in the department, to be located near Juliaca.[26] Construction of a long-projected rail link around Lake Titicaca between Puno and Guaqui, Bolivia, was also asked.[27] Still other work projects were suggested, including the development of Lake Titicaca's hydroelectric and irrigation potential, construction of a cement plant, and countless school construction and other work projects.

The Drought Affair

As the economic and political interests behind these various projects struggled to obtain both public and private support for them, economic conditions continued to worsen in the altiplano, especially at the level of the peasantry. The initial manner of food distribution was exceedingly awkward, supplies being available only at the provincial capitals

[23] See, for example, "Chamber Debates," *EC*, September 12 and 27, 1956, and December 19, 1956, p. 4.

[24] "Senate Debates," *ibid.*, September 20, 1956, p. 4.

[25] "Chamber Debates," *ibid.*, October 4, 1956, p. 12.

[26] "Senate Debates," *ibid.*, August 23, 1956; "Senate Debates," October 1, 1956, p. 4; "Chamber Debates," September 13, 1956, p. 4.

[27] "Senate Debates," *ibid.*, January 17, 1956, p. 6.

and a few other urban centers, where they were sold by bagloads only, and not at all on Sundays.[28] If peasants had the money for such purchases, they had to travel a considerable distance to get them. Late in October, 1956, the Lions Club of Puno offered to make deliveries to outlying districts, and to operate a small store in Puno, in the back of the warehouse where the supplies were stored, selling the foodstuffs in any amount at the official prices.[29] Because of the inadequacy of the railways to ship the food rapidly, some of it was reported to be rotting in storehouses in Arequipa and Mollendo.[30] But even when the supplies reached the altiplano, they were slow in being sold because of the peasants' limited purchasing power. Most sales reportedly went to *hacendados*, who used the foods both to keep their *colonos* content and to feed their livestock.[31]

Powdered milk, which was given to the peasants in CARE packages distributed by the Seventh Day Adventists, was said to be unpopular, and was looked upon with distrust. In one case, a group of American tourists, fishing along the Ramis River, were attacked and beaten by peasants who accused them of trying to poison their children with the powder.[32] Because of inadequate instruction, much of the milk was wasted. In some cases, peasants fed the milk to their starving cattle, whereupon the cattle died of diarrhea.[33] Everywhere, peasants were reported to be living on roots, seed, and, if they were fortunate enough, fish.[34] A sample survey of thirteen thousand families throughout the department found that 54 percent had no money, no work, and no food.[35] According to Senator Chávez Molina, cattle-rustling was becoming a major problem.[36] Indians mortgaged and sold their lands in desperation; some went so far as to sell their children.[37] Handicrafts

[28] *Ibid.*, September 11, 1956, p. 15; September 18, 1956, p. 15.
[29] *Ibid.*, October 28, 1956, p. 15.
[30] *Ibid.*, November 17, 1956, p. 3.
[31] *Ibid.*, May 22, 1960, p. 6.
[32] *Peruvian Times*, October 4, 1957, p. 2.
[33] *EC*, February 22, 1957, p. 13.
[34] *Ibid.*, February 11, 1957, p. 11; March 22, 1957, p. 13.
[35] *Ibid.*, April 19, 1957, p. 3.
[36] "Senate Debates," *ibid.*, December 18, 1957, p. 4.
[37] *Ibid.*, January 19, 1957, p. 11.

flooded the markets of the altiplano, Cuzco, Arequipa, and even Lima, as Indians turned their hands to whatever might bring them money for food. But there were few buyers. In Cuzco, peasants with alpaca wool were forced to sell it at one-fifteenth of the price it formerly had commanded to be able to buy cornmeal.[38] Perhaps the most alarming story from this period was the report from Pilcuyo (located between Ilave and Juli in the province of Chucuito), that in a nearby village a twelve-year-old girl had been tied to a huge funeral pyre and burned to death to appease the gods and to persuade them to bring rain.[39]

Criticism of the food relief program in the altiplano was widespread. Spokesmen for the landowners' associations demanded to know why the public works projects to provide employment for the peasants had not begun.[40] They were particularly motivated in these demands by the fear that the peasants, especially those of the neighboring villages, would seize the haciendas or sack them.[41] Roadwork jobs for 6,000 had been promised at the end of the first year of the drought.[42] But a year later, after another year of drought, the number of people employed in roadwork was only 2,046, and they had not worked or been paid continuously because of machinery breakdowns and delays from Lima.[43]

In Congress, the minority Opposition, composed of the followers of Odría and Belaúnde, the Christian Democrats, and the Communists, condemned the *prado-aprista* administration (now called the *convivencia*, or "common-law marriage") for its mishandling of the crisis. The leader of the attack, Puno Senator Juan Chávez Molina, repeatedly demanded a strict accounting of the foodstuffs, their shipment and storage costs, and the use made of the net income from their sale.[44]

[38] *Ibid.*, January 21, 1957, p. 11.

[39] *Ibid.*, November 17, 1956, p. 3.

[40] *Ibid.*, January 15, 1957, p. 15; January 16, 1957, p. 3; June 6, 1957, p. 13; June 26, 1957, p. 3; January 26, 1958, p. 3.

[41] Interview, Atalo Gutiérrez, Puno, April 12, 1965; *EC*, April 1, 1960, p. 15.

[42] *EC*, June 15, 1956, p. 17.

[43] *Ibid.*, June 26, 1957, p. 3.

[44] See the "Senate Debates," *ibid.*, September 26, 1957, pp. 4, 12; November 13, 1957, p. 4; December 17, 1957, p. 4.

Because of the government's prolonged silence, two *pradista* deputies from Puno renounced their membership in the MDP and became Independents, "convinced that their efforts to serve their region had been in vain."[45] Taking advantage of the intensified political atmosphere, a wealthy landowner and *belaundista*, Juan Zea Gonzales, established the first radio station in the department, *Radio La Voz del Altiplano*, on March 1, 1957. Although claiming that "its doors are open for all political viewpoints,"[46] Zea's radio served to focus attention on the economic crisis and its political ramifications. This was also the function of the department's daily newspaper, *Los Andes*, whose editor, Samuel Frisancho, was imprisoned for seven months during the Prado Administration, for his bitter critiques.[47]

As the second year of drought drew to a close, 24,000 tons of foodstuffs were reported to be still undistributed in the department.[48] But in the third year, after a season of normal rainfall, the United States declared that it would discontinue its aid shipments on April 1, 1958, at the start of the harvest season. This was condemned throughout southern Peru, since many families had been unable to buy seed and fertilizer and had planted little or nothing.[49] The United States, however, apparently judged the area to be without need on the basis of the undistributed foodstuffs. Unable to force the Peruvians to give the food away, the Americans probably had no alternative. With the discontinuation of food deliveries, the special machinery for relief distribution was scrapped, and the remainder of foodstuffs was put under the authority of the PRPDSP. However, the attack on the Prado Administration and the former Executive Committee in charge of supplies to the south greatly intensified after the new session of Congress began in mid-August.[50] On October 21, 1958, the coordinator general of sup-

---

[45] *Ibid.*, December 19, 1958, p. 3, my translation.

[46] Interview, Juan Zea Gonzales, Lima, May 6, 1965.

[47] Interview, Samuel Frisancho, Puno, April 13, 1965.

[48] *EC*, December 8, 1957, p. 15. As *Caretas* later reported, of the 23,000 tons of grain sent to southern Peru, "22,000 was destined for . . . the mills of Arequipa and Cuzco, and only 1,000 was sent to the center of the affected zone" (no. 179 [June 12–25, 1959]: 22).

[49] *EC*, March 23, 1958, p. 13.

[50] See, for example, the almost daily accounts of *la affaire sequía* (the

plies to the south, Ingeniero Rodolfo Collantes, was replaced (*subro-gado*) by the Minister of Agriculture, for "errors committed by him in the performance of his duty."[51] But Chávez Molina and the Opposition were not willing to see the matter closed so easily. After a fierce debate in the Chamber of Deputies, it was finally agreed that an investigating committee should be established to look into the many charges that had been made.[52] However, the only deputies from Puno or Cuzco on the committee as it was later set up were loyal *pradistas*.[53] Despite the opportunity the committee might have had to defend the Administration's handling of the foodstuffs in the face of the continuing attack, it never issued a report and still had not met by mid-1961.[54]

On March 25, 1959, *El Comercio* reported that seven men involved in the relief operations had been arrested in Cuzco, charged with irregularities in the milling and resale of the American grain.[55] At first it was announced that the trial would be carried out by the Cuzco Provincial Council's Committee against Speculation and Monopoly.[56] Later, it was announced that the Superior Court of Cuzco would try the seven and would subpoena six others, including three ex-Ministers of State.[57] Immediately, the chief of fiscal police (*jefe de policía fiscal*) was sent to Cuzco to conduct his own investigation. In the meantime, the men had been released.[58] Early in June the Peruvian Supreme Court took charge of the case, appointed an *ad hoc* judge to review the papers as collected in Cuzco and to pronounce final judgment.[59] Although issuing occasional statements that the papers were under careful scrutiny and that a decision was near, the subpoenas were never

drought affair) in *ibid.*, October 15, 1958, p. 4; October 20, 1958, p. 15; October 21, 1958, pp. 2, 3; October 25, 1958, pp. 3, 4.

[51] *Ibid.*, October 22, 1958, p. 3; October 25, 1958, p. 3.

[52] "Chamber Debates," *ibid.*, December 13, 1958, p. 4; December 16, 1958, p. 4.

[53] *Ibid.*, January 17, 1959, p. 4.

[54] *Ibid.*, May 15, 1961, p. 4; August 11, 1961, p. 4.

[55] *Ibid.*, March 25, 1959, p. 3.

[56] *Ibid.*, April 5, 1959, p. 4.

[57] *Ibid.*, April 13, 1959, p. 3.

[58] *Ibid.*, April 16, 1959, p. 15.

[59] *Ibid.*, June 6, 1959, p. 4.

issued, and the case entered a limbo until it was declared officially closed by the military junta that seized power after the elections of 1962.[60]

If the charges of corruption and irregularities in the distribution of foodstuffs were never cleared up, the Administration of Manuel Prado at least tried to give a partial accounting of its use of the "net" income from the food sales. Of the S/268,000,000 ($13,900,000) of foodstuffs admittedly received from the United States, the Treasury Minister (Ministro de Hacienda) reported in 1961 that S/127,000,000 had been obtained from sales, of which S/61,000,000 had been spent on a variety of public works projects. Another S/8,800,000 had been returned to the peasants in food donations. Another unspecified amount had gone into the construction of eight large houses in Puno. And the balance had been used to defray shipment, storage, and other handling costs.[61] But what had happened to the other half of the foodstuffs, for which there was no reported sale? This strategic omission brought the immediate criticism of El Comercio.[62]

The "drought affair" (la affaire sequía) was significant as a general phenomenon that forced many conflicting interests in the altiplano to make a common front against the national government in Lima. It was also important for the timing of some of its twists and turns. For that reason, our narrative will return to the "affair" in the next chapter. However, before we begin a discussion of the specific events leading to the creation of the Puno development corporation (Corpuno), it is useful to review the course of the various proposals for development made in the wake of the great drought.

[60] Ibid., August 21, 1962, p. 4. It is worth noting that even the American official in charge of supervising the foodstuffs had not escaped the scandal. He was removed from his post in 1958, after buying a hacienda and utilizing ICA technicians to make improvements in the area. After leaving his post, he remained in Peru, taking a job as a technical advisor in the Peruvian Ministry of Agriculture. This information was reported by Sam Coon, a former congressman from Oregon (1953–1957, Republican), who had been deputy director of the ICA mission in Peru at the time (reported in ibid., July 24, 1959, p. 1).

[61] Ibid., May 31, 1961, p. 4.

[62] Ibid., June 1, 1961, p. 2.

ATTEMPTS TO INITIATE LOCAL DEVELOPMENT PROJECTS

The Peru-Bolivia Plans

The most extensive set of proposals was presented by Puno's *pradista* senator, Enrique Torres Belón, for a massive hydroelectric and irrigation project utilizing the waters of Lake Titicaca. With apparent support from the Prado government, a Mixed Peruvian-Bolivian Commission was arranged to discuss these and other Peru-Bolivia development projects, including a Puno-Guaqui railroad (finally linking the tracks of both countries); a highway connecting Desaguadero and the Peruvian port of Ilo (providing La Paz with more direct access to the coast); and an oil pipeline from Bolivia to Ilo along the same route.

Senator Torres Belón was asked to preside over the Mixed Commission, which began its deliberations on January 30, 1957, in La Paz.[63] Within three weeks an agreement (*convenio*) was signed to initiate studies on all the proposed projects.[64] On November 20, 1957, the Peruvian Congress approved the agreement. The Christian Democrats, who had their greatest political support in Arequipa, were the only major group voting against the agreement. Presumably the La Paz-Ilo road and oil pipeline, by bypassing Arequipa, would adversely affect that city's commerce.[65] Nevertheless, in subsequent years, little was heard of these joint projects.

In 1961 technicians from the General Electric Corporation conducted an exhaustive study of the altiplano's watershed and Lake Titicaca, to provide an estimate of the hydroelectric-irrigation project. Their estimate of between $250,000,000 and $300,000,000 was so prohibitive as to cause the project to be left dormant to the present.[66] The Puno-Guaqui railroad proposal has also been quiescent. After lengthy studies and new meetings, another agreement was signed with Bolivia approving construction of the La Paz-Ilo road.[67] However, by 1967, the

[63] *Ibid.*, January 30, 1957, p. 2.
[64] *Ibid.*, February 20, 1957, p. 3.
[65] At least this was the explanation given by deputies from Moquegua in Congress ("Chamber Debates," *ibid.*, November 21, 1957, p. 4; November 23, 1957, p. 4).
[66] *Ibid.*, July 19, 1961, p. 3.
[67] *Ibid.*, October 15, 1963, p. 1.

only concrete result of the Peru-Bolivia negotiations has been the construction of a new one-lane concrete bridge on the main road between
Puno and La Paz over the Desaguadero River, inaugurated in August,
1964.[68]

Road Construction

The remainder of the road-building and -maintenance program in
the department fared a little better, although it was frequently snarled
by regional rivalries over competing routes. Some money had gone into
improvements of the Puno-Moquegua road, which was almost impas-
sable except to pack trains and pedestrians.[69] After repeated delays, the
Ministers of Agriculture and Interior finally reported that two thousand workers were being employed on the road.[70]

Several months later, the "progress" on the Puno-Moquegua road
was reported to be so "great" that in Arequipa a demand arose for a
direct road link between Cuzco and Arequipa, bypassing the altiplano,
"to balance the situation."[71] The chambers of commerce of both cities
sought to set up ad hoc committees to mobilize support for such a road,
which, besides providing work for thousands of destitute Cuzco and
Arequipa peasants, would cut 165 kilometers off the altiplano route
(through Juliaca).[72] Curiously enough, a month later, construction on
the Puno-Moquegua road halted and the heavy machinery was transferred to another road project in Trujillo, in northern Peru.[73] The out-
cry of Puno and Moquegua congressmen was immediate and furious.[74]
Yet nothing was done to renew operations. After heavy rains damaged
the old Arequipa-Puno road,[75] demands were heard for its widening
and paving as well.[76] When only minor maintenance work was per-

---

[68] Los Andes (Puno), August 22, 1964, p. 6 (hereinafter cited in this chapter as LA).

[69] A little over a million sols were set aside for improvements on election
day, 1956 (EC, June 17, 1956, p. 3).

[70] Ibid., January 20, 1957, p. 4.

[71] Ibid., September 11, 1957, p. 15.

[72] Ibid., January 5, 1958, p. 11; January 10, 1958, p. 15.

[73] Ibid., February 11, 1958, p. 4.

[74] "Chamber Debates," ibid., February 12, 1958, p. 4.

[75] Ibid., March 2, 1959, p. 13.

[76] Ibid., March 6, 1959, p. 13; March 14, 1959, p. 11; May 1, 1959, p. 11.

formed to reopen, but not improve, the road, demands were renewed in Arequipa and Cuzco for a direct Arequipa-Cuzco road.[77] The opposition in the altiplano to such a road was undoubtedly as sharp as the opposition in Arequipa to the Puno-Moquegua and La Paz-Ilo roads, which would bypass Arequipa (see Map 4).

During the Congressional debates on these programs, the *belaundista* senators from Cuzco (Antonio Astete Abril and Sixto Coello Jara) accused the Peruvian Corporation (operators of the Southern Railways) of playing upon these rivalries to maintain their own predominance in transport in southern Peru.[78] By the mid-sixties there had still been no approval for an Arequipa-Cuzco road, and the approval for major construction on the Puno-Moquegua road was finally given only in July, 1964, at the insistence of the Puno development corporation.[79] However, as we shall see in Chapter 8, the step-up in road construction on the Puno-Moquegua road contributed to the aggravation of Juliaca-Puno relations within the altiplano and led to a new postponement of construction. Clearly, the rivalries of all the major cities in southern Peru for preferential treatment in road-building constituted a vicious circle that could tempt (or frustrate) a national government into ignoring the problem altogether.

Road-building in the selva was every bit as sporadic and frustrating. In June, 1956, S/370,000 had been promised for road work on the Sandia-Tambopata road, and S/270,000 were promised for the Macusani-San Gabán road[80] (see Map 5). Although work was soon initiated on these roads, tropical weather conditions, machinery breakdowns, and bureaucratic delays in establishing routes and providing wages for the crews frequently caused work suspensions.[81] In August, 1957, the United States signed an agreement with Peru to provide a $2,000,000 loan for selva access roads in the departments of Cuzco and Puno.[82] But, although several hundred workers were utilized on the two roads

[77] *Ibid.*, July 16, 1959, p. 19.
[78] "Senate Debates," *ibid.*, October 27, 1959, p. 4.
[79] *LA*, July 28, 1964, p. 1.
[80] *EC*, June 17, 1956, p. 3.
[81] *Ibid.*, March 7, 1957, p. 15; October 17, 1958, p. 13; January 30, 1959, p. 12.
[82] *Peruvian Times*, April 26, 1957, p. 3.

MAP 4. ACCESS ROUTES: ALTIPLANO TO COAST

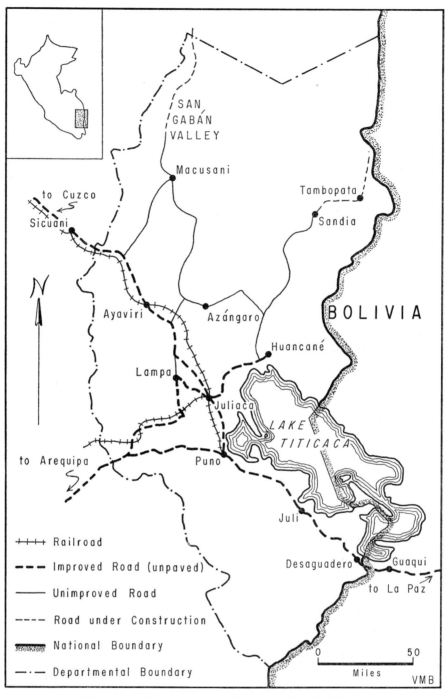

SAN
GABÁN
VALLEY

Macusani

Tambopata

to Cuzco

Sicuani

Sandia

BOLIVIA

Ayaviri

Azángaro

Huancané

Lampa

Juliaca

LAKE
TITICACA

to Arequipa

Puno

Juli

+++ Railroad

- - - Improved Road (unpaved)

—— Unimproved Road

- - - Road under Construction

National Boundary

-·- Departmental Boundary

Desaguadero

Guaqui

to La Paz

0   50

Miles

VMB

MAP 5. ACCESS ROUTES: ALTIPLANO TO SELVA

in Puno, preference by the Peruvian government was given to the Cuzco roads. By late November, 1957, only seven kilometers of an estimated eighty had been completed on the Tambopata road.[83]

Because of the desperate conditions on the altiplano, thousands of peasants poured into the selva area, following the various road crews. But, if their intention was to find and claim new parcels of land near the road, they were disillusioned. Although the government had set aside seventeen thousand hectares in the Tambopata Valley for "Indians," the formalities involved in obtaining title to the land were reportedly so complicated that the claimants often had to mortgage at least a part of their future crops to get the skilled legal assistance needed to properly process their claims.[84] Furthermore, it was reported that job preference, at least on the San Gabán road crews, was given to peasants from Cuzco.[85]

In May, 1959, work on the San Gabán road temporarily came to a halt over charges that it had wandered off route.[86] With the $2,000,000 from the United States reportedly spent, it seemed that construction would be permanently suspended. As a disastrous flood had struck the altiplano, leaving thousands homeless, demands were heard throughout the department that the San Gabán road construction be resumed, utilizing the unemployment and homeless peasants from the altiplano.[87] A delegation from the province of Carabaya went especially to Lima to state its case.[88] Work was resumed a month later, continued for a year, and then discontinued again.[89] Work was resumed sporadically in 1962 and 1963. But the San Gabán road was still unfinished in 1965.[90]

A higher priority was given to the Tambopata road.[91] Instead of re-

---

[83] EC, November 29, 1957, p. 15.
[84] Ibid., January 28, 1958, p. 3.
[85] Ibid., October 17, 1958, p. 13.
[86] Ibid., December 6, 1960, p. 4.
[87] Ibid., May 28, 1960, p. 15.
[88] Ibid., June 8, 1960, p. 7.
[89] Ibid., August 3, 1960, p. 9.
[90] Ibid., April 18, 1965, section two, p. 1.
[91] Interview, Senator Juan Zea Gonzales, Lima, May 6, 1965; interview, Earl Smith, A.I.D., Lima, March 26, 1965.

lying on private contractors to do the job, the government deployed the Fourth Engineer Battalion of the Peruvian Army into the Sandia area in 1961 to organize and supervise the work on the Tambopata road. A $1,000,000 loan from the United States provided equipment, while American foodstuffs were supplied to the workers and their families, all of whom were from the altiplano. By early 1965, work was progressing so well that limited automotive transport was finally possible from Sandia to San Juan del Oro, at the head of the Tambopata Valley. Over sixty kilometers had been opened in four years.[92] Cost of transport to and from the Tambopata Valley was expected to drop from 2 sols to less than 0.10 sols per quintal[93] per kilometer, with the opening of the road to regular truck transport.[94]

The Protection and Processing of Wool

Because of the competition of synthetic fibers and the rising costs of forage crops as a result of the drought, livestock-raising *hacendados* had demanded the removal of the 20-percent export duty on alpaca wool and the 10-percent duty on sheep wool, as well as technical assistance to all stock-raisers for quality improvements.[95] The export duties were subsequently removed for one year, but, at the same time, import duties on synthetic fibers were removed at the insistence of the Lima textile industry.[96] As the wool export duties were about to be reimposed a year later, the landowners' associations, as well as Senators Chávez Molina and Peña Prado, spoke out for import duties on the wool substitutes.[97] Spokesmen for the textile industry responded with dire predictions that important factories would be closed if the government taxed the wool substitutes.[98] Frequent advertisements appeared in *El Comercio* in February, 1958, from both sides, trying to show the extent of suffering that victory of the one side would inflict

92 John G. Waggener, "Army Civic Action in Southeastern Peru," *Peruvian Times*, March 5, 1965, pp. 4–5.

93 One quintal equals 220.46 pounds.

94 Waggener, "Army Civic Action," p. 5.

95 *EC*, May 18, 1956, p. 3; "Senate Debates," September 20, 1956, p. 4.

96 *Ibid.*, October 21, 1956, p. 4.

97 *Ibid.*, July 8, 1957, p. 13; August 1, 1957, p. 13; "Senate Debates," December 4 and 5, 1957, p. 4.

98 *Ibid.*, February 12, 1958, p. 9.

upon the other. *El Comercio's* editors cautiously sided with the wool growers,[99] but no support was given the *hacendados* by the government on this issue. By June, 1958, the *hacendados'* attack had shifted to a demand that artificial wool be labeled as such,[100] and a continued demand for lifting the export duties and other taxes on wool.[101] At the same time, the government was requested to aid the transformation of the sheep industry from wool to meat production.[102]

In December, 1958, it was reported that six thousand quintals of wool were stored in Ayaviri without a buyer.[103] Thus, Puno congressmen promptly supported a demand by Senator Torres Belón that the government facilitate the installation of an American wool-processing plant in Ayaviri, by permitting the importation of the plant's used machinery (from Texas, where it was then established).[104] The Administration, however, refused to grant the permit, after a debate in which it is said that the Ministers of Agriculture and the Treasury were overruled by President Prado and the Ministers of Labor and Development.[105] In the fight that preceded (and followed) this decision, the National Agrarian Society actively supported the altiplano's cause, while the National Textile Committee and the Peruvian Labor Federation opposed it.[106] Although originally a member of the Pradista Party, and never officially severing his ties with it, Senator Torres Belón appears to have passed more and more frequently into the Opposition after this conflict. As we shall see below, his fight for the processing plant continued into other contexts, and contributed to the successful passage of the Corpuno bill.

The Slaughterhouse and Freezing Plant

The possibility that sheep raisers might reorient their efforts to meat production provided some momentum to the plan for a local slaughter-

[99] *Ibid.*, February 15, 1958, p. 2; February 17, 1958, p. 2.
[100] *Ibid.*, June 13, 1958, p. 13.
[101] *Ibid.*, July 18, 1958, p. 15.
[102] *Ibid.*, April 6, 1958, p. 13; May 23, 1958, p. 13.
[103] *Ibid.*, December 2, 1958, p. 15.
[104] "Senate and Chamber Debates," *ibid.*, February 10, 1959, p. 4.
[105] *Ibid.*, June 5, 1959, p. 13.
[106] *Ibid.*; April 24, 1959, p. 13.

house and freezing plant along the Southern Railways line in Cabanillas, near Juliaca. The attempt to raise money for it had begun in 1953, under the impetus of the local landowners' associations.[107] Such a plant, it was estimated, would save over a million kilos of meat lost in the shipping of live cattle to Lima, which at the market prices then prevailing would amount to at least S/7,000,000 a year.[108] In September, 1958, a loan of S/2,500,000 was announced by the Agropecuarian Development Bank for the project.[109] Almost immediately, however, the plans were stalled by the organization of a group in Arequipa seeking their own freezer plant.[110] Although they did not also seek construction of a slaughterhouse, their attempts to finance the separate freezer plant evidently slowed the Puno group's progress.

After great effort, the goal of S/8,000,000, needed for the Puno venture, was reached in 1959.[111] Significant among the funds was a loan of S/90,000 from the Maryknoll fathers' peasant-financed savings cooperative.[112] In April, 1960, the plant commenced operations.[113] However, by the end of 1962, it was bankrupt. The reasons given were shortage of funds and mismanagement.[114] Operations remained paralyzed until October, 1964, when the Puno development corporation (Corpuno) bought the plant and proceeded to reorganize and remodel it for ultimate resale to private enterprise.[115]

The Cement Plant

A similar private industrial venture, the construction of a cement plant in Caracota, near Juliaca, was likewise slow in reaching fruition. The high costs of Lima cement were blamed partly on transportation costs and partly on the monopoly control of the Portland Cement Com-

---

[107] *Ibid.*, July 24, 1957, p. 17.

[108] *Ibid.*, August 10, 1957, p. 13.

[109] *Ibid.*, September 1, 1958, p. 13.

[110] *Ibid.*, September 28, 1958, p. 13.

[111] *Ibid.*, October 3, 1959, p. 15.

[112] *Ibid.*, April 12, 1959, p. 13.

[113] *Ibid.*, April 7, 1960, p. 13.

[114] *Ibid.*, February 10, 1964, p. 9; interview, Donald Jackson, Stanford Research Institute, Cuzco, May 3, 1965.

[115] *EC*, October 10, 1964, p. 15.

pany, which operated the two plants in Lima (and three others in northern and central Peru).[116] All of southern Peru shared these grievances, but the formation of a united political front in the south was impeded by the demands of each major department for its own cement plant.[117] However, in May, 1957, it was announced that the Caracota plant had obtained financing from the House of Rothschild and from a Danish source, which would furnish the equipment for the plant.[118] Production within two years was promised.

But after the disastrous Arequipa earthquake of January 15, 1958, demands for Arequipa's own cement plant intensified. Portland Cement "generously" lowered its prices to aid in reconstruction, thus confounding plans for both the Arequipa and Puno plants.[119] Soon thereafter, Portland bought a large share of the Caracota stock.[120] J. V. Salazar, a frequent contributor from Puno to *El Comercio*, wrote that the shareholders of the Caracota plant had been systematically subjected to "the fear of ruinous competition," and placed in "the dilemma of giving a majority share in the planned regional factory to the coastal enterprise . . . or of having its prices ruined."[121]

Development of the Caracota plant seemed to be paralyzed for several years. In late 1961, when shipments of cement from Venezuela and Bolivia arrived in southern Peru, prices from Lima briefly dropped again.[122] At this time, it appears that the Portland Company either got its majority share of the plant's stock, or made a deal with its owners, for construction began in Caracota in December, 1961, and proceeded rapidly through 1962. After the military *coup* of 1962, demands were heard from Arequipa that the plant be nationalized.[123] In Puno a rumor was heard that the plant would be moved to Arequipa.[124] But, although work had been completed, the plant had still not opened by mid-

---

116 *Ibid.*, April 30, 1957, p. 13.
117 *Ibid.*
118 *Ibid.*, May 9, 1957, p. 5.
119 *Ibid.*, February 13, 1958, p. 15; February 26, 1958, p. 3.
120 *Ibid.*, August 28, 1958, p. 15.
121 *Ibid.*, September 7, 1960, p. 9, my translation.
122 *Ibid.*, November 14, 1961, p. 9; December 3, 1961, p. 11.
123 *Ibid.*, December 26, 1962, p. 7.
124 *Ibid.*, July 18, 1963, p. 11.

1963.[125] The first law promulgated by incoming President Belaúnde was the liberation of foreign cement from import duties.[126] A few months later, presumably because of the threat of cheaper imports into southern Peru, the Caracota plant was finally opened.[127]

The Asillo Irrigation Project

One of the Peruvian government's public works financed with the moneys from the sale of American foodstuffs, was the Asillo irrigation project in the provinces of Melgar and Azángaro, begun late in 1956.[128] In mid-1958, after the discontinuation of American aid, the project was halted and seven hundred workers were laid off.[129] However, work was later resumed and the project was completed in 1959, at an estimated cost of $525,000.[130] Ironically, the completion of the project was greeted with criticism, because the workers were let go.[131] A Cornell University research team later reported that the new irrigation canals remained practically unused until 1961, because of high taxes for usage combined with inadequate instruction on their use, conflicts over which Peruvian agency should administer the project, and general distrust and ignorance of the program's goals.[132] Those few families that chose to participate in the program tended to use the water for family needs and for their animals, rather than to irrigate their lands.[133] However, careful technical assistance was subsequently planned to help the beneficiaries of the project use the water more productively, and irrigation committees were formed in several communities to supervise and assist these programs.[134] Also, an extension of canals to new parcels, as well as new projects of a similar type in the

---

[125] *Ibid.*, August 9, 1963, p. 11.
[126] *Ibid.*, August 10, 1963, p. 4.
[127] *Ibid.*, November 9, 1963, p. 13.
[128] Hernán Castillo *et al., Accopata: The Reluctant Recipient of Technological Change,* p. 68.
[129] *EC,* July 2, 1958, p. 13.
[130] Castillo, *Accopata,* p. 68.
[131] *EC,* November 18, 1959, p. 15.
[132] Castillo, *Accopata,* pp. 69–72.
[133] *Ibid.*, p. 70.
[134] *Ibid.*, p. 69.

pampas of Ilave and Taraco, were made possible by new American loans in 1964.[135]

The Juliaca Airport

The remaining project of importance actively sought in this period was the opening of air communications from the department to the outside world. A field in the hills above Puno had once been a landing stop for occasional Lufthansa flights to La Paz before the Second World War. The field had not been used since 1939 and was deemed too small for use in the 1950's.[136] After the war Puno and Juliaca continually fought over the site of a new airport, with the result that none was ever built.[137] With the emergency created by the drought, the congressmen of the altiplano unanimously urged construction of a field in the flatlands near Juliaca.[138] Work was begun in 1957 at a cost of S/1,500,000, with an opening planned for 1958.[139] However, although work was completed, the field's inauguration was held off until an airline could be persuaded to provide service to the area. Finally, after no commercial lines showed an interest, the Peruvian Military Air Transport agreed to provide once-a-week service, and the field was opened in an impressive ceremony on September 9, 1959.[140]

CONCLUSIONS

There was an apparent unity of the altiplano's major groups (expressed at least in fairly unified action on the part of the department's congressmen) in a common cause that appeared to make of the department a highly integrated and demanding actor in the national system, seeking, by reason of domestic disaster, a partial and temporary redistribution of the nation's resources. The major exceptions to this departmental cohesion were the peasants who emigrated from the area,

[135] United States, Agency for International Development, *Cooperation for Progress*, (Lima, 1965), p. 16.

[136] *EC*, October 26, 1957, p. 15.

[137] *Ibid.*, September 10, 1959, p. 13.

[138] "Chamber Debates," *ibid.*, September 13, 1956, p. 4; "Senate Debates," October 1, 1956, p. 4.

[139] *Ibid.*, December 22, 1957, p. 15.

[140] *Ibid.*, September 10, 1959, p. 13.

and those among the merchants, lawyers, and public functionaries who may have had something to gain, either from the remaining groups' general misfortune, or from loyalty to the outside groups in control of the national system.

The altiplano's cause was made more potent by the alliance of other southern departments also suffering (although to a lesser degree) from the drought. In this conflict between southern Peru and the rest of Peru, a partial resolution was achieved with the emergency injection of resources from wholly outside the Peruvian system. The premature discontinuation of this aid (i.e., before many families could recoup or build up the necessary capital for resumption of normal agricultural production, and before any projects or enterprises to aid the department's economic growth could be developed) left the department apparently as vulnerable economically and cohesive politically as it had been during the peak of the drought. With national elections drawing near and a new economic disaster about to befall the department, Puno's hand might be strengthened in obtaining some of the sought-for concessions.

Nevertheless, the altiplano's geopolitical position in southern Peru complicated her utilization of the general opposition sentiment in that region. Within the "alliance" of southern departments, some of the common interests (e.g., work projects, new roads, wool- and meat-processing plants) were crosscut by the specific preferences of each department. Parties and groups elsewhere in Peru, attempting to maintain the *status quo*, could play upon these cleavages to divide and conquer the demanding south. Even in the altiplano, signs of potential divisiveness were apparent. Conflicting priorities with regard to different coastal (or selvatic) access roads, or airport sites, had the effect of dissipating the effectiveness of the region's demands as a whole upon the national system.

Party loyalties, which could be expected to crosscut regional loyalty to some extent, did not appear to do so. At least no interdelegation fighting was reported at this time among Puno congressmen, although it was to become extensive at a later date. In contrast, some defections (both formal and informal) from the Administration's party were reported. Even the cleavage between *hacendado* and Indian was minimized, as *hacendados* led the battle to get public works projects, food-stuffs, and other benefits for the desperate (and dangerously restive) peasants. Although, at a later time, land seizures were again to take place in the altiplano, none were reported during the period of the drought and its aftermath.

6

THE CREATION OF CORPUNO, 1960–1962

NEW DOMESTIC CRISES—floods and heavy frosts—renewed the demand for action in improving economic and social conditions in the altiplano. A bill was proposed in Congress to set up an autonomous local development agency. Debates on the proposal took place both in Puno and in Lima. Cleavages in the local system, which were exploited from the national level to some extent, delayed final approval of the bill. But, as new elections neared, accompanied by unfavorable foreign publicity, the national administration was obliged to grant support to the bill.

A NEW WEATHER CRISIS

The rains of the 1959–1960 agricultural season were exceedingly heavy. On February 2, 1960, it was reported that seventeen thousand hectares in the province of Huancané had been flooded by the Ramis River, affecting the crops and homes of over fifteen thousand peasants.[1] As no roads in the altiplano were paved, many of the major thorough-

[1] *El Comercio* (Lima), February 2, 1960, p. 1 (hereinafter cited in this chapter as *EC*).

fares were closed or seriously damaged by the heavy rains.[2] The Puno congressmen unanimously urged a resumption of American relief and of public works programs.[3]

Then, in the middle of March, a premature end of rain was followed by a series of disastrous frosts, which destroyed an estimated 90 percent of the crops in the province of Chucuito, according to the SCIPA (agricultural extension) agent in Puno.[4] *El Comercio* estimated that the damage in Puno caused by the "black frost" might be worse than that which the area suffered in 1956–1957.[5] Indians from the province of Chucuito were reported to be pouring into Puno for help and proceeding on to Juliaca and Arequipa. Children were again reported being sold by their parents. *Hacendados* in the Huancané and Azángaro areas expressed the fear that, as in the early 1920's, the Indians would resort to sacking the haciendas in order to survive.[6] According to SCIPA calculations, the losses from the frosts amounted to over S/200,000,000, and yields in the department as a whole were only a third or fourth of the amount normally harvested.[7]

In response to this latest crisis, the Minister of Agriculture, in August, 1960, announced that the Prado Administration was trying to get more foodstuffs from the United States, and that the Agropecuarian Development Bank was applying for an American loan for broadening its credit operations.[8] Renewed demands for the investigation and trial of the administrators of the earlier relief program were ignored, but the Minister declared that the remaining foodstuffs and income from that program had all been allocated for use in the devastated area.[9]

Another direct effect of the new crisis was the enactment of the Corpuno (Puno development corporation) bill. Before these debates

[2] *Ibid.*, February 5, 1960, pp. 1, 5.
[3] "Senate Debates," *ibid.*, February 4, 1960, p. 4; "Chamber Debates," February 10, 1960, p. 4.
[4] *Ibid.*, March 26, 1960, p. 11.
[5] Editorial, *ibid.*, March 28, 1960, p. 2.
[6] *Ibid.*, April 1, 1960, p. 15.
[7] *Ibid.*, May 2, 1960, pp. 1, 13.
[8] *Ibid.*, August 27, 1960, p. 1.
[9] *Ibid.*

can be discussed, however, a review of the other post-1956 development programs and agencies should be made.

OTHER DEVELOPMENT PROGRAMS IN PERU

The first of these development programs, the American-sponsored Regional Plan for the Development of Southern Peru (PRPDSP), although aimed at establishing an overall development program for the region, largely degenerated into a research project, with a few public works administered with the funds derived from the sale of American foodstuffs. Separate Peruvian funds were never allocated to the program, although some of the findings and recommendations in the PRPDSP's final report were useful for later programs. The joint supervision and planning of these larger projects, envisioned when the PRPDSP was first set up under the regime of outgoing President Odría, were evidently objectionable to the incoming Prado Administration. Prado chose instead to set up a separate fund for development projects of nationwide scope. Thus, the major result of the PRPDSP's endeavors was a report of twenty-nine volumes, published in 1959, which catalogued and analyzed the physical and human resources of southern Peru.[10]

As a nationwide version of the American-sponsored Southern Peru Plan, the National Economic Development Fund (FNDE) was proposed by the Prado Administration and passed by Congress in December, 1956. In its first year of operations, there was a bitter struggle between the managers of the FNDE and the departmental public works councils over the development programs for each region. As a result of this conflict, an amendment was offered in the next session of Congress to the law establishing the FNDE, that would close the councils altogether.[11] After considerable debate, and protest from the departments against bureaucratic centralism, the Senate changed the amendment so that it suspended the councils' operations for a year only, during which time the Fund could plan and carry out a year's operations independently. This was the version that finally passed both houses in November,

[10] PRPSDP, *Informes.*
[11] *RC,* October 5, 1957, p. 2.

1957.[12] *El Comercio* doubted that the FNDE could efficiently organize its operations within even this one year's time, judging by the difficulties it had had in the first year of operations.[13]

A year later, it reported that, of the S/18,000,000 allocated for works in Puno in 1958, not a single centavo had been spent in the department.[14] In March, 1959, after the FNDE and the councils were again in joint operation, Samuel Frisancho, the editor of *Los Andes*, told *El Comercio* that "of the total funds assigned to [Puno] by the Fund, only about 60 percent is being invested, and this in a direct form, without the knowledge of the Council . . ."[15] The fear that the FNDE could not be held locally accountable for its projects, combined with a general distrust of centralized administration, created a widespread opposition to the FNDE in many regions.

CORPUNO—AN AUTONOMOUS LOCAL DEVELOPMENT CORPORATION

About the same time that the FNDE bill was originally passed, another bill was passed in the Peruvian Congress to create an autonomous, self-financing Corporation for Reconstruction and Development (CRYF) in Cuzco. On February 10, 1957, CRYF was installed.[16] One of the first projects that the new entity undertook was a study for a massive hydroelectric project on the Urubamba River at the foot of the fabled ruins of Machu Picchu, north of Cuzco.[17] The magnitude of the project undoubtedly captured the imagination of many *puneños*, who soon were asking that a similar autonomous corporation be set up for Puno.[18] *El Comercio* gave editorial support to such a proposal,[19] but nothing was done about it at the time.

However, after the Administration's frustration of the series of projects mentioned above—especially the failure to get approval for the

[12] *Ibid.*, November 19, 1957, p. 4.
[13] Editorial, *ibid.*, November 20, 1957, p. 2.
[14] *Ibid.*, November 24, 1958, p. 15.
[15] *Ibid.*, March 31, 1959, p. 6, my translation.
[16] *Ibid.*, February 11, 1957, p. 3.
[17] *Ibid.*, March 18, 1957, p. 13.
[18] *Ibid.*, April 6, 1957, p. 13.
[19] *Ibid.*, April 8, 1957, p. 2.

transfer to Puno of the wool-processing plant from Texas, attitudes among the Puno delegation to Congress were more prepared for such a legislative proposal. When Deputy Róger Cáceres presented his bill for the creation of a development corporation in Puno, he had their immediate and enthusiastic support.[20]

The Proposed Bill

Cáceres' proposal was to set up an autonomous, semirepresentative agency, the Corporación de Fomento y Promoción Social y Económico de Puno (Corporation of Development and Social and Economic Promotion of Puno, popularly nicknamed "Corpuno"), which would operate with its own resources to plan and execute development projects of all kinds. Its goals were broadly characterized as "economic technification" and "cultural and social integration." More specifically, they included agrarian reform, colonization projects, industrialization, promotion of savings and credit cooperatives, craft development, rural and urban housing development, improved animal husbandry, aid to agricultural, mining and commercial growth, and "socioeconomic programs to benefit the peasant communities and to actively integrate them into the social life of the country."[21] To carry out these ambitious goals, the Corporation would be authorized to make international financial agreements, contract loans and credits in Peru or abroad, expropriate urban or rural lands, organize and finance enterprises and colonization projects for peasants, participate in private corporations, administer public aid in cases of emergencies, organize cooperatives, construct public works, and protect local products.[22]

The Corporation could also act as representative or partner of national banks, and international or national programs, such as the FNDE, SCIPA, the Puno-Tambopata Program, and the Peace Corps.[23] But, in addition to outside aid, the Corporation was authorized to fi-

[20] "Chamber Debates," *ibid.*, November 6, 1959, p. 4.
[21] *Proyecto de Ley*, Article 3, as passed by the Peruvian Chamber of Deputies, October 5, 1960, reprinted in Róger E. Cáceres Velásquez, *Puno: Universidad y Corporación*, pp. 93–95, my translation.
[22] *Ibid.*, Article 6, pp. 96–97.
[23] *Ibid.*, Articles 8 and 9, p. 98.

nance its broadly conceived operations with the following incomes (*rentas*), as proposed by Cáceres:

    a. A 0.25-percent *ad valorum* tax on imports into the department,
    b. A 0.10-sols tax on each pack of nationally produced cigarettes; and a 0.50-sols tax on foreign cigarettes,
    c. A 2.5-percent tax on cattle sales in the department,
    d. A 2.5-percent tax on *auquénido* wool exports from Peru, (i.e., ⅛ of the total export duty would be returned by the national government to Puno's Corporation),
    e. Donations from private or public entities, and
    f. The proceeds from all investments made by the Corporation.[24]

These funds would belong exclusively to the Corporation, being directly consigned to the Corporation's accounts by the collection agencies involved. The only partial control was the requirement that these accounts be made available for public scrutiny.[25] Cáceres estimated that the Corporation's income from taxes alone would exceed S/50,000,000.[26] In addition, the Corporation would take over all of the former Public Works Council's activities, including the theoretical administration and planning of the FNDE's financial allotments to the department.

Perhaps the most interesting aspect of the proposed new Corporation was its internal structure. The Corporation was to be governed by an elective, functionally representative Departmental Assembly. Although administered by a manager (*gerente*), with the assistance of an appointive Technical Committee, both would be under the supervision of a Directorate elected by and responsible to the Assembly. The Assembly was to be composed of thirty-seven delegates, organized into five committees, as follows:

    1. Committee of Public Services, formed by seven delegates from the field offices of the Ministries of Development, Agriculture, Education, Health, and War, as well as from the Technical University of the Altiplano and the national Charity [Beneficencia] Society.

---

[24] *Ibid.*, Articles 10–14, pp. 98–99, my translation. See below for changes to this section of the bill.
[25] *Ibid.*, Articles 15 and 16, p. 100.
[26] *EC*, October 6, 1960, p. 17.

2. Committee of Municipal Delegates, formed by representatives from each of the nine provincial councils in the department.

3. Committee of Production Delegates, formed by elected representatives of the departmental associations of commerce, industry, landowners (*grandes y medianos productores agropecuarios*), labor, white-collar workers (*empleados*), and peasants (one elected each from the Quechua and Aymará sectors), for a total of seven.

4. Committee of Professional Delegates, formed by the elected representatives of the departmental societies of agronomists, civil engineers, doctors, primary school teachers, secondary school teachers, lawyers and economists (and accountants), for a total of seven.

5. Technical Committee, formed by six delegates appointed by the President of the Republic, chosen from among the nominees of seven national organizations: the Agrarian Reform Institute, the Peruvian Association of Agronomy Engineers, the Peruvian Indian Institute (Instituto Indigenista), the Peruvian Society of Economists, the Technical University of the Altiplano, the Peruvian Association of Civil Engineers, and the Peruvian Federation of Cooperatives. A seventh appointee would exercise the presidency of the Assembly and preside as well over the Directorate of the Corporation.[27] Members of the Technical Committee would, unlike the others, be salaried, although the other delegates would be paid during the period in which the Assembly was to meet.[28]

The Assembly's duties would include approval of the annual budget and report of the president, and study and approval of plans, programs, and all other activities of the Corporation during each year, as well as the annual election of the six members of the Directorate.[29] The Directorate was to be composed of two members chosen from the Technical Committee, and one from each of the other committees.[30] The Directorate would meet regularly to execute all accords of the Assembly and to supervise administrative matters.[31]

Passage of the Corpuno bill promised a fairly substantial redistribu-

[27] Cáceres, *Puno*, Article 34, pp. 104–106.
[28] *Ibid.*, Articles 35, 41, pp. 106, 107–108.
[29] *Ibid.*, Article 46, p. 109.
[30] *Ibid.*, Article 37, p. 106.   [31] *Ibid.*

tion of national resources to Puno's benefit. Compared to the Public Works Council, which the Corporation was intended to replace, the new organism would enjoy approximately ten times the former's income, as well as being able to engage in activities of far broader scope than strictly public works. In addition, none of the members of the Public Works Council were responsible locally for their actions. All were appointees, removable only by the President of the Republic.[32] The Puno Public Works Council admitted in 1960 that its operations had been irregular because of the Administration's frequent withdrawal of funds to cover budgetary deficits, and that the allotments to Puno under the FNDE had never corresponded to the level guaranteed by the FNDE law.[33] Nevertheless, the Council's members criticized the new Corpuno bill as unrealistic in both its goals and its expectation that it would actually generate any more money than the Public Works Council had.[34] Cáceres' position was that the representative nature of the Corporation's Assembly would make the Administration more hesitant to hold back or withdraw funds from the Corporation, while the ability to seek foreign aid would substantially increase these revenues.[35] In fact, the proposed Corporation resembled a kind of state within a state—a unique method of decentralizing a unitary political system without embracing outright the federal principle.

Debate and Passage

After presentation of the bill by Cáceres, and its endorsement by Puno deputies and others, the bill passed to the Chamber's specialized committees for review. During this time, a public assembly was held in Puno to discuss the new project. Criticism of the Prado Administration and the Public Works Council was evidenced, and general support was shown for the more autonomous proposed Corporation.[36] After further discussions among themselves, the Puno deputies agreed upon

[32] *Ley 11908*, summarized in "Comunicado de la Junta de Obras Públicas," reprinted in *Los Andes* (Puno), January 19, 1960, p. 4 (hereinafter cited in this chapter as *LA*).

[33] *Ibid.*, January 19, 1960, p. 4.

[34] *Ibid.*, January 21, 1960, p. 3.

[35] Interview, Róger Cáceres, Lima, May 7, 1965.

[36] *LA*, September 27, 1960, p. 1.

some changes to the bill, which were incorporated in the Congressional committees. [37]

The first half of 1960 was marked with flood and frost disasters and the demand of congressmen from Puno for aid and new public works. The Administration's response, in the next session of Congress, was to release the Corpuno bill from its several committees. It was passed by the Chamber without any apparent opposition on October 5, 1960, and sent to the Senate.[38]

Later in October, a round-table debate was called in Puno by leaders of the radical Society of Lawyers, challenging the Corporation bill as not going far enough in terms of finance and popular representation. The officers of the Public Works Council joined in the attack, questioning, as noted above, the Corporation's unrealistic goals and ability to obtain the expected funding.[39] Most important, however, was the criticism of Cáceres' "personalist ambitions."[40] A few days later, a town meeting (cabildo abierto) was called, and, before a much larger audience, the Corpuno bill was debated for seven hours. Finally, it was given a vote of confidence.[41]

Part of the opposition to Cáceres can be attributed to the maneuvering of other political groups in the altiplano, trying to build up support for their electoral campaigns in 1961–1962. Róger Cáceres' brother, Néstor, was at this time actively organizing a series of peasant unions, using the extensive resources of his family. This development clearly threatened the traditional bases of political strength in the department.

But hostility to the Cáceres brothers received its greatest expression with regards to Róger Cáceres' maneuvering on another bill that was considered of importance to the department's mestizos, the bill to create the Technical University of the Altiplano. Cáceres, who had originally proposed the University's creation in 1957, had been es-

[37] The most important of these was the addition of the Committee of Production Delegates described above. Interview, Victor Sotomayor, secretary of Corpuno, Puno, April 5, 1965.
[38] "Chamber Debates," EC, October 6, 1960, p. 17.
[39] LA, October 17, 1960, p. 1.
[40] Ibid.
[41] EC, October 23, 1960, p. 9.

pecially critical of the revisions made by Senator Torres Belón and approved by the Senate in February, 1959.[42] Instead of closing ranks to support the Senate's version, Cáceres continued to push for his own version, giving credence to the charge that he wanted credit for the bill more than he wanted the bill passed.[43] He was supported, however, by other Christian Democrats, including Senator Chávez Molina, who put the blame on the *apro-pradistas* for delays in bringing *either* version of the University bill to a vote in the Chamber.[44] In coverage of the University and Corporation issues in *El Comercio* and *Los Andes*, it is the former issue that commanded the attention of newsmen and congressmen alike, although in terms of total cost or potential socioeconomic development its impact would appear to be far more limited than that of the Corporation. Late in December, 1960, the Chamber passed the University bill, with the Torres Belón revisions. All the Puno deputies, including Cáceres, supported it.[45]

In the Senate, Chávez Molina opened the campaign for passage of the Corpuno bill in January, 1961, with an attack on the political interests in the nation who had opposed the wool-processing plant and who were now opposing the Corpuno bill.[46] "A popular clamor," said Chávez Molina, had arisen in Puno for passage of the bill, yet the Administration ignored it.[47] Although he was exaggerating his case somewhat, it is true that a petition, urging passage of the bill, was circulated throughout the province of San Román and signed by more than half of the estimated fourteen thousand adults of the province. A delegation of fifteen then journeyed to Lima to present the petition to the Senate.[48] A Frente Departamental Pro-Corporación was formed under the leadership of one of Cáceres' lieutenants, Atalo Gutiérrez, a *cholo*, and secretary-general of the Peasant Union Front (Frente Sindical de Campesinos, FSC) that the Cáceres brothers had organized.

[42] See his analysis of the Torres Belón bill in Cáceres, *Puno*, pp. 13–40.
[43] *LA*, October 31, 1960, p. 4; *EC*, December 2, 1960, p. 9.
[44] "Senate Debates," *EC*, December 19, 1960, p. 4.
[45] "Chamber Debates," *ibid.*, December 29, 1960, p. 4.
[46] "Senate Debates," *ibid.*, January 21, 1961, p. 4.
[47] *Ibid.*
[48] *Ibid.*, March 7, 1961, p. 9.

Gutiérrez prepared a series of peasant demonstrations in Puno and other provincial towns in support of the bill.[49]

Although the popular base for this movement was possibly as wide as Chávez Molina and Cáceres claimed, the real impetus for passage of the bill appeared to come from outside of Peru altogether. On April 7, 1961, *Time* published an account of the mismanagement of the United States relief to Puno that bore the title "Stealing from the Starving."[50] This reopened the old drought affair with a vengeance. *El Comercio* claimed that the "name of Peru has been sullied by the cynicism and evil of the *convivientes* [i.e., APRA and the *pradistas*]."[51] Fresh data and allegations on the relief irregularities came from Puno,[52] and the fiscal investigators handling the legal case in Lima announced that their pronouncement on the case was almost ready.[53]

At about the same time, the Puno agencies of SCIPA, the Agropecuarian Development Bank, and the Puno-Tambopata Program announced that the 1961 losses from frosts were S/138,000,000, or about half of the expected crops.[54] Food reserves were almost used up, and a new wave of emigration, crime, and general misery was predicted.[55]

On May 3 it was announced that the special congressional investigating committee would have its report on the relief irregularities ready by the time Congress would meet again.[56] In the meantime, it was reported from Washington that an auditor of the United States International Cooperation Administration had reported to an American house investigating committee that the *Time* charges were basically true.[57] Soon afterward, however, the United States State Department declared that the news stories were exaggerated and that the relief

---

49 *Ibid.*, May 27, 1961, p. 4.
50 "Stealing from the Starving," *Time*, April 7, 1961, p. 36.
51 *EC*, April 11, 1961, p. 2.
52 *Ibid.*, April 13, 1961, p. 9.
53 *Ibid.*, April 18, 1961, p. 1.
54 *Ibid.*, April 27, 1961, p. 9.
55 "Editorial," *ibid.*, April 28, 1961, p. 2.
56 *Ibid.*, May 3, 1961, p. 4.
57 "Editorial," *ibid.*, May 19, 1961, p. 2.

supplies had averted serious unrest. But the State Department also made it clear that the Peruvian government's choice of commercial sale of the foodstuffs had been its own responsibility, as was the selection and administration of public works projects.[58] Thanking the State Department for its "expression of confidence," the Peruvian Treasury Minister proceeded to issue an accounting of public works expenditures from the relief moneys.[59] As we saw above, however (Chapter 5), he left over half the foodstuffs unaccounted for and prompted a renewed attack by the editors of *El Comercio*.[60]

In this atmosphere, the Corpuno bill finally reached the Senate floor on July 1, 1961. However, a series of attempts to initiate debate failed for lack of a quorum. In a bitter speech on July 17, Senator Torres Belón attacked the Administration, denouncing its cynical discrimination against Puno and demanding that action be taken on the Corpuno bill.[61] These sharp words by a member of Prado's own party achieved their effect, and debate on the bill began two days later.[62] After opposition was expressed to the funding provision establishing a 2.5-percent tax on cattle sales (which allegedly would raise the price of meat in Lima and other urban areas), a compromise was reached, raising the direct share that the Corporation would get of the 20-percent national *auquénido* wool tax (from 12.5 percent to 50 percent), and deleting the cattle sales tax. The bill was then passed on July 20, 1961.[63] Five months later the bill was promulgated into law by President Prado.[64]

A special commission, set up in accordance with the law, prepared a set of supplementary statutes, which were approved in Lima, April 27, 1962.[65] The official installation of the Corporation was held off until after the June elections of 1962. But nine days after the military

[58] United States, Department of State, "Press Release 350" (May 26, 1961), *The Department of State Bulletin*, 44 (June 12, 1961): 923.

[59] *EC*, May 31, 1961, pp. 4, 7.

[60] *Ibid.*, June 1, 1961, p. 2.

[61] "Senate Debates," *ibid.*, July 18, 1961, p. 1.

[62] "Senate Debates," *ibid.*, July 20, 1961, p. 4.

[63] "Senate Debates," *ibid.*, July 21, 1961, p. 4.

[64] *Ibid.*, December 21, 1961, p. 4.

[65] *Ibid.*, April 28, 1962, p. 4.

coup of July 17, 1962, the Corporation was formally installed by Colonel Miguel Salas, the acting military prefect of Puno.[66]

CONCLUSIONS

The attempt by Puno legislators (Róger Cáceres and Juan Chávez Molina, in particular) to cast aside the older Public Works Council for the creation of a more ambitious and broadly based development corporation was successful only after it had passed through a number of political trials and been aided by continued internal disaster and by embarrassing propaganda from completely outside the Peruvian system.

The political trials emanated from a series of cleavages within the Puno system, some of which were exploited from the national level, others naturally dividing the *puneños*. Among the natural cleavages were resentments of local aspirants for political office against the energetic and personalist behavior of Róger Cáceres (who boasted, for example, that he had introduced more legislation than all the other deputies from Puno combined).[67] In addition, his brother's organization of the peasants into unions had awesome political implications. Clearly, unless Cáceres' impressive record could be sullied somehow, he would not only be re-elected, but he might also be able to get some of his followers elected.

Another cleavage was between issue areas and the differential priorities given them by groups in the Puno system, for example, mestizos valuing a new university more than the proposed Corporation, and *cholos* and entrepreneurial *forasteros* (represented, for example, by the Juliaca petitioners) who valued the Corporation. As both of these new institutions would be located in the city of Puno, there might appear to be no geopolitical cleavage involved. However, the broader development goals of the Corporation, as compared to the Public Works Council, may have meant a relative cutback in urban public works in Puno relative to rural and provincial projects. In addition, substantial economic development might be of greater benefit to Juliaca than Puno unless it was carefully controlled. The provisions for demo-

66 *Ibid.*, July 27, 1962, p. 9.
67 Róger E. Cáceres Velásquez, *Mensaje a los Puneños*, p. 23.

cratic participation (however indirect), which were written into the Corpuno law by Róger Cáceres, may have constituted a potential threat to such traditional central control.

This apparent preference by many residents in the city of Puno for the Public Works Council was exploited by the national government, which resumed funding the Council in 1960.[68] The Council aggravated the divisiveness in the department by focusing on traditional rather than economic development projects. Its first decision was to authorize the construction of a municipal theatre for Puno.[69]

The Corpuno bill's two victories, in the Chamber and the Senate, ultimately owed much of their success, it seems, to the timing and nature of events quite apart from the merits of the legislation itself. In the Chamber, passage followed a year of extremely severe crop losses in the altiplano, the final defeat of the textile plant project, and the national scandal over relief irregularities stemming from the 1956–1957 droughts. The bill's passage in the Senate, and presidential promulgation soon thereafter, followed repeated serious crop losses and embarrassing publicity given Puno's troubles in *Time*. Without these external pressures and local disasters, it seems possible that continued manipulation of the potential cleavages within the Puno system would have made passage of the Corpuno bill politically unnecessary for the Prado Administration.

In any case, the creation of Corpuno loosened the cohesion of the department and made political cleavages once more inevitable. Henceforward, politics in the Puno subsystem would not be so easily manipulated from outside the altiplano.

[68] *LA*, January 21, 1960, p. 4.
[69] *EC*, December 23, 1960, p. 15.

THE ELECTIONS OF 1962 AND 1963

THE ELECTIONS OF 1962 and 1963 were accompanied by the organization of peasant syndicates and a considerable enlargement of the electorate. Events from 1956 to 1962 had an apparent impact upon local voting, as leftist Opposition candidates won easily over their more conservative opponents, including those who had been identified with the incumbent Administration. However, deepening differences among the leftists over personal and other matters caused considerable bitterness and conflict.

THE 1962 NATIONAL ELECTIONS

In June, 1962, Peru was to have a national election. By late 1961 it was becoming clear that there would be a wide field of parties contending for the Presidency, as well as for seats in Congress. The *apristas*, whose party had been legalized by the Prado Administration in return for their support of his legislative program, were running a full slate of candidates, headed by Víctor Raúl Haya de la Torre, their candidate for President. The supporters of former President Manuel Odría, had reorganized themselves as the Unión Nacional Odriísta (UNO), preparing a slate of candidates headed by Odría, who had returned from abroad to seek the Presidency. Fernando Belaúnde Terry, the young architect and leader of the Acción Popular party (AP), had continually toured the country during the Prado regime, organizing committees and urging a program of decentralized economic development, especially in the sierra and selva. His candidacy in 1962 was a foregone conclusion as early as 1956. The Christian Democrats (Partido Demócrata Cristiano, PDC) entered a separate slate of candidates, although they had run on the Belaúnde ticket in 1956. Their candidate for President was Héctor Cornejo Chávez.

The Communists, although still outlawed as such, organized a popular front party called the Frente de Liberación Nacional (FLN). (The organizational meeting of the FLN was reportedly held in the home of Ernesto More, the Puno Communist who had been elected to Congress in 1956 on the *pradista* ticket.)[1] Their Presidential candidate was a retired general, César Pando Egúsquiza. Other parties running Presidential candidates included the Socialist Party (PSP) and the Social-Progressive Movement (MSP). President Prado's own party, the Movimiento Democrático Pradista (MDP), briefly tried to regroup around the candidacy of Pedro Beltrán, Prado's controversial Prime Minister for three years. But, because of Beltrán's unpopularity and Haya de la Torre's determination to run for President himself, a coalition was formed, called the Alianza Democrática (AD), which incorporated a few *pradistas* into the basically *aprista* Congressional list, seeking thereby to legitimize the *apristas*.

In Puno, Congressional tickets were put forth by the AP, PDC, AD, UNO, FLN, and two other groups calling themselves the Unión Departamental Puneñista (UDP) and the Movimiento Agrario Departamental (MAD), both loosely organized conservative parties, representing landowning interests. This profusion of political candidates and activity was prompted in part by the general opposition in the department to the Prado Administration, and in part by the increased voter registration in the department from 43,312 in 1956[2] to

[1] Salomón Bolo Hidalgo, *Cristianismo y Liberación Nacional*, p. 20.
[2] *El Comercio* (Lima), June 16, 1956, p. 6 (hereinafter cited in this chapter as *EC*).

69,132 in 1962.[3] Both factors seemed to invite the politically ambitious to try out for themselves the new conditions for getting elective offices.

The Organization of the Peasants

The most dramatic departure from previous campaigns was the organization of rival peasant fronts by the Communists and the Christian Democrats. Although the number of voters in the department was limited by a literacy requirement, virtually eliminating the peasantry as an electoral force, the disasters and scandals of the 1956–1962 period were accompanied by attempts to organize the peasants for other ends. In November, 1958, the Federación Departamental de Campesinos (FDC) was formed as an affiliate of the Peruvian Peasant Confederation, a Communist group.[4] Its member syndicates were found mostly on large foreign-owned haciendas and in small lakeside communities in the provinces of Puno and Huancané. Apparently, there was little effort expended in recruiting new syndicates to the FDC or in pressing political action on its behalf. However, its members were reportedly active in the harassment of the United States relief program, allegedly for no other purpose than to embarrass the United States.[5] Nevertheless, no mention of them appeared in the Puno papers until the 1962 elections were approaching and the local affiliate of FLN was formed, of which the FDC became a founding member.[6] One of the FLN candidates for deputy in 1962 was a former secretary-general of the FDC, Honorio Morales Arce.

In 1960 a rival peasant front, the Frente Sindical de Campesinos (FSC), was established with the sponsorship of the Christian Democrats. The organizers of the FSC, as mentioned earlier, were Róger Cáceres' younger brother, Néstor, and Atalo Gutiérrez, a *cholo* who was fluent in Quechua, Aymará, and Spanish. Néstor Cáceres, after

---

[3] Hermogenes Vera Salazar, *El Proceso Electoral de 1962 en el Departamento de Puno*, p. 20.

[4] *El Campesino* (Puno), February 14, 1965, p. 1.

[5] United States, Department of State, "Press Release 350" (May 26, 1961), *The Department of State Bulletin*, 44(June 12, 1961): 923.

[6] *Los Andes* (Puno), December 2, 1961, p. 1 (hereinafter cited in this chapter as *LA*).

graduating in economics at the University of San Agustín in Arequipa, had gone to work for the PRPDSP as a member of one of its research teams. Seeing an opportunity to advance his own political ambitions, as well as to help mobilize support for the Corpuno bill, he set to work with Gutiérrez, who at that time was employed in the Cáceres emporium, organizing the peasant front, using the extensive resources and facilities of his father's mercantile trade, as well as those of the PDC, to which both he and Gutiérrez belonged. Róger Cáceres, who at this time was the secretary-general of the Christian Democratic Youth in Lima, was able to send university students and others to the altiplano to help in the organizing.

In early 1961 the FSC engaged in its first political activities: a series of demonstrations in support of the Corpuno bill and the collection of signatures for a petition. In December, 1961, the First Departmental Convention of Puno Peasants was held, presided over by Atalo Gutiérrez. Among the resolutions passed by the Convention were demands that the Corpuno law (already passed by both houses of Congress) be promulgated, that free services on haciendas by *colonos* be eliminated, that an agrarian reform be carried out immediately, and that social security be made available to peasants.[7]

Local Candidates and the Campaign

Both Néstor Cáceres and Atalo Gutiérrez were placed on the PDC ticket as candidates for the Chamber of Deputies. Juan Chávez Molina and Róger Cáceres headed the ticket, seeking re-election as senator and deputy, respectively.

Other congressmen seeking re-election in 1962 included Teófilo Monroy (AP) and Emilio Frisancho (AD), now running for Senate seats, and deputies Guillermo Briceño (AD), Fernando Manrique (FLN), Ernesto More (FLN), and Humberto Eduardo (UDP). Among the new candidates for office were Samuel Frisancho, editor of *Los Andes*, who was running for a deputy seat on the FLN ticket, and Juan Zea Gonzales, owner of Radio La Voz del Altiplano who was running for the Senate on the AP ticket.

[7] *EC*, December 16, 1961, p. 11; December 17, 1961, p. 12.

Little has been reported about the campaign in 1962 in the altiplano, except for the brief appearances made by several of the Presidential contenders, including Haya de la Torre, Belaúnde, Cornejo Chávez, and the FLN's Pando Egúsquiza. Belaúnde, who had visited the altiplano in both 1960 and 1961,[8] was the most popularly received of the candidates, according to *El Comercio*.[9] Haya de la Torre's appearance in Puno was disrupted by rock-throwing and whistling. His speech was cut short and numerous arrests were made.[10] Cornejo Chávez had the bad fortune to be both whistled down *and* rained out.[11] But in February, at the outset of the campaign, the FLN provided the most explosive political incident of any that were to follow. It took place in Juliaca.

The events [reported *El Comercio*] began at 11:00 A.M. when around one thousand persons gathered in the main plaza to hear the voice of General Pando Egúsquiza. No sooner had he begun his speech than around three thousand persons, mostly women, appeared in the plaza, setting off an extraordinary tumult. Tomatoes, vegetables, and even stones accompanied the voices of protest over the visit of the FLN and silenced the voice of the speaker. The police found themselves helpless to restore order, and things ended about noon when the FLN leaders left the city.[12]

In contrast, that night in Puno the FLN candidates spoke in the Plaza de Armas without incident from 7:00 to 9:00 P.M. with an estimated five thousand in attendance.[13]

The Election and Military Coup

In June, as election day neared, reports reached *El Comercio* of extensive machinations and pressures by the *prado-aprista* authorities throughout the department to assist the candidates of the AD ticket.[14] Four parties—the AP, PDC, FLN, and UNO—denounced these ac-

[8] *Ibid.*, February 21, 22, 23, 1960, p. 4; August 17, 18, 19, 1961, p. 4.
[9] *Ibid.*, May 26 and 27, 1962, p. 4.
[10] *Ibid.*, May 6, 1962, p. 4.
[11] *Ibid.*, April 18, 1962, p. 4.
[12] *Ibid.*, February 12, 1962, p. 9, my translation.
[13] *Ibid.*, February 12, 1962, p. 9.
[14] *Ibid.*, June 3, 1962, p. 4.

tions.[15] Even so, election day, June 10, 1962, passed without incident in the altiplano. In the nation as a whole, however, it produced a major crisis. No Presidential candidate, according to official returns, received the one-third of votes constitutionally required to be elected.[16] Haya de la Torre, who led in the official returns by less than thirteen thousand votes, had only 32.9 percent of the votes, while Belaúnde had 32.2 percent and Odría 28.4 percent. The four remaining Presidential candidates had less than 6.5 percent altogether.[17]

Throughout June and into July, the official tabulations proceeded at a snail's pace, accompanied by frantic negotiations among the three front-runners and denunciations by Belaúnde and members of the Armed Forces that the election had been rigged. *El Comercio* reported charges of irregularities in over half of Peru's voter precincts. (In Puno, for example, complaints of irregularities were filed in 268 of 387 precincts.)[18] On July 17, therefore, the Armed Forces seized the Presidential Palace in a *coup d'état*, annulled the elections, sent the Congress home, and promised new and honest elections in June, 1963.[19] Thereupon, a year of military government and rule by decree began.

Results of the Election in Puno

Accepting the election results at their face value, however, the Presidential outcome in Puno was a clean sweep for Belaúnde, as the following results show:[20]

Belaúnde Terry (AP)	32,503
Odría (UNO)	7,459
Haya de la Torre (AD)	5,757
Cornejo Chávez (PDC)	1,687
Pando Egúsquiza (FLN)	1,422
Ruíz (MSP)	359
Castillo (PSP)	150

[15] *Ibid.*, June 8, 1962, p. 4.
[16] *Peruvian Constitution* (1933), Article 138.
[17] *Peruvian Times*, July 20, 1962, p. 2.
[18] *EC*, July 15, 1962, p. 4.
[19] *Ibid.*, July 18, 1962, p. 1.
[20] Vera Salazar, *Proceso Electoral*, p. 21.

In both the Senate and Chamber races, the *belaundista* tickets swept to victory intact, with individual members of the FLN, Christian Democrats, and others fighting it out for the remaining seats. (In the Senate race, each party had been allowed to run only two candidates for the three available seats; in the Chamber race, they could run eight candidates for a total of eleven seats). The Senate results were as follows:[21]

Juan Zea Gonzales (AP)	22,430
Teófilo Monroy (AP)	17,168
José Macedo Mendoza (FLN)	10,142
Juan Chávez Molina (PDC)	7,982
Darío Palacios (AD)	6,748
Emilio Frisancho (AD)	5,867
Honorio Ponze (UNO)	4,554
Gustavo Zegarra (FLN)	3,985
Guillermo Záa (UNO)	3,978
Abdón Valdez Pino (PDC)	3,621
Vladimiro Bermejo (MAD)	2,290
Amadeo Landaeta (UDP)	1,914
Adrián Cáceres Olazo (MAD)	1,778
Washingtón Cano (UDP)	1,718

In the Chamber race, the first twenty finalists (of 56) were as follows:[22]

Jaime Serruto (AP)	21,743
William Barriga (AP)	19,906
Gustavo Salcedo (AP)	19,386
León Cárdenas (AP)	19,215
Mario Franco (AP)	18,475
César Aníbal Vera (AP)	17,611
Julio Mita (AP)	16,951
Alberto Enríquez (AP)	16,623
Róger Cáceres (PDC)	12,952

[21] *Ibid.*, p. 22.
[22] *Ibid.*, p. 25.

Rubén Chambi (PDC)	8,831
Nicanor Tinajeros (UDP)	7,538
Juan Deza Galindo (PDC)	7,010
Guillermo Briceño (AD)	6,793
Alfredo Rivera (AD)	6,049
Samuel Frisancho (FLN)	5,832
Luís Quintanilla (PDC)	5,807
Aurora Paredes de T. (UDP)	5,633
Santiago Ortega (UNO)	5,607
Néstor Cáceres (PDC)	5,558
Alfredo Alberoni (UDP)	5,546

Farther down the list were Fernando Manrique (FLN), the former *belaundista* deputy (in twenty-fifth position, with 5,288 votes), Ernesto More (FLN), the former *pradista* deputy (in forty-second place, with 3,681 votes), and Humberto Eduardo (UDP), a former *pradista* deputy (in forty-eighth place, with 2,316 votes). In the competition between the peasant syndicate leaders, Néstor Cáceres finished in nineteenth place, as we saw, followed by Atalo Gutiérrez (in thirty-sixth place, with 4,378 votes) and, finally, Honorio Morales Arce (FLN) (in forty-first place, with 3,842 votes).[23]

It is also interesting to note the remarkable success of the radio station's owner, Juan Zea Gonzales, in contrast to the local newspaper owner, Samuel Frisancho. However, as no candidate outpolled Belaúnde, he undoubtedly provided a strong coattail influence for the other AP candidates. In this light, it is interesting to see that Frisancho, whose name was at the bottom of the FLN deputy list, nevertheless outpolled the other FLN candidates, including two former deputies, themselves.

THE 1963 NATIONAL ELECTIONS

Preparations

In the interim between elections, there was a scramble for positions, especially on the *belaundista* ticket, which had been so successful locally in 1962. An error of judgment, whereby five of the newly elected

[23] *Ibid.*

AP deputies had decided to enter Parliament against Belaúnde's orders on the eve of the military *coup d'état*,[24] led to their expulsion from the party by Mario Villarán, the secretary-general of the AP. Although Belaúnde intervened to restore the five to full party status,[25] Puno *belaundistas*, anxious for a place on the AP ticket, joined in the condemnation of the five, whereupon an extremely bitter exchange of denunciations took place in the pages of *Los Andes*.[26]

On January 5, 1963, the Military Government briefly arrested hundreds of Communists and leftists throughout Peru, charging them with plots against the government.[27] In Puno, this roundup included not only FLN members, but also some Socialists, *belaundistas*, and Christian Democrats. One of these was Atalo Gutiérrez, the FSC organizer.[28] Perhaps to appease the military, the national FLN leaders agreed not to run a Presidential candidate in 1963 and urged their followers to support Belaúnde.[29] However, FLN supporters organized their own Congressional ticket in Puno, this time calling themselves the Frente Patriótica (FP).

Like the FLN, the smaller Socialist and Social Progressive parties stayed out of the Presidential race in 1963. However, both the *apristas* and *odriístas* defied speculation that they might draw together by announcing the candidacies once again of Haya and Odría. This time, the *apristas* eschewed the dubious help of the *pradistas* and ran their slate of candidates under the name Partido Aprista Peruano (PAP). Thus, besides the three front-runners of the year before, the only new figure in the Presidential race was a Lima engineer, Mario Samamé Boggio, who had formed a compromise party called the Union del

[24] *EC*, July 18, 1962, p. 4.

[25] Interview, Gustavo Salcedo, prefect, Puno, April 14, 1965.

[26] *LA*, August 26, 1962, pp. 1, 4; September 7, 1962, p. 1; September 9, 1962, p. 2; September 13, 1962, p. 1. Puno's mayor from 1963 to 1966, Remigio Cabala (one of the denouncers), and the prefect from 1963 to 1966, Gustavo Salcedo (one of the five expelled), later referred to the affair as merely "a personal misunderstanding" (interviews, Puno, April 12 and 14, 1965).

[27] *EC*, January 6, 1963, p. 1.

[28] *Ibid.*, p. 11.

[29] *LA*, May 22, 1963, p. 1.

Pueblo Peruano (UPP). In Puno, the UPP proposed a full slate of Congressional candidates.

The AP-PDC Alliance

The most striking event of the new campaign was the formation in Lima of a new alliance between the Christian Democrats and *belaundistas* to back Belaúnde and a merged Congressional ticket. This merger of leading candidates was particularly difficult in Puno because of the relative success of the *belaundistas* the year before and because of the general resentment against Róger Cáceres. In October, 1962, before the Alliance was announced, this resentment had found expression in formal critiques by the Puno AP of Cáceres' (unsuccessful) attempt to take over Corpuno (see next chapter).[30] Thus, it was a bitter pill for the *belaundistas* when, in January, 1963, they found themselves faced not only with admitting Róger Cáceres to their ticket, but with admitting his brother Néstor, as well.[31] The situation was aggravated still more by the new electoral code promulgated by the Military Government in November, 1962, which gave Puno only eight seats in a smaller Chamber of Deputies, instead of the eleven she had had in 1956 and 1962.[32] If half of the Congressional candidates on the AP-PDC ticket in Puno were to be Christian Democrats, as the terms of the Alliance decreed, then four of the winning *belaundistas* of 1962 would have to be striken from the 1963 ballot. Several *belaundistas* protested the pact, by forming a group called Acción Popular Rebelde.[33] One of these went on to run for Congress on the new UPP ticket.[34]

When the AP-PDC ticket was announced on March 12, it was found that Néstor Cáceres' name had been replaced by that of a *belaundista*.[35] His immediate reaction was to form the Independent Peasant Party (Partido Independiente de Campesinos, PIC), with

[30] *Ibid.*, October 9, 1962, p. 4; October 23, 1962, p. 1.
[31] *Ibid.*, January 25, 1963, p. 1.
[32] *EC*, November 13, 1962, p. 1.
[33] *LA*, March 5, 1963, p. 1.
[34] Mario Franco (*ibid.*, June 12, 1963, p. 1).
[35] *Ibid.*, March 12, 1963, p. 1.

a slate of candidates for the Chamber of Deputies.[36] His brother Róger surprised some by retaining his place on the AP-PDC list.

The national Christian Democratic Party was particularly embarrassed and confused by these events, as less than a week before they had sponsored an impressive convention of the FSC in Puno, inviting observers from Lima, Bolivia, and Paraguay. *La Prensa* reported that the delegates to the convention represented 550 peasant unions with 150,000 members.[37] The delegates had approved resolutions asking for the immediate expropriation of four big haciendas in the provinces of Azángaro, Lampa, and Puno, as well as resolutions demanding schools, technical assistance, social and economic welfare, and other benefits.[38] On the final day of the convention, 30,000 peasants had reportedly filled the streets of Puno to witness the closing ceremonies.[39] Utilizing the momentum of this movement for their own purposes, the Cáceres brothers sponsored a trip by 15 representatives of the FSC to Lima in May, 1963, to visit the offices of AID, where they requested $60,000,000 for projects in Puno.[40] By this time, the FSC claimed 650 member syndicates, representing 200,000 peasants.[41]

This vigorous and aggressive program of the FSC, as well as the extensive campaigning of Néstor Cáceres, bore electoral results, as he more than doubled his strength from the year before. This was all the more remarkable in that a reregistration of voters, carried out by the Military Government, had reduced the number of voters in the altiplano to 59,618, a drop of almost 10,000 from the year before.[42] This undoubtedly cut the hardest into the ranks of the group most likely to support the candidates of the PIC: the barely literate *cholos* and peasants.

[36] *Ibid.*

[37] *La Prensa* (Lima), March 6, 1963, n.p. (shown to me by Earl Smith, AID).

[38] *LA*, March 10, 1963, p. 1.

[39] *Expreso* (Lima), March 10, 1963, n.p. (shown to me by Earl Smith, AID).

[40] *La Prensa* (Lima), May 17, 1963, n.p. (shown to me by Earl Smith, AID).

[41] *Ibid.*

[42] *LA*, March 16, 1963, p. 4.

The Election and Local Results

On June 9, 1963, Peruvians gave Belaúnde a clear-cut victory of 708,662 votes, compared to 623,501 for Haya de la Torre, 463,085 for Odría, and only 19,320 for Samamé Boggio.[43] In Puno the sentiment for Belaúnde was even stronger than the year before, with Belaúnde polling 38,100 votes to Haya de la Torre's 6,115, Odría's 6,184, and Samamé Boggio's 731.[44]

The AP-PDC ticket swept the Senate race in Puno, but was only partly successful in the Chamber race, because of the competition of the Independent Peasant and other tickets. (In the Senate race, there were three seats available with each party permitted to run three candidates; in the Chamber race eight candidates were presented by each party for the eight available seats.) The leaders in the Senate race were as follows:[45]

Juan Zea Gonzales (AP)	32,052
Juan Deza Galindo (PDC)	16,026
Rafael Miranda (AP)	10,683
José Macedo Mendoza (FP)	6,714
José Luís Lescano (PAP)	6,115
Santiago Ortego (UNO)	5,248

The leaders for the eight Chamber seats were as follows:[46]

Jaime Serruto (AP)	22,830
Néstor Cáceres (PIC)	11,525
Róger Cáceres (PDC)	11,415
Teófilo Monroy (AP)	7,611
Darío Palacios (PAP)	5,786
Julio Arce Catacora (PIC)	5,752
León Cárdenas (AP)	5,707
Fernando Manrique (FP)	5,155
José Antonio Sardón (UNO)	4,348

[43] *Hispanic American Report*, 16, no. 6 (August, 1963): 597.
[44] *LA*, June 12, 1963, p. 1.
[45] *Ibid.*
[46] *Ibid.*

The reaction of the *belaundistas* to the outcome of the election in Puno was extremely bitter. On July 13, 1963, they held a departmental convention, at which they declared Róger Cáceres a traitor to the AP-PDC Alliance and demanded his expulsion from the PDC for having sabotaged the ticket by his alleged aid to his brother's peasant ticket.[47] Darío Vidangos, the secretary-general of the PDC in Puno, responded with an attack on the local leaders of the AP, accusing them of being Marxists trying to destroy the Alliance, and asking for their own expulsion from the AP.[48] In regard to the Cáceres brothers and the Independent Peasant ticket, Vidangos expressed confidence that they were all good Christian Democrats and that they would return to the party soon.[49] Nevertheless, the attack on Róger Cáceres continued, prompting him on one occasion to ask for police protection on a visit to the altiplano after threats had been made on his life.[50]

In the meantime, the Cáceres brothers had founded their own newspaper in Puno, *El Tiempo*, appointing as its managing editor an *odriísta*.[51] Although *El Tiempo*'s appearance was sporadic, its extensive coverage of the Cáceres brothers' activities in Congress must have antagonized their enemies still further. In Congress, although the developing conflict between the AP-PDC and *aprista-odriísta* forces dominated the nation's attention, the Cáceres brothers and their peasant party colleague were extremely active, presenting a "sea of bills,"[52] including twenty bills on the first day of Congress.[53] One of these was a controversial bill proposing universal suffrage for Peruvians. Although it was never passed, it earned the Cáceres brothers some notoriety. Finally, in November, 1963, Róger Cáceres renounced his membership in the PDC, joining his brother and the other peasant-party deputy as Independents in Congress.[54]

[47] *Ibid.*, July 13, 1963, p. 1.
[48] *El Tiempo* (Puno), July 27, 1963, p. 3.
[49] *Ibid.*
[50] *LA*, August 2, 1963, p. 1.
[51] *El Tiempo* (Puno), July 10, 1963, p. 2.
[52] *LA*, September 23, 1963, p. 1.
[53] "Chamber Debates," *EC*, August 13, 1963, pp. 1, 4.
[54] *Ibid.*, November 17, 1963, p. 4.

THE 1963 MUNICIPAL ELECTIONS

One of the first acts of President Belaúnde, after his inauguration on July 28, 1963, was to announce that nationwide municipal elections would be held later in the year, for the first time in forty years.[55] Once again, political activity intensified throughout the country, this time becoming of direct relevance to each province and district, where mayors and councils would be elected on December 15, 1963. *Apristas* and *odriístas*, having banded together to control Congress in opposition to the AP-PDC administration of Belaúnde, decided to run fusion tickets in these elections, as did the AP-PDC Alliance.[56]

In Puno, slates were entered in each provincial election by the APRA-UNO Coalition, the AP-PDC Alliance, and the leftist Frente Patriótica. The Cáceres group, now called the Independent Party of Workers and Peasants (Partido Independiente de Trabajadores y Campesinos, PITC), defied the expectations of local Christian Democrats and ran their own lists throughout the department. *Los Andes* expressed concern about the holding of municipal elections, as they might elevate an illiterate to mayor someplace.[57] Charges that the PITC was Communist were accompanied by accusations that the Cáceres brothers were exploiting the peasants "on behalf of the oligarchy."[58]

Although the AP-PDC Alliance won majorities in six of the nine provincial councils (Huancané, Chucuito, Melgar, Sandia, Azángaro, and Puno), the PITC won seats in most of the councils and controlled two of them (Lampa and San Román). In the ninth province (Carabaya), a local party controlled the council. The elections were noteworthy, not only for the continued influence of the Cáceres group, but also for the political debut of a third Cáceres brother, Luís, who was elected mayor of the San Román provincial council (whose capital, Juliaca, was the seat of the family's economic power).[59] In the province of Puno, the AP-PDC Alliance won eight of fifteen council seats (in-

[55] *Ibid.*, July 30, 1963, p. 4.
[56] *Hispanic American Report*, 16, no. 10 (December, 1963): 990.
[57] *LA*, September 25, 1963, p. 4.
[58] *Ibid.*, November 28, 1963, p. 3; December 1, 1963, p. 4.
[59] *Ibid.*, December 20, 1963, p. 1.

cluding that of the mayor), while the Frente Patriótica won three, the PITC won three, and the APRA-UNO Coalition won only one.[60]

CONCLUSIONS

Despite the fact that less than 10 percent of the Puno population was allowed to vote, the dramatic events of the 1956–1962 period had a marked impact on voting. Although the leftist *belaundista* candidates did well in 1956, so did the candidates of the more conservative *pradista* ticket. Only the ticket identified with the incumbent regime (the *odriístas*) did poorly. In 1962 the party identified with the incumbent's regime (the *aprista*-dominated Alianza Democrática) again suffered. But so did the other conservative parties. Only the leftists (*belaundistas*, Christian Democrats, and a few FLN candidates) did well. The most dramatic change between the 1962 election and the national and municipal elections of 1963 was the increasing strength of the independent peasant movement, especially when measured against the reduced size of the local electorate.

It is difficult to explain cleavages among groups that seem to share similar programmatic and ideological viewpoints except in terms of personal rivalries for political power. A brief cleavage, for example, in the *belaundista* ranks was incredibly bitter, although it is now sluffed off as an unimportant thing of the past.

On the face of it, the alienation of the Cáceres brothers from the PDC appeared also to be a personal matter—the result of the exclusion of one of them from the AP-PDC ticket. This would seem to be supported by the similar ideological and programmatic orientations of the AP-PDC and Cáceres groups even to this day. However, in spite of the reform orientation of both, the cleavage between them is more than personal. It relates to the socioeconomic differences between Puno's peasants and elite and the peculiar position of the merchant in between them.

We have seen that the entrepreneurial role in the altiplano was usually taken by *forasteros* (outsiders) or lower-class *cholos*. Transforming economic mobility into social or political mobility was vir-

[60] *Ibid.*

tually impossible in the mestizo-dominated capital of the department, Puno. But in a busy commercial center like Juliaca, where economic opportunities were much more abundant, it was not so difficult to be accepted socially or politically. The Cáceres family, economically successful in Juliaca, suffered a certain isolation and disdain elsewhere in the altiplano, as we have seen. Róger Cáceres' insistence on studying law may have originated in his feeling of social exclusion and a desire to be accepted by becoming a typical mestizo lawyer. Luís, the second son, sought to study medicine, another mestizo-esteemed field. He was overruled and forced to become the manager of his father's store. Néstor Cáceres' desire to study law was also frustrated by his father, who insisted that he study economics instead.

Dissatisfaction with the careers planned for them by their father, combined with their social exclusion in altiplano society, must have aided their decision to utilize the extensive family resources to enter politics, something their father had never done. Electoral office, the ultimate expression of mestizo status, was undoubtedly considered a preserve of the social and cultural elite, to which entrance by outsiders would be controlled by the exclusive nature of the literate electorate. Encountering difficulty organizing a following among the mestizos, the Cáceres brothers felt no hesitation to experiment with the increasingly literate *cholos* and peasantry (toward whom their father had oriented his economic activity before them). Not only did this relationship serve the Cáceres brothers well in 1962 and 1963, but it also would continue to serve them well, until the politically ambitious but tradition-oriented mestizos (including the altiplano's leftist *belaundistas* and Communists) should seriously attempt to bridge the gap between the region's two castes.

THE BATTLE OVER CORPUNO'S
PROGRAM, 1962–1965

THE UNPRECEDENTED EXTENSION of development projects to benefit all regions and social groups of the department seemed to engender
more conflict than it resolved. Much of this, of course, was the expression of conflicting interests in the destination of Corpuno moneys.
At first, the criticisms were aimed at the administrative expenses of
the new organization. Later, a number of demands for specific kinds
of large-scale programs were made—and frustrated—by the organization's leaders. Crosscutting interests at this time prevented any serious
cleavages from emerging. However, after a series of decisions at both
the local and national levels seemed to favor Puno over Juliaca in
regards to a number of development issues, violence erupted, producing a political crisis of national proportions.

THE FIRST YEAR

The Cáceres Affair

On July 26, 1962, the military prefect of Puno installed the Corpuno
Assembly and its first president, Juan Luís Mercado, the recently de-

posed prefect of the department.[1] Two months later, the Assembly was called by Mercado into an extraordinary session and presented with the candidacy of another unemployed politician for Corpuno's managership, Róger Cáceres. Along with Cáceres' name was submitted a list of nominees for the Corporation's Directorate. Although the Assembly was not as yet intact (several groups still had to appoint their representatives to it), and in spite of many abstentions reported by those in attendance, Cáceres and the proposed Directorate were elected.[2] Many protests were heard against this maneuver and the rapidity with which Cáceres allegedly proceeded to place his followers and friends in other positions throughout the organization.[3] After the local branch of the AP party attacked Cáceres for attempting to transform Corpuno into his own political machine,[4] the Military Government removed both Cáceres and Mercado from their posts. Mercado was replaced by Andrés Romero Portugal, a landowner who had been closely associated with Enrique Torres Belón, the former senator from Puno.[5] A new manager was not chosen at this time—one member of the Technical Committee taking that post on an interim basis until the next meeting of the Assembly.[6]

New Officers and the Demand for Reorganization

In November a new extraordinary session of the Assembly was called, at which the presidency of Romero was approved and a new Directorate elected.[7] The man elected as manager was Oscar Espinoza Bedoya,[8] a twenty-three–year–old civil engineer, who, while an archi-

[1] *El Comercio* (Lima), July 27, 1962, p. 4 (hereinafter cited in this chapter as *EC*).

[2] *Los Andes* (Puno), September 19, 1962, p. 1 (hereinafter cited in this chapter as *LA*).

[3] *Ibid.*, September 20, 1962, p. 1; September 27, 1962, p. 1; September 28, 1962, p. 4; September 30, 1962, p. 1.

[4] *Ibid.*, October 9, 1962, p. 4.

[5] *Ibid.*, October 17, 1962, p. 1.

[6] *EC*, October 25, 1962, p. 9.

[7] Andrés Romero Portugal, *Texto de la Memoria Leída Ante la Asamblea Departamental de Delegados* (March 4, 1963), p. 18 (hereinafter cited as Romero, *Report for 1962*).

[8] *Ibid.*, p. 19.

tecture student of President Belaúnde, had been president of the National Student Federation.[9] As a Christian Democrat, Espinoza had become a close friend of Róger Cáceres, and, when the latter allegedly tried to take over Corpuno, Espinoza was one of those for whom he found a place in the organization. The ostensible reason for Espinoza's election as manager was his impressive performance as technical delegate in charge of the Department of Public Works, Housing, and Urbanism during the first few months of operation.[10] However, Espinoza's selection was also due to the continued influence of Cáceres in the Assembly.

The failure of the Military Government to thoroughly reorganize Corpuno or to purge it of its allegedly pro-Cáceres elements meant that criticism of the new organization, especially in the city of Puno itself, was fairly strong. One of the major foci of attack was the high salaries and other perquisites enjoyed by the personnel, especially by the principal officials. However, the high salaries established by the Corporation were defended as absolutely essential to attract skilled personnel away from the lucrative opportunities on the coast.[11] As Espinoza put it, "most people prefer working in a ministry where the salaries are higher and where there is less of a spotlight on you."[12] To prove this point, President Romero, in his annual reports of Corpuno's activities in 1962 and 1963, pointed to the fact that two posts on the Technical Committee had remained unfilled, in spite of repeated requests to Lima for qualified appointees.[13] In response to criticisms that Espinoza was drawing a double salary, that of a technical delegate and that of manager, Espinoza renounced the manager's salary, although he continued to perform both jobs.[14] But criticism continued. The travel expenses of Romero and Espinoza, who made frequent

[9] EC, October 7, 1959, p. 4.

[10] Romero, Report for 1962, p. 19.

[11] Andrés Romero Portugal, Memoria Anual 1964, p. 10 (hereinafter cited as Romero, Report for 1964).

[12] Interview, Oscar Espinoza Bedoya, Puno, April 20, 1965.

[13] Romero, Report for 1962, p. 18; and Texto de la Memoria Leída Ante la Asamblea Departamental de Delegados (March 3, 1964), p. 26 (hereinafter cited as Romero, Report for 1963).

[14] Romero, Report for 1962, p. 19.

trips to Lima in connection with their work came under attack.[15] Finally, in May, 1963, *Los Andes* announced with satisfaction that the Corpuno salary scales had been lowered.[16]

Other Criticisms

A second source of criticism concerned the slowness of Corpuno to initiate any projects. The ambitious character of the Corporation, as spelled out during the campaign for its enactment, had prompted a flood of requests for public works and other projects from communities throughout the department, once it was made a reality. Thus, there was considerable dismay when it was learned that virtually all of Corpuno's first year's income of S/43,000,000 was allowed to pass unspent into the 1963 budget.[17] President Romero defended this action in his Annual Report for 1962, saying that "it wasn't technically advisable to start any works without previously relying on studies, plans, and budgets, whose attainment is a delicate and laborious task."[18]

A third source of criticism was Corpuno's relationship with the Puno Municipal Council. Among the first projects the Council requested of the Corporation was the extensive pavement of Puno streets and sidewalks and resumption of work on a municipal theatre, which had been planned under the Odría regime, and authorized by the Public Works Council, but never built.[19] Corpuno put the theatre proposal under study and, upon the request of the Council, drew up a contract (*convenio*) whereby the Council was provided with S/1,000,000 to carry out a specified number of paving projects.[20] Two months later, after charging the Council with irregularities in its use of the money, Corpuno rescinded the contract and took over supervision of the work itself.[21] The mayor, an appointee of the Military Government, thereupon announced his resignation in a bitter attack upon Corpuno.[22]

[15] *EC,* January 10, 1963, p. 11; LA, April 16, 1963, p. 1; April 29, 1963, p. 4.
[16] *LA,* May 17, 1963, p. 1.
[17] *Ibid.,* February 16, 1963, p. 1.
[18] Romero, *Report for 1962,* p. 12, my translation.
[19] *LA,* November 30, 1962, pp. 1, 4.
[20] *Ibid.,* February 5, 1963, p. 1.
[21] *Ibid.,* April 13, 1963, p. 1.
[22] *Ibid.,* April 16, 1963, p. 1.

Emergency Relief

Complicating Corpuno's challenge was yet another heavy rainstorm that hit the area at the end of January, 1963, causing serious floods that ravaged the pampas of Taraco and Ilave.[23] Continued heavy rains throughout February kept the flood waters from receding, and even led to floods of the Puno waterfront and the higher pampa between Puno and Juliaca.[24] Runways of the Juliaca airport were reported damaged because of inadequate drainage from the rains.[25] Subsequently, in April, a devastating frost hit many parts of the altiplano, threatening to destroy the remaining crops that the floods had not already affected.[26] Representatives of the Ministry of Agriculture immediately toured the area and confirmed the reports of crop damage.[27]

Corpuno's first action in these disasters was to provide money to the local authorities in the Taraco area for building defenses along the banks of the Ramis River. The peasant delegates in the Corpuno Assembly (both of them FSC leaders) helped organize the work forces from among the ranks of their local followers.[28] Corpuno then solicited S/4,400,000 from the FNDE for more permanent work on the Ramis defenses.[29] A project of peasant resettlement, to be discussed in the next chapter, was also begun among the affected population at this time. Finally, extensive road work was provided in both the Ilave and Taraco areas to peasants whose needs were established by local Maryknoll Fathers in collaboration with a Corpuno commission composed of the two peasant delegates and a member of the Technical Committee.[30] As no criticism appeared in the press concerning Corpuno's emergency aid, its performance of these works must have been

[23] *EC*, January 30, 1963, p. 1; February 3, 1963, p. 1; February 6, 1963, p. 1; February 7, 1963, p. 1.

[24] *Ibid.*, February 23, 1963, p. 11; February 28, 1963, p. 1.

[25] *Ibid.*, February 22, 1963, p. 4.

[26] *Ibid.*, April 20, 1963, p. 1.

[27] *Ibid.*, April 21, 1963, p. 1.

[28] Romero, *Report for 1962*, p. 20.

[29] *Ibid.*

[30] *Ibid.*, p. 21.

relatively circumspect in comparison with past emergency aid programs.

Corpuno and the 1963 Elections

In the campaign preceding the national elections of 1963, Communist and *belaundista* criticism of Corpuno was directed primarily at the "ring" (*argolla*) of *caceristas* still holding high positions in the organization, and at their high salaries.[31] However, during the Corpuno General Assembly of March, 1963, Róger Cáceres and Oscar Espinoza had privately fought over the matter of an immediate and extensive agrarian reform program, which Cáceres was pushing for electoral purposes. The Assembly supported Espinoza's recommendations that studies should be undertaken first and that the initiative and financing of an extensive reform should be the responsibility of the national government. This led to a bitter rupture in relations between Espinoza and Cáceres.

Nevertheless, after Belaúnde's victory in the national elections, his followers in Puno, and others, continued their demand for a reorganization of Corpuno.[32] It was surprising to many, therefore, when Cáceres himself joined in the attacks on the Corporation.[33] In a public assembly in July, 1963, Cáceres proposed that the president of Corpuno be elected by the department and not appointed by the president. He also reiterated his demand for immediate expropriation of vast landholdings by Corpuno's Agrarian Reform Department.[34] In late July, just before the inauguration of Belaúnde, in an extraordinary session of the Corpuno General Assembly, Espinoza answered Cáceres' and the others' criticisms, defending Corpuno's programs and policies in detail and proclaiming that the Corporation "was above politics."[35] A few days after the inauguration of Belaúnde, *Los Andes* reported

---

[31] *LA*, April 29, 1963, p. 1; May 6, 1963, p. 1; May 8, 1963, p. 1; May 15, 1963, p. 1; May 29, 1963, p. 1.

[32] *Ibid.*, June 12, 1963, p. 1; June 25, 1963, p. 1.

[33] *Ibid.*, June 28, 1963, p. 1; July 4, 1963, p. 1; *El Tiempo* (Puno), July 10, 1963, p. 1 (hereinafter cited in this chapter as *ET*).

[34] *ET*, July 12, 1963, p. 1; *LA*, July 12, 1963, p. 4.

[35] *LA*, July 25, 1963, p. 1.

that Espinoza had just gotten married in Lima, at a wedding attended by all the high dignitaries of the Christian Democrat Party. "With this support," complained *Los Andes'* editor, "it will be difficult to get him out of the *gerencia* [managership]."[36] Nevertheless, criticism continued through August and September, and demands were voiced by both the *belaundistas* and the *caceristas* for Corpuno's reorganization.[37]

However, as the municipal election campaign became more intense, and as it became clear that Belaúnde had no intention of interfering with Corpuno, criticism died out. *Los Andes* was prompted to editorialize, on the eve of the election, that "for fear of losing three or four votes, none of the candidates for mayor has said a blessed thing [*no ha dicho esta boca es mía*] regarding Corpuno."[38]

CORPUNO'S PROGRAMS

The chief reason for the reduced hostility toward Corpuno was undoubtedly the latter's large resource base, which few had probably expected and fewer still wished to jeopardize their access to by antagonizing Corpuno's officials. In the December, 1962, Assembly, a budget of almost S/100,000,000 had been approved, which included an unprecedented S/47,000,000 in public works projects, with the balance allocated to loans, investments, studies, and emergency reserves. Salaries accounted for S/3,700,000 and other administrative costs (rentals, equipment, travel) came to S/2,000,000.[39] In addition to Corpuno's own funds, S/22,000,000 had been promised by the FNDE, of which a little over S/7,000,000 was actually received.[40]

Primary among Corpuno's work projects were sewerage and potable water installations or improvements in twenty-seven towns of the altiplano (including all the provincial capitals).[41] Twenty-three road-

[36] *Ibid.*, August 5, 1963, p. 1, my translation.
[37] *Ibid.*, September 18, 1963, p. 1; September 21, 1963, p. 1; *ET*, September 19, 1963, p. 1.
[38] *LA*, December 14, 1963, p. 1, my translation.
[39] Romero, *Report for 1963*, pp. 30–34.
[40] *Ibid.*, p. 35.
[41] Romero, *Report for 1962*, pp. 7–10; *Report for 1963*, p. 47.

building or improvement projects were undertaken, including work resumption on the Macusani-San Gabán and Puno-Moquegua roads.[42] In addition, there were nine electrification projects, including the long-awaited expansion of the power network in Puno.[43]

One of the principal criticisms of Corpuno during 1964 was its unwillingness to undertake a massive hydroelectrification project such as the Cuzco Corporation (CRYF) was doing at Machu Picchu.[44] Electrification of the department by diesel-run plants was criticized as expensive and limited in its capacity to aid industrial growth, to say nothing of providing minimal urban needs. One critic insisted that Corpuno's dispersion of its extensive funds to small, unrelated and "unproductive" investments was politically motivated and exceedingly shortsighted.[45]

President Romero answered these critiques in his Annual Report for 1964, in which he argued that

> although it is the Assembly that approves the budget programs and that in the last analysis could atomize the resources into an infinite number of works, the absence of large scale public works projects in our first two budget programs is not the result of an improvisation. We know perfectly well, for example, that any plan of industrial growth presupposes electrical services at low cost and that that in turn presupposes heavy investments that must be made with great foreplanning. We know that we are not doing this; nevertheless, we think that an entity with limited resources like Corpuno . . . cannot mortgage its very life on a single financial operation . . . neglecting all those things without which a great quantity of kilowatts would be meaningless (primary resources, local markets, infrastructure, etc.).[46]

The Corpuno Assembly's judgment against a hydroelectric project has been, in part, sustained by the growing controversy surrounding the expense and nonproductivity of the Machu Picchu project itself.[47]

[42] Romero, *Report for 1963*, pp. 45–46.

[43] *Ibid.*, p. 47.

[44] *LA*, May 22, 1964, p. 4; May 30, 1964, p. 4; October 25, 1964, p. 4; November 20, 1964, p. 2.

[45] Interview, José Luís Lescano, Puno, April 13, 1965.

[46] Romero, *Report for 1964*, p. 28, my translation.

[47] *Caretas*, no. 327 (February 25, 1966): 18–19.

New Criticism

A large budget and an unprecedented capacity for a kind of pork-barrel in public works projects were not enough to bury criticism of the Corporation. In early 1964, just after the municipal elections, the Corpuno Directorate decided to approve a six months' leave with pay for Oscar Espinoza to accept a study grant awarded him by the Italian government.[48] This incurred the bitter criticism of the Cáceres brothers and others, including Samuel Frisancho, the editor of *Los Andes* and self-proclaimed watchdog over Corpuno's affairs.[49]

While Espinoza was gone, Frisancho and the Cáceres brothers allegedly collaborated in an attempt to take over the Corporation.[50] In April, 1963, Frisancho had been elected the dean of the Society of Lawyers.[51] The following March, he was chosen as their delegate to the Professional Committee in the Corpuno Assembly.[52] Then, after reportedly spending a great deal of money entertaining other representatives to the Assembly, and after the Cáceres brothers directed their followers (the two peasant delegates and the Municipal Council representatives of Juliaca and Lampa) to support him, Samuel Frisancho was elected to the Directorate.[53]

During the remainder of the Assembly, Frisancho and the Cáceres brothers (who were in attendance through most of the sessions) attacked the program, personnel, and structure of the Corporation.[54] Especially bitter was Néstor Cáceres' attack on the Agrarian Reform Department for its continued refusal to sponsor any programs of expropriations.[55] The Department's only activity thus far had been the Chijnaya resettlement project (to be discussed below). Another proj-

[48] Romero, *Report for 1963*, p. 26.
[49] *LA*, March 17, 1964, p. 1.
[50] Interview, Russell Scarato, Stanford Research Institute-AID, Puno, March 31, 1965.
[51] *LA*, April 18, 1963, p. 1.
[52] *Ibid.*, March 1, 1964, p. 1.
[53] Interview, Scarato, March 31, 1965. A contributing factor to the *rapprochement* between Frisancho and the Cáceres brothers may have been the cessation of publication of the Cáceres newspaper, *El Tiempo*, after the February 1, 1964, issue. Publication was not resumed until November 4, 1964.
[54] *LA*, March 13, 1964, p. 1; March 17, 1964, p. 1; March 18, 1964, p. 1.
[55] *Ibid.*, March 17, 1964, p. 1.

ect, about to be initiated, involved a land-consolidation program in a densely populated area near the lake (also mentioned below). But, as neither of these involved expropriations or many families, they were viewed as a betrayal of Corpuno's original goals. The leaders of the FSC had earlier demanded the resignation of the technical delegate in charge of the Agrarian Reform Department.[56] Finally, after a vote of no confidence narrowly passed the Assembly, he resigned.[57]

Frisancho's hand was also seen in the plans for public works outlined in the March, 1964, Assembly. In the budget approved on March 31, 1964, were a number of projects for the city of Puno, including the long-awaited initiation of work on the municipal theatre, auditoriums for two local schools, construction of a new fire station, the completion of a new covered market, and a new road (*vía de circunvalación*) in the hills above Puno, providing both a bypass and a basis for urban expansion.[58] Over S/20,000,000 were also allocated for programs benefiting the peasantry—the most, according to Néstor Cáceres, ever accorded to that sector of the department's population.[59] "In this fashion," editorialized *Los Andes*, "a chapter has been closed in the history of the Corporation of Puno, and new perspectives are being opened for the development and progress of the department . . ."[60]

The Puno-Juliaca Cleavage: Genesis

"The Historical Unity of the Department of Puno"

Events took a strange new twist two months later, however, when a rumor was spread that a committee was being formed in Arequipa to seek the division of the department of Puno into two departments, one with its capital in Puno and the other with its capital in Juliaca.[61] Immediately, all manner of eulogies and defenses of the "historical unity of the Department of Puno" began to appear in the pages of

[56] *ET*, January 15, 1964, p. 1.
[57] *LA*, March 17, 1964, p. 1.
[58] *Ibid.*, April 2, 1964, p. 1.
[59] *Ibid.*
[60] *Ibid.*, my translation.
[61] *Ibid.*, May 14, 1964, p. 1.

Los Andes from the Society of Lawyers,[62] the Chasky Intellectual Society [of Puno],[63] the Puno Society of Public Accountants, the Federation of Students at the Technical University, the Federation of Workers,[64] the [Communist] Federation of Peasants,[65] and other groups.

On May 23 a town meeting (*cabildo abierto*) was held in Puno, sponsored by the recently elected *belaundista* mayor, Remigio Cabala.[66] Róger Cáceres appeared before the meeting, assuring the hostile crowd that he had always worked for departmental unity and would continue to do so. Mayor Cabala then proposed, and Cáceres supported, the creation of a Committee for the Defense of the Unity and Interests of the Department of Puno, to be chaired by Dr. David Frisancho, the president of the Puno Lions Club and brother of the editor of *Los Andes*.[67] Cáceres later said that the rumor about a plan to divide the department had been spread by his enemies in the Puno Society of Lawyers.[68] Although a specific motive is not clear, the rumor marked the end of the brief collaboration between Samuel Frisancho and the Cáceres brothers.

New Programs Considered

On June 6 and 7, 1964, a public forum was held under the sponsorship of the recently appointed departmental prefect, Gustavo Salcedo, to prepare a list of requests to be made by the Prefect in his audience with President Belaúnde, later in the month. In attendance at the forum were "representatives of the municipal councils of the department, Corpuno, the Society of Lawyers, the National Planning Institute, the Technical University of the Altiplano, the Departmental Agropecuarian Association, and other official and private entities, as well as representatives of the local press."[69] The list of "initiatives

---

62 *Ibid.*
63 *Ibid.*, May 21, 1964, p. 1.
64 *Ibid.*, p. 6.
65 *Ibid.*, May 24, 1964, p. 6.
66 *Ibid.*, p. 1.
67 *Ibid.*
68 Interview, Róger Cáceres, Lima, March 27, 1965.
69 *LA*, June 10, 1964, p. 1, my translation.

approved by the forum" included demands for a Puno airport and an industrial park in Juliaca, along with the more familiar demands for national assistance to artisan, mining, and agropecuarian development, hydroelectric projects, and the reopening of the Cabanillas freezing plant.[70]

In late July, 1964, the FNDE budget was announced with S/40,000,000 allocated to Puno for various projects, including the construction of bridges on the Puno-Moquegua road, and further work on the Macusani-San Gabán road.[71] Samuel Frisancho assured readers of *Los Andes* that, as a member of the Corpuno Directorate, he would insist upon a prompt execution of the FNDE-financed projects, especially the Puno-Moquegua road improvements.[72]

In August, 1964, after the return of Espinoza from Italy, Corpuno announced its intention of establishing an industrial park in Juliaca, in accordance with the Prefect's forum proposals. Its purpose would be "to prepare (*acondicionar*) a special zone for the establishment (*radicación*) of industries to which all manner of facilities will be provided."[73] On August 28 it was reported that Corpuno had applied to AID for S/6,200,000 to finance the project.[74] Studies by representatives of the Stanford Research Institute (on loan to Corpuno through AID) were made for an optimal site on the outskirts of Juliaca, and, when one was decided upon, Corpuno proceeded to prepare zoning and installation studies, while at the same time requesting that the Ministry of Development sponsor a Presidential decree exonerating investors in the proposed park from taxes.[75]

In response to the support given by Corpuno to the Juliaca industrial park, David Frisancho demanded that the city of Puno have its own industrial park, as well as its own airport, and even suggested that a new railroad be built from Puno directly to Arequipa.[76] The proposal

---

[70] *Ibid.*

[71] *Ibid.*, July 28, 1964, p. 1.

[72] *Ibid.*

[73] Romero, *Report for 1964*, p. 123, my translation.

[74] *LA*, August 28, 1964, p. 2.

[75] Romero, *Report for 1964*, p. 124.

[76] *LA*, September 11, 1964, p. 1.

for a separate Puno airport, already endorsed in the Prefect's forum in June, received considerable support from the local Lions Club.[77] In October a Comité pro-Aeropuerto Ventilla was formed by David Frisancho, to organize volunteer labor in Puno to clear a road to the Ventilla hacienda, which had been selected as the best site to propose for the airport.[78] At the same time, it was reported that Samuel Frisancho had obtained the formal approval of his fellow Corpuno directors to support the Ventilla Committee, and that Senator Rafael Miranda, a *belaundista* from Puno, was preparing a bill to submit in Congress authorizing the airport.[79]

These events took on a national scope when the *aprista-odriísta* majority in Congress, looking for popular causes that would bring support to the Coalition in its running conflict with the Belaúnde administration, decided to help Puno in its demand for an airport and for construction of the Puno-Moquegua road. In November, 1964, Darío Palacios, the only Coalition deputy from the altiplano, announced that the Congressional majority would support requests for a S/150,000,000 loan to complete the Puno-Moquegua road.[80] When Senator Miranda encountered opposition from among his fellow *belaundistas* to the Ventilla bill as wasteful, the *aprista-odriísta* Coalition took the lead and passed it in the Senate[81] and in the Chamber.[82] However, President Belaúnde refused to promulgate the bill. When a demand for additional funds from Corpuno was made by supporters of the Ventilla project, Espinoza refused to grant them.[83]

In the meantime, thousands of peasants were trucked into Puno every Sunday, where they joined volunteer work brigades from the city itself in constructing an access road to the Ventilla field on the plateau above the city.[84] A year later, the road was finished and inaugurated

[77] *Ibid.*, September 17, 1964, p. 1; September 21, 1964, p. 1.
[78] *Ibid.*, October 17, 1964, p. 1.
[79] *Ibid.*
[80] *Ibid.*, November 18, 1964, p. 1.
[81] *Ibid.*, March 22, 1965, p. 1.
[82] *Ibid.*, April 19, 1965, p. 1.
[83] Interview, Espinoza, April 20, 1965.
[84] *LA*, January 10, 1965, p. 1 and *passim*; also personal observation during March and April, 1965.

with a pilgrimage of cars and trucks to the field, where numerous speeches were made.[85]

Throughout the year, there had been demands in *Los Andes* for passage and promulgation of the Ventilla bill, under the slogan ¡Alas para Puno! (Wings for Puno). Emphasis, curiously, was not so much on the economic gains that would accrue to the *puneños*, as on the pride and glory of having their own airport. Under pictures of jets flying in formation, or lined up on an immense paved runway, arguments such as the following appeared from time to time:

In the future, the Ventilla field will be the dwelling place for thousands of winged craft . . .
Magical Promise! . . .
that has filled our hearts with excitement; that has inspired our hope of soaring into the infinite; that has awakened the sleeping and noble spirit of cooperativism in our race.
Magical Promise! . . .[86]

But, although there was a great tendency to romanticize the Ventilla issue, this did not make it any less important to the *puneños*, nor less threatening to the *juliaqueños*. The urgency of getting the Ventilla airport open was increased by the announcement in July, 1965, that Faucett Airlines, a privately owned Peruvian firm, would join the Peruvian military line in servicing Juliaca, beginning sometime later in the year.[87]

Trouble over the Proposed Industrial Park

In the meantime, the projected industrial park for Juliaca had run into difficulties. The Juliaca Municipal Council, which had promised to donate the land for the park, delayed in doing so while the Cáceres brothers hurriedly tried to buy up the surrounding land, for which they were planning a large-scale privately financed housing project. In October, 1964, Corpuno had granted a loan of S/1,500,000 to the Council for construction of a civic center and for a paving project.[88]

---

[85] *Ibid.*, October 11, 1965, p. 6.
[86] *Ibid.*, September 23, 1965, p. 1, my translation.
[87] *Peruvian Times*, July 23, 1965, p. 22.
[88] Press Release, October 14, 1965, Corpuno, printed in *LA*, October 15, 1965, p 6.

Instead of investing the money as agreed upon, the Council proceeded to buy a hacienda for the industrial park.[89] Accusing the Council of misappropriating the money (as the Puno Council had done two years before, regarding a paving project), Corpuno demanded to see the Council's accounts.[90] Espinoza, in a public letter to Corpuno's president, wrote that:

Unfortunately, the ambition of the "reigning" family in Juliaca has forced an excessive delay of the conclusion of this accord [to establish an industrial park in Juliaca], by their unending speculations on how to obtain the greatest political benefits with the operation. Finally, on the fourteenth of this month [September, 1965], and perhaps in response to the movement that has been produced in this city, the Council has been hurried into sending a written form ceding the lands for the industrial park. That cession differs from the original plan of Corpuno and offer of the Council, making clear the interest of using this project for the known ends of the family that controls the destinies of Juliaca.

For all of these reasons . . . we consider that the negotiations with the Juliaca Council must be given up as definitely closed, and that we must continue with our studies for a [new] location for the department's industrial zones.[91]

While Juliaca's industrial park seemed to slip from her grasp, Puno's demands for one increased. Reports that a Japanese plastics firm and a Belgian bicycle assembly plant were willing to establish branch plants in the altiplano spurred interest in both cities.[92] Senator Rafael Miranda and Deputy Darío Palacios both presented bills in Congress to establish an industrial zone in or near the city of Puno.[93] With the support of the *aprista-odriísta* majority, the Miranda bill was passed in the Senate in September, 1965.[94] As the pressure was built up for Corpuno to join in support of the Puno site, Espinoza was prompted to declare that he

[89] *Ibid.*

[90] *Ibid.*

[91] Letter from Oscar Espinoza Bedoya to Andrés Romero Portugal, September 16, 1965, reprinted in *ibid.*, September 18, 1965, p. 4, my translation.

[92] *Ibid.*, January 28, 1965, p. 2; interview, Espinoza, April 20, 1965.

[93] *LA*, March 2, 1965, p. 1; March 30, 1965, p. 1.

[94] *Ibid.*, September 4, 1965, p. 1.

viewed with terror the sudden and virulent campaign that has been initiated in this city [Puno] regarding the long-standing industrial park project . . . I consider that the Corporation must again avoid being converted into a banner of the incapable few who are looking for causes to find popular acceptance with their eyes on future political events.[95]

In response to Espinoza's critique of the irrational actions of local agitators, a *Los Andes* correspondent reported that a "Magnum Assembly" had been held by the Puno Municipal Council on September 27, 1965, with the motive of discussing plans for the city's three-hundredth anniversary, which was approaching in 1968. Foremost among the suggestions were the industrial park and the airport. But, instead of reporting the content or decisions of the discussions, the reporter repeatedly emphasized the objectivity, maturity, and intelligence of the participants. "There were none," he wrote, "who were confused in their thinking or conduct, in that negative way that is so characteristic of an underdeveloped people . . ."[96] Another columnist, however, from Melgar Province, wrote that the debates between Puno and Juliaca were sterile and dangerous, serving to delay the needed industrial growth of the department as a whole.[97] In fact, it was reported at about the same time that Arequipa's plans for an industrial park were advancing rapidly, and that she had been assured of the participation of at least three large Japanese firms (including the Sony electronics and Suzuki motorcycle companies).[98]

Other Aggravations

Besides the debates and activities concerning the industrial parks and the Ventilla airport, other events were occurring at this time that also helped to aggravate relations between Puno and Juliaca and between the Cáceres brothers and their enemies. On September 20, 1965, *Los Andes* reported the arrests of Atalo Gutiérrez and Elias Pacho Huanca, two of the FSC's most influential leaders and the delegates

[95] Letter from Espinoza to Romero, *ibid.*, September 18, 1965, p. 4, my translation.
[96] *Ibid.*, October 1, 1965, p. 2, my translation.
[97] *Ibid.*, p. 8.
[98] *Ibid.*

to the Corpuno Assembly from the Quechua and Aymará peasants, respectively. Gutiérrez was arrested in regard to a long-standing dispute between one of the FSC syndicates and an Azángaro *hacendado*.[99] Pacho Huanca, who had been elected mayor of the district of Chucuito (province of Puno) in the 1963 elections, was charged with misappropriating money from the municipal treasury.[100]

Word also reached *Los Andes* at this time of the government's intention of carrying to completion the work on the Puno-Moquegua road. On September 21, Deputies Jaime Serruto (AP) and Darío Palacios (PAP) wired *Los Andes* that a law had been promulgated by President Belaúnde authorizing the improvement *and pavement* of this alternative route to the coast.[101]

Then, on October 2, 1965, it was announced that S/500,000 had been allocated by Congress to the prefect of Puno to initiate construction work on the Ventilla field.[102] Shortly thereafter, Faucett Airlines announced that its service from Lima and Arequipa to Juliaca would begin October 24, the anniversary of the founding (in 1929) of San Román Province.[103] On October 28, the *aprista-odriísta* majority, using the constitutional provision whereby the president of Congress can promulgate laws passed by Congress but rejected by the President,[104] promulgated the Ventilla law.[105]

The explosion of violence that followed soon afterward in Juliaca had at its base one additional issue. It will be recalled that in May, 1964, the citizens of Puno had become exercised over the rumor that Arequipa interests were preparing to divide the department of Puno in two. The Cáceres family had been linked with this scheme, although denying it vehemently. Yet, it was believed that there would be much gain politically and economically for Juliaca by separation.

On February 26, 1965, the rumor was given new life. During the early morning hours, leaflets were dropped throughout the city of

99 *Ibid.*, September 20, 1965, p. 1.
100 *Ibid.*
101 *Ibid.*, September 21, 1965, p. 6 (*Ley 15604*).
102 *Ibid.*, October 2, 1965, p. 1.
103 *Ibid.*, October 18, 1965, p. 1.
104 *Peruvian Constitution* (1933), Article 129.
105 *Peruvian Times*, November 26, 1965, p. 1 (*Ley 15719*).

Puno, urging a revolt of the seven northern provinces against Puno and proposing their secession from the department.[106] Although the culprit was quickly found to be a young Communist,[107] the affair caused a sensation in Puno, reopening the bitter attacks on the Cáceres brothers' treasonous hostility to the "historic traditions of the altiplano."[108]

THE PUNO-JULIACA CLEAVAGE: EXPLOSION

The Threat of Secession

Seven months later, as the campaign for the Ventilla airport and the industrial park intensified, *Los Andes* announced that a plan was underway for the annexation of Juliaca to the department of Arequipa.[109] If the rumors of other schemes may have lacked any basis in fact, this story was soon proven to be true. On October, 24, 1965, the anniversary of Juliaca's promotion to provincial capital, Luís Cáceres, Juliaca's mayor, announced that the Municipal Council was ready to separate itself from the department of Puno and to annex itself to the department of Arequipa. The mayor of Arequipa, Ulrich Neisser, was in attendance at the meeting, and, in an emotional ceremony, he presented the Council with a cobblestone from the streets of Arequipa and announced that "Arequipa would receive Juliaca with open arms."[110] To climax the "madness" of the meeting, *Caretas* reported that

the *cacerista* leader, Nancy Soto, spoke with energy that "the people of Juliaca were tired of the humiliations and delays that they have suffered on the part of Puno" and warned that there were *juliaqueños* ready to set up barricades and to use dynamite "to liberate themselves."[111]

In the days that followed, the momentum of the Juliaca protest

---

[106] *LA*, February 27, 1965, p. 1. Why the leaflets were dropped in Puno, instead of the capitals of the seven northern provinces, was a question that did not seem to temper the fury that followed in Puno.

[107] *Ibid.*

[108] *Ibid.*, March 2, 1965, p. 6; March 4, 1965, p. 2; March 5, 1965, p. 2.

[109] *Ibid.*, October 15, 1965, p. 1.

[110] *Caretas*, no. 321 (November 10, 1965): 11, my translation.

[111] *Ibid.*, my translation.

grew inexorably. On October 29, in a town meeting attended by over twelve hundred, Luís Cáceres presented four demands to the Puno authorities: the resignation of Oscar Espinoza, manager of Corpuno; the resignation of the chief of the Health Area (for neglecting Juliaca's health services, while opening a new hospital in Puno); the resignation of the chief of the Office of Roads (for favoring work on the Puno-Moquegua and Puno bypass roads over all others); and the execution of "various works" in Juliaca.[112] If these demands were not met, declared Cáceres, a general strike would be called. The next day a strike committee was established, headed by one of the Juliaca councilmen. The commandant of the local police (*guardia civil*) post sought to arrange a meeting between Cáceres and the mayor of Puno to propose a settlement, but met with no success.[113]

The Strike and Blockade

With intransigence apparent on both sides, no more dramatic opportunity existed for spotlighting Juliaca's grievances before the department and nation, than the anniversary (November 4) of the founding of the city of Puno. On that day, Corpuno was going to dedicate a number of works carried out during the past few years, including the municipal theatre, the covered market, a new hospital, extensive paving projects, and a housing development, all of them in the department's capital.[114] Belaúnde's Minister of Government, Javier Alva Orlandini, arrived in the altiplano ahead of the ceremonies for consultations with local officials and several public appearances. A group of *aprista* leaders, headed by the president of the Chamber of Deputies, was expected to arrive by plane from Lima on November 4 at the Juliaca airport.

On November 3, Alva Orlandini arrived in Juliaca. Invited to meet with the Municipal Council in the Town Hall, Alva Orlandini declined, asking to meet instead in the offices of the *guardia civil*, since a large crowd had gathered in front of the Town Hall, and he was afraid that they would try to kidnap him.[115] In the meeting that fol-

[112] *Oiga*, no. 149 (November 12, 1965): 3.
[113] *Ibid.*
[114] *LA*, October 22, 1965, p. 3.
[115] *Oiga*, no. 149 (November 12, 1965): 4.

lowed, the Minister read the Council's four-point memorandum and stated that he was unable to do anything himself to satisfy them. Finally, he warned them to abstain from any acts they might later regret. The councilmen returned to the Town Hall, where the crowd had grown. After discussing the matter among themselves, they reduced the demands to one demand: the resignation of Oscar Espinoza.[116] However, by this time, Alva Orlandini had left Juliaca on a visit to Azángaro with the *belaundista* deputy, León Cárdenas.[117] Thus ignored, the *juliaqueños* decided to call the threatened strike at midnight and to cut off all communications to Puno for forty-eight hours.[118]

According to the press, both in Lima and in Puno, the organizers had broad support in and around Juliaca, where hundreds of Indians and *cholos* volunteered to dig trenches across the roads and to collect rocks and boulders to block the roads and railroads.[119] Local Juliaca radio stations, Radio Sol de los Andes (owned by the Cáceres family) and Radio Juliaca (owned by Juan Zea Gonzales and operated by local *belaundistas*), *both* were reportedly organizing and encouraging the masses to actions against the authorities.[120]

The Violence

Local police and a detachment of assault guards (*guardia republicana*), which had been ordered to the area by Alva Orlandini, were on hand, but did nothing as the makeshift barricades went up. Peasants and *cholos* gathered along all the roads, especially the one leading to Puno, where they kept a vigil through the night, reportedly drinking heavily.[121] At around 9:00 A.M., November 4, six vehicles appeared on the road from Puno on their way to meet the delegation of *apristas* at the airport. This, according to *Caretas,*

[116] *Ibid.*

[117] *La Prensa* (Lima), November 5, 1965, p. 2.

[118] *Ibid.*

[119] *Caretas*, no. 321 (November 10, 1965): 12; *La Prensa* (Lima), November 6, 1962, p. 2; *LA*, November 5, 1965, p. 4; *Oiga*, no. 149 (November 12, 1965): 4.

[120] "Comunicado de la Dirección General de la Guardia Civil y Policía," Puno, November 5, 1965, reprinted in *La Prensa* (Lima), November 6, 1965, p. 2, and *LA*, November 8, 1965, p. 3.

[121] *Ibid.*

was considered as the test of [Juliaca's] planned defiance. The crowd stoned the drivers, turned over the vehicles and even burned two of them. They belonged to the Technical University of the Altiplano and to Corpuno.

The police tried to impede the attack against the vehicles, but without much success. At 10:00 A.M. it rained heavily, forcing a large part of the crowd to flee. The police took advantage of this to clear the road and remove the stones.[122]

When the rain stopped, and the *juliaqueños* saw that the road was being cleared, a crowd of them, headed by Luís Cáceres, pursued the troops to their command post, waving firearms, throwing stones, and exploding molotov cocktails. The troops responded with tear gas and shots fired in the air. But the crowds persisted.

Informed of this by radio, the Minister of Government (in Puno) then ordered the mayor arrested, along with other leaders of the disorders. He also ordered the two radio stations closed.[123] These acts further infuriated the masses, who in the streets and from the hills above the city continued to attack the military and police troops throughout the day with sniper fire and explosives, as well as with rocks fired with deadly accuracy from pre-Incaic slingshots.[124] The toll from the rioting, as of November 8, was five dead, twenty-seven demonstrators and twenty-two officials and troops wounded, twenty-nine arrested, and over twenty missing.[125]

Although a state of siege was declared in the province of San Román by President Belaúnde,[126] demonstrations, especially by masses of women dressed in black, continued for a week thereafter, accompanied by repeated incidents of violence. An American journalist, passing through Juliaca by train almost a week after the fighting had begun, made these observations:

Alongside the tracks a human chain, long and deep, was already taking formation. The links of that chain looked at us as though we were creatures from another world. . . .

122 *Caretas*, no. 321 (November 10, 1962): 12, my translation.
123 *Ibid.*
124 *Ibid.*
125 *LA*, November 8, 1965, p. 1.
126 *La Prensa* (Lima), November 5, 1965, p. 1.

At one point, with the station still a good distance away, a chorus of strident voices shouted "Muera! Muera!"—death to us. But no-one made a move toward the train. Two truckloads of heavily armed troops prevented them from doing so . . .

A few tracks away from us [in the stationyard], people were angrily encircling two green coaches. . . . A woman explained that the coaches contained new troop arrivals. This proved to be false, but . . . sadly, one remembers them contorting their faces and shaking their fists at those empty coaches.[127]

Juliaca: A National Issue

The Juliaca events, serious enough in themselves, quickly became an issue of nationwide proportions, as the AP-PDC Alliance and the *aprista-odriísta* Coalition accused each other of responsibility for the bloodshed. The Administration was accused of putting down the riots with excessive violence, while the Coalition leaders were charged with having promoted the secession in the first place by trying to manipulate public opinion in the area through irresponsible bills and political promises.

Both sides were critical of the Cáceres brothers. But the latter received an enormous amount of publicity in their emotional defenses of Juliaca and their charges that the "feudal bosses" of Puno and the "cynical officials" of Corpuno and the Belaúnde government were neglecting Juliaca. These charges undoubtedly fell upon sympathetic ears in many parts of Peru.[128]

Because of a recent law, passed by the *aprista-odriísta* majority in relation to guerrilla activities elsewhere in the country, any acts of violence against representatives of the state were now subject to military trial and a possible death penalty.[129] City leaders in Puno demanded that Róger and Néstor Cáceres be ousted from Parliament

---

[127] Robert Carl Hirschfield, "Passing through Juliaca," *The Minority of One,* 8, no. 3 (March 1966): 25.

[128] At least one provincial council elsewhere in Peru (the province of Tayacaja in the department of Huancavelica) announced its solidarity with the Juliaca rioters, for reasons of being mistreated by its own departmental authorities (*La Prensa* [Lima], November 6, 1965, p. 8).

[129] *Caretas*, no. 317 (August 19, 1965): 16.

and included in the trial as the intellectual authors of the violence.[130] But the *aprista-odriísta* majority ignored these demands, and not only proposed amnesty for all the prisoners (except Luís Cáceres) but also moved to censure Alva Orlandini and force his resignation.[131]

After over sixty hours of explosive debates, a deal was made between the *aprista-odriísta* majority and the AP-PDC Alliance, whereby the censure of Alva Orlandini would be removed in exchange for the amnesty of the prisoners.[132] In protest against the amnesty, a general strike was called in Puno, and a committee of five *puneños*, including Mayor Cabala, Samuel Frisancho, the leaders of the *odriísta* and Christian Democratic parties, and a representative of the Puno Association of Industries and Commerce, travelled to Lima to ask that the amnesty be withdrawn and that all the prisoners be tried. This request was ignored.[133]

Conclusions

To residents of the city of Puno, it was a bitter irony to see the major parties of the country fighting among themselves rather than joining to punish the Cáceres brothers and their followers. Yet, since Belaúnde's election two and a half years before, and the formation of the *aprista-odriísta* Coalition to control Congress, the battle between the Alliance and the Coalition had taken precedence over almost every issue in Peru. Thus, in the Juliaca crisis, the Cáceres brothers emerged virtually unscathed. Luís Cáceres, who was still to be tried, had been released from jail and assured by the members of the Municipal Council of Arequipa that they would pay for his legal expenses and otherwise support him in any way they could.[134]

In subsequent weeks, Corpuno and several government ministries assured Juliaca of generous new investments in a number of areas, including housing,[135] sewerage improvements,[136] and drinking water

130 *La Prensa* (Lima), November 10, 1965, p. 2.
131 *Ibid.*, November 13, 1965, p. 1.
132 *Ibid.*; *Oiga*, no. 150 (November 19, 1965): 4–5.
133 *LA*, November 20, 1965, p. 1.
134 *La Prensa* (Lima), November 7, 1965, p. 8.
135 *LA*, November 24, 1965, p. 1.
136 *Ibid.*, November 26, 1965, p. 6.

facilities.[137] In regard to the industrial park, Darío Palacios, the *aprista* deputy, reported in December that a bill would soon be passed to make the entire department of Puno an industrial zone, free of taxes for incoming industries.[138] Work momentum was slowed on both the Puno airport and the Puno-Moquegua road projects. In March, 1966, it was reported that Oscar Espinoza had resigned the managership of Corpuno.[139] On these counts, then, it appeared as if the rioters had achieved most of their goals.

Caretas concluded its account of the riots with the comment:

> What has happened can be a political blow to the provincial empire of the Cáceres family. In their attempt to "Juliacanize" Puno or "Arequipanize" Juliaca without awaiting the natural growth of that city to give it the importance that it merits, they have certainly won the hostility of the 61,000 electors throughout the rest of the department. In Juliaca there are only 4,000.[140]

The test of this prediction came in the municipal elections of December, 1966, in which FSC-sponsored candidates again sought election in every province and district in the department. If class loyalties were to prevail over regional loyalties, at least at the lower-class levels (*cholo* and peasant), then such a reverse in the political fortunes of the peasant movement might not be forthcoming.

The campaigns throughout the province were bitter and hard fought. The enemies of the PITC used every weapon possible to combat the Cáceres brothers and their followers. In Juliaca a common "front to oppose the bossism [*caciquismo*] of the peasants" was formed by all other political parties to run a single slate of candidates against Luís Cáceres.[141] Similar fronts were organized elsewhere in the department. In fact, one columnist decried the fact that while, "in all the provinces . . . there exists a marked spirit of unity in confronting the peasant mass [*campesinado*] . . . in Puno there is no such atti-

[137] *Ibid.*, November 30, 1965, p. 2.

[138] *Ibid.*, December 9, 1965, p. 1.

[139] Letter to author from Irwin Zagar, Peace Corps volunteer, Puno, March 10, 1965.

[140] *Caretas*, no. 321 (November 10, 1965): 14, my translation.

[141] *LA*, July 1, 1966, p. 1.

tude . . . toward the common enemy."[142] Five separate lists were filed in the Puno provincial elections—by the Coalición, the Alianza, the PITC, a local "united left" front, and a local conservative party. Such partisan divisiveness, some felt, might pave the way for a plurality victory by the Cáceres group.

This fear was not borne out in the November, 1966, elections. The *cacerista* candidate for mayor came in third in the balloting, which was easily won by the Alianza slate for the second straight time. The fourteen Council seats were distributed as follows (according to the procedures of proportional representation followed in Peru's municipal elections): the Alliance won eight, the leftists three, the PITC two, and the Coalition one.[143]

But elsewhere in the department, the PITC candidates scored a series of impressive victories, picking up two additional provincial councils (in Chucuito and Huancané)[144] and narrowly losing two others (Azángaro and Melgar),[145] while firmly holding their original two (San Román and Lampa).[146] Only the selvatic provinces (Carabaya and Sandia)[147] and the province of Puno were able to withstand the wave of sentiment for the peasant movement.

At the district level, many of the new councils were also PITC-dominated. In the proud colonial town of Pomata (province of Chucuito), a member of the local elite protested the "fatal disgrace" by which Pomata "is going to be in the hands of an illiterate."[148] "What is apparent," wrote a *Los Andes* columnist, "is that there exists political anarchy" throughout the department.[149]

But the anarchy worsened in December as an active throng, estimated at four thousand people, met in the central plaza of Lampa to protest the election of an Indian as mayor and to demand that he, and

[142] *Ibid.*, July 15, 1966, p. 1, my translation.
[143] *Ibid.*, November 14, 1966, p. 6.
[144] *Ibid.*, November 19, 1966, p. 8; November 22, 1966, p. 3.
[145] *Ibid.*, November 21, 1966, p. 5.
[146] *Ibid.*, November 14, 1966, p. 6; November 18, 1966, p. 8.
[147] *La Prensa* (Lima), December 13, 1966, p. 7.
[148] *LA*, December 5, 1966, p. 6.
[149] *Ibid.*, November 17, 1966, p. 3.

all the other lackeys of the Cáceres brothers leave town at once.[150] A few days earlier, a manifesto by "the Lampa residents in Puno" had declared that

the *cacerista* list is filled with semicivilized Indians. They scarcely know how to read and write, and some can scarcely print their own names. We are not enemies of the Indian like the Cáceres [family]. But we are enemies of ignorance, incompetence, and inexperience, which the little masters of demagogery love and value so highly . . .[151]

Two weeks later, after the mayor-elect refused to leave town, he was arrested on charges of sexually molesting a fifteen-year-old girl.[152] With legal and political aid from the Cáceres brothers, he was finally released from jail and duly installed in office.[153]

This incident dramatically illustrates the depth of class animosity that exists throughout the department and that has finally found its inevitable expression in the legally sanctioned process of electoral conflict. Whatever the national issues, parties, or candidates may be in any future elections, the local class conflict will probably overshadow all else in the altiplano.[154]

---

[150] *Ibid.*, December 6, 1966, p. 1.

[151] Published in *ibid.*, December 2, 1966, p. 3; my translation.

[152] *Ibid.*, December 19, 1966, p. 1.

[153] Letter to the author from Laura Rosenberg, Peace Corps Volunteer, Lampa, February 2, 1967.

[154] The immediate prospect of Presidential and Congressional elections, which had been scheduled for June, 1969, was dimmed by the military *coup d'état* of October, 1968. Unlike the 1962 military junta, the junta that took power in 1968 avoided making any promises regarding an early return to constitutional government.

9

THE LINGERING PROBLEM OF
AGRARIAN REFORM

At the basis of the altiplano's social and economic development problem is the use and ownership of land. Both principal groups in the area, landowners and peasants, are so traditionally dependent upon the land that neither is adequately equipped either psychologically or educationally to envisage any other kind of economic activity. Yet, as population pressures and personal expectations regarding living standards have increased, the tension between the groups has also increased. The organization of peasant unions by the Cáceres brothers and the Communists, while intended for broader and more diverse purposes, undoubtedly has had the effect of further aggravating this tension. In many cases, in recent years, *hacendados* have been reported as selling their lands, or portions thereof, to their *colonos*, or to neighboring *comuneros*.[1] Nevertheless, these actions do little to improve the general conditions of *minifundia* and *latifundia* in the altiplano and the ever present and growing demand by the peasant union leaders for a sweeping agrarian reform.

[1] Hernán Castillo *et al., Accopata: The Reluctant Recipient of Technological Change,* p. 26; Pedro Ortiz V. and Raúl Galdo P., *El Indígena de la Isla de Amantaní,* pp. 35–37.

ATTITUDES TOWARD AGRARIAN REFORM

Agrarian reform in the altiplano, as in any other part of the underdeveloped world, means different things to the different people who demand (or say they demand) it. To the peasants, it may often mean the expropriation of large estates and their parcellation and redistribution among those peasants actually working the land and/or the relatively landless peasants of neighboring villages. Indirectly, it may also mean an end to social and economic abuses among classes. To many landowners, the ideal agrarian reform may mean technical assistance, more available credit, infrastructural development (e.g., road-building, irrigation), and colonization projects in virgin lands to which an excess peasant population may be siphoned. To others, agrarian reform means the problem of increasing agricultural productivity and rural well-being by the change of a number of conditions, all of which are interrelated in a complex web. This may involve such measures as increased land taxation (to discourage unproductive practices and landholding for purely social reasons, and to force the intensification of cultivation on larger landholdings), the consolidation of smaller parcels (to permit economies of scale in the use of machinery, purchases of seeds, fertilizer, and insecticides), the formation of consumer and marketing cooperatives (to eliminate costly middleman services), and a whole series of social and educational aids to improve the general conditions within which the farmer can maximize his productivity and well-being.[2]

Because of their conflicting interpretations of agrarian reform, both the landowners and the peasants of the altiplano have been able to

[2] The complexity of the agrarian reform problem and the need for a broadly diversified approach to land productivity is best discussed by Theodore W. Schultz in *Transforming Traditional Agriculture*. See also Richard P. Schaedel, "Land Reform Studies," *Latin American Research Review*, 1, no. 1 (Fall, 1965): 75–122; Thomas F. Carroll, "The Land Reform Issue in Latin America," in *Latin American Issues: Essays and Comments*, ed. Albert O. Hirschman, pp. 161–201; Oscar Delgado, "Revolution, Reform, Conservatism: Three Types of Agrarian Structure," *Dissent*, 9, no. 4 (Autumn, 1962): 350–363; Thomas R. Ford, *Man and Land in Peru*, pp. 118–143; Albert O. Hirschman, *Journeys toward Progress: Studies of Economic Policy-Making in Latin America*, pp. 131–213; and Edmundo Flores, *Land Reform and the Alliance for Progress*.

declare themselves in favor of it and to criticize the performance of the governmental agencies (Corpuno and the National Agrarian Reform Office, ONRA) that are charged with responsibility for carrying it out. Corpuno soon antagonized peasant leaders by refusing to carry out a program of expropriations; and ONRA upset many middle- and large-scale landowners by the zeal and speed with which it initiated its studies and preparations for expropriations.

Landowners, it will be recalled, were particularly enthusiastic supporters of public works and industrialization programs during the times of droughts and floods. Presumably, such programs reduced the potential friction between the landowners and the hard-hit peasantry by providing the latter with temporary work. Also, the most vocal champion of the hydroelectrification of the department has been the leader of the local federation of landowners, José Luís Lescano.[3] However, the landowners expect the financing of these programs to come either from outside the department, or from the producers of *auquénido* wool (mostly peasants), who share, with outside buyers, the burden of the export taxes that go toward financing the operations of Corpuno.

On the other hand, the leaders of the peasantry, while sharing the interest in industrialization and public works, have constantly pressed in recent years for the expropriation of a number of haciendas, and have used a variety of means to push for improved treatment of peasants on still other haciendas. A wave of land seizures in the departments of Cuzco and Junín, beginning in 1960, spread the fear of revolution throughout the sierra.[4] In Puno, a serious clash took place between police and peasants on a disputed piece of land near the city of Puno, in December, 1960. As a result, two peasants were killed and a number arrested.[5] In the first convention of the FSC, held later in the month, the expropriation of a number of haciendas was demanded, as

[3] *Los Andes* (Puno), May 22, 1964, p. 4 (hereinafter cited in this chapter as *LA*); May 30, 1964, p. 4; March 5, 1965, p. 6; June 8, 1965, p. 2.

[4] Hugo Neira, *Cuzco: Tierra y Muerte*; see also *Peruvian Times*, May 6, 1960, pp. 1–2; December 15, 1961, p. 1; January 26, 1962, p. 4; March 9, 1962, p. 1; March 23, 1962, pp. 6, 8–9.

[5] *El Comercio* (Lima), December 1, 1960, p. 1 (hereinafter cited in this chapter as *EC*).

well as the release of the arrested peasants. In addition, solidarity with the peasants in revolt elsewhere in the country was expressed.[6]

Incidents took place in 1962 and 1963 on five other haciendas, most of them involving local branches of the FSC.[7] In March, 1963, during the departmental congress of the FSC, demands were again formulated for the expropriation of haciendas, but this time the demand was directed to the new local development corporation.[8] These requests were denied by Corpuno, as we saw above, with the result that FSC-Corpuno relations deteriorated considerably.

Reactions to the Agrarian Reform Bill

Soon after the election of Belaúnde, his Minister of Agriculture visited Puno and approved Corpuno's policy of promoting an integrated agrarian reform program in conjunction with the national government, instead of isolated expropriations that could only serve political purposes.[9] Two months after the Corpuno Assembly forced the resignation of the chief of the Agrarian Reform Department of Corpuno, an Agrarian Reform bill was passed in Congress. Although it was not as progressive as the one sought by President Belaúnde and the AP-PDC Alliance, it was promulgated by Belaúnde and preparations were rapidly made to implement it on as wide a scale as was financially possible.[10]

During the eight months of debate that preceded the passage and promulgation of the Agrarian Reform bill,[11] both peasant and landowner groups in Puno were critical of the proposed legislation, the former calling it too conservative, the latter saying that it was not conservative enough. Néstor Cáceres, speaking for the FSC, demand-

---

[6] *Ibid.*, December 17, 1961, p. 12.

[7] *LA*, November 20, 1962, p. 4; July 16, 1963, p. 4; August 29, 1963, p. 4; *El Tiempo* (Puno), August 27, 1963, p. 7 (hereinafter cited in this chapter as *ET*); September 8, 1963, p. 6.

[8] *LA*, March 10, 1963, p. 1.

[9] *Oiga*, no. 149 (November 12, 1965): 5.

[10] *Hispanic American Report*, 18, no. 5 (July, 1964): 438–440; *Peruvian Times*, May 29, 1964, pp. 11–13.

[11] See *Caretas*, no. 274 (September 17, 1963): *passim.*

ed that the Agrarian Reform bill be amended to enable lands to pass directly to those who work them, without cost.[12]

The hacienda owners, on the other hand, declared that the maximum land sizes permissible under the proposed AP-PDC bill were far too small for efficient cattle-raising, and that payment for expropriated lands in bonds would be a severe burden for many landowners, as well as being unconstitutional.[13] When the *aprista-odriísta* Coalition offered a more conservative counterproject (*contraproyecto*), local landowners immediately supported it as being "more integral."[14]

In regard to the Cáceres demand of "land to those who work the land," the landowners, in a cleverly worded communique, declared that "we have always defended [the notion] that the land is for him who works it, because we are direct administrators, that is, we use our intellectual and technical labor, which is the critical force in any enterprise, in order to fulfill efficiently the social and economic function of the land, making it more productive."[15] In the same communique, they continued as follows:

We declare with pride that we form part of the abandoned peasant class that finds itself faced on one side by demagogic attacks by the new racist redeemers and on the other by the permanent menace of economic crisis that is being increased daily by the discouragement provoked by uncertainty.[16]

After the *aprista-odriísta* Agrarian Reform bill had passed and been promulgated, local landowners were dismayed by the speed with which Belaúnde proceeded to set up branches of the National Agrarian Reform Office (ONRA), and to initiate cadastral surveys and socioeconomic investigations of land tenure conditions in the sierra.[17]

[12] *ET*, January 14, 1964, p. 1; *LA*, January 25, 1964, p. 2.
[13] *LA*, September 13, 1963, p. 4; September 14, 1963, p. 4. The constitutionality problem involved the requirement of previous indemnification for expropriated property (*Peruvian Constitution* [1933], Articles 29 and 47), for which, it was argued, bonds would be considered inadequate.
[14] *LA*, January 7, 1964, p. 6.
[15] "Comunicado de las Asociaciones Agropecuarias de Puno," April 11, 1964, printed in *ibid.*, April 19, 1964, pp. 2–3, my translation.
[16] *Ibid.*, my translation.
[17] *Ibid.*, July 23, 1964, p. 1; August 10, 1964, p. 4.

In the department of Puno, ONRA began its studies in the provinces of Chucuito and Puno, photographing the land by air and sending teams of young social scientists and agronomists to every hacienda to study conditions, demarcate holdings, and perform other services.

During this time, incidents between peasants and *hacendados* were less frequently reported and involved strikes or legal suits rather than land seizures or violence. Part of the credit for this widespread change in tactics was given, by friend and foe alike, to the FSC and its leadership. A key reason for the switch was the provision in the Agrarian Reform Law whereby "persons who instigate or foment or promote or execute acts of invasion or usurpation of lands owned by the State, Corporations or private persons, or execute acts disturbing possession, are hereby excluded from the benefits of the allotment of lands under the Agrarian Reform . . ."[18]

On May 21, 1965, the altiplano was declared an Agrarian Reform Zone by the Minister of Agriculture, and a list was published of eighty holdings, belonging to fifty-one owners (or groups of owners), that were to be affected by the Agrarian Reform in Chucuito and Puno.[19]

By the end of 1966, the only lands in the process of expropriation were those of the Puno office of the Beneficencia Pública (a national charity organization whose self-sufficiency rested upon vast landholdings ceded to it in the past by the government, partly as an attempt to weaken the political influence of the Catholic Church). The fact that private properties were avoided in the first ONRA expropriation was probably dictated by a number of factors: (1) a sharp cutback in funds allocated to ONRA in the national budget after 1965, (2) expectations of less legal and political resistance from the Beneficencia, and (3) expectations that one prompt and deliberate expropriation might spur private owners to either improve their lands or abandon them—easing ONRA's problems of selecting holdings for later expropriations. It is too early to say at this time (1968) whether these calculations would eventually prove correct. At any rate, after several

[18] Special Provision, Law No. 15037, *Agrarian Reform Law*, translated by U.S. AID, July 16, 1964.
[19] Published in *LA*, August 2, 1965, pp. 4–5.

months of disputing the land's value, the Beneficencia and ONRA came to terms. In the meantime, however, the local director of the Beneficencia complained that the "renters, seeing the impossibility of working [the land] because of the attitude of the peasants . . . are abandoning their holdings . . . [and] that on finding them in the hands of the peasants, ONRA is not going to be able to fulfill its objectives . . ."[20]

Undaunted, ONRA proceeded soon thereafter to publish a new list of sixteen more holdings subject to possible expropriation in the Puno-Chucuito area.[21] The engineers were apparently determined to maintain the psychological pressure on the landholders while they awaited the day when more resources would be forthcoming or popular pressures for expropriations would become more irresistible.

POLITICAL ACTIVITY AMONG THE PEASANTS

In the altiplano, whether the Belaúnde regime pressed hard or cut back in the matter of expropriations, the FSC and the Cáceres brothers appeared to have the most to gain. The harder the ONRA engineers pushed for a meaningful reform, the more the peasant leaders claimed that none of this would have been possible without the FSC. And as ONRA's and SIPA's funds were cut to the bone in the fiscal crises of 1966 and 1967,[22] the peasant leaders reaffirmed their traditional grounds for distrust of all national programs.

One of the reactions of the *belaundistas* in the altiplano to the political "nutcracker" of the FSC movement was to enter the competition for more tangible influence among the peasantry, first by their program of Cooperación Popular, and later by outright alliance with the Communist peasant federation, the FDC.

Cooperación Popular

The Executive Interministerial Commission of Popular Cooperation, begun in 1963 at the outset of Belaúnde's administration, was an

[20] "Comunicado, Sociedad de Beneficencia Pública de Puno," published in *ibid.*, September 16, 1966, p. 2, my translation.

[21] *Ibid.*, December 9, 1966, p. 1.

[22] *EC*, July 21, 1966, p. 2; *Caretas* no. 338 (September 11–23, 1966): 10–

extremely popular organization offering direct material aid (popularly visualized as "picks and shovels") to communities that were willing to plan and volunteer labor for self-improvement projects, such as irrigation, school construction, road-building, plaza improvement, and other programs. In Puno, 118 such projects had been undertaken by August, 1964, and 252 more were under consideration.[23] In addition to material aid, Cooperación Popular instituted a kind of domestic Peace Corps, called Cooperación Popular Universitario, through which university students spent their summer vacations living and working in sierra peasant communities, providing technical assistance or just manual labor to the projects planned by the communities. A number of such volunteers worked in the altiplano during the summers (January–March) of 1964 and 1965.

The FDC

However, as a program to advance the political influence of Belaúnde's Acción Popular party, Cooperación Popular had a serious shortcoming. This was the absence of any continuing contact with the community leaders after a program was completed. In fact, it is reported that the best organized and most demanding communities for Cooperación Popular programs in the altiplano were those that were already controlled by the FSC.[24]

As a result of this situation, therefore, local AP leaders were given directions to initiate negotiations with the Federación Departamental de Campesinos, the local branch of the Communist Confederación de Campesinos Peruanos. In February and March, 1965, a tremendous battle took place within the ranks of the FDC, which resulted in its division into two separate organizations, the FDC-*ortodoxos,* who sought collaboration with and assistance from the AP, and the FDC-

---

13; *Oiga,* no. 191 (September 16, 1966): 4–5, 34; no. 192 (September 23, 1966): pp. 4–11, 22; and *New York Times,* Hemisphere Business Review, January 22, 1968, p. 71.

[23] República del Perú, Comisión Ejecutiva Interministerial de Cooperación Popular, *El Pueblo Lo Hizo,* pp. 42, 46–52.

[24] Interview, Alejandro Nuñez, director of Cooperación Popular, Puno, April 19, 1965.

auténticos, who condemned the idea and purged those leaders who espoused it.[25] A convention, planned for February, 1965, was postponed indefinitely, while a struggle went on between the two factions for control of the individual syndicates.[26] The number of active syndicates in the FDC before the split was estimated variously at from ninety to three hundred.[27]

The FSC

In contrast to the confusion and division in the ranks of the FDC, the FSC continued to grow, claiming 1,184 syndicates in April, 1965[28] and 1,326 in November, 1965.[29] According to Puno's Communist deputy in Congress, Fernando Manrique, the FSC owed its success to the considerable wealth of the Cáceres family, which enabled them to have a salaried organizer in every FSC-affiliated community.[30] Atalo Gutiérrez admitted to the salarying of only a "handful" of FSC leaders, in charge of regional activities. The community leaders, he said, were paid from dues collected from the union members, themselves.[31] Others criticized the salarying of any leaders as "immoral" and "a violation of the tradition of the labor movement."[32] Nevertheless, Manrique's argument was probably correct—the FSC's strength stemmed from the salarying of organizers who knew the area and were willing to work in it.

But, besides the organizational skills and resources of the leaders,

---

[25] *El Campesino* (Puno), February 14, 1965, mimeographed newsletter, supporting *ortodoxo* position; Federación Departamental del Campesinos de Puno, *Boletín Informativo,* March 15, 1965, news release supporting *auténtico* position; also *LA,* March 10, 1965, p. 6; March 12, 1965, p. 4; *La Voz de Puno,* no. 12 (April 9, 1965): p. 3.

[26] *El Campesino* (Puno), February 14, 1965.

[27] The lower figure is the estimate of Atalo Gutiérrez, secretary-general of the FSC; the higher figure is that of Roberto Bautista, the former secretary-general of the FDC, and president of the Organizing Commission of the FDC-*ortodoxo* (Interviews, Puno, April 12 and 14, 1965).

[28] Interview, Gutiérrez, April 12, 1965.

[29] *La Prensa* (Lima), magazine supplement, November 14, 1965, p. 13.

[30] Interview, Fernando Manrique, Lima, May 7, 1965.

[31] Interview, Gutierrez, April 12, 1965.

[32] Interviews, Senator Juan Zea Gonzales (AP), Lima, May 6, 1965; Rosendo Aza, labor leader, Puno, April 14, 1965.

the FSC owed its popularity to the programs and accomplishments of its Congressional representatives. The three deputies, Róger and Néstor Cáceres and Julio Arce Catacora, were active in presenting countless bills (*proyectos*) and solicitudes (*pedidos*) for ministerial action or investigation. In the legislative year beginning July 28, 1964, through the spring of 1965, they jointly or separately sponsored 77 bills and 217 solicitudes, 6.5 and 7.5 percent, respectively, of the total number in the Chamber of Deputies. This represented a productivity for each man three times greater than the average for Peruvian congressmen.[33]

The orientation of the bills and solicitudes was clearly toward the peasant population, focussing on educational deficiencies at the village level; inequitable conditions on the haciendas; inadequate medical, agricultural, technical, and other services to the villages; and the mistreatment of peasants by public authorities.[34] With respect to the latter, the Cáceres brothers frequently introduced bills creating new districts or provinces—smaller administrative units—in response to peasant complaints of public abuse or inattentiveness. The creation of new districts was decried by other politicians as the needless expansion of governmental bureaucracy. In fact, however, this process gave rural populations greater access to the national government by drawing its representatives out into the villages, and by selecting some of their own leaders for official positions. The sustained electoral successes of the Cáceres brothers and their PITC candidates for local offices confirms the political value of these actions.

It is said that Communist or other leftist intellectuals, especially students, are notorious for their ability to "talk revolution," and equally notorious for their inability or aversion to actually work in a sustained manner among peasants or slum dwellers without becoming disillusioned. In the altiplano the peasants have been considerably

---

[33] República del Perú, Cámara de Diputados, *Relación de los Proyectos Presentados, Conjunta y Separadamente por los Señores Diputados Róger y Néstor Cáceres Velásquez y Julio Arce Catacora, Durante las Legislaturas de 1964 Hasta la Fecha;* and *Relación de los Pedidos Presentados, Conjunta y Separadamente por los Señores Diputados Róger y Néstor Cáceres Velásquez y Julio Arce Catacora, Durante las Legislaturas de 1964 Hasta la Fecha.*

[34] *Ibid.*

mobilized, far more than in any other area of the sierra. But they have
been mobilized, largely, by their own people. Common economic interests, rather than ideological visions, provided the linkage between
merchants and *cholos*, and *cholos* and peasants, that enabled this mobilization. Other groups, such as the mestizo lawyers and intellectuals,
were weighted down with a heritage of exploitation and prejudice,
depriving them of an opportunity to direct their relationships with the
peasants toward any lasting, positive ends. Any investment by the
Belaúnde regime, through its program of Cooperación Popular or
other devices, in trying to establish a peasant political bloc to rival the
FSC may be bound, ultimately, to boomerang in the FSC's favor because of the enormous expense involved in satisfying every community relative to the modest expense for the FSC to organize neglected
peasants into protest groups.

Corpuno's Programs

As an illustration of the expense of developing peasant productivity,
it is worth reviewing the programs of Corpuno carried out by its
Agrarian Reform Department—programs that prompted great criticism from the FSC when they were undertaken, but that have subsequently received praise in the national press.

Chijnaya

The first of these programs was the Chijnaya project, involving the
purchase of a hacienda near the town of Pucará (province of Lampa)
for the resettlement of approximately seventy families made homeless
by the February, 1963, flood of the Ramis River. In charge of the
project was a young Peace Corps volunteer, Ralph Bolton. A detailed
description of the project by a Cornell University research team studying Peace Corps operations in Peru is worth quoting at some length, to
illustrate the difficulties and complexities inherent in even a carefully
planned and well-financed program of peasant improvement.

[Ralph Bolton] drew up a lengthy questionnaire with which to survey the
zone. With the aid of the Puno Development Corporation's personnel, the
questionnaire was administered to nearly 300 persons. This served as a tool

to begin talking to people about the possibility of moving to another area, sounding out local opinion.

At first, most of the people were very suspicious of the offers to help. The landowners, Mestizo merchants, unenlightened clergy, persons with vested interests in the Taraco area, circulated malicious rumors that this was a Communist plot, or that the Indians would be slaughtered by the gringos to make grease for their machines or carried off to work in the jungles. Despite the problems created by rumor mongering, and the general social structure of the District [of Taraco], plans were developed, and the Bishop of Puno agreed to sell an estate owned by the Church called Chijnaya, located near the town of Pucará, one hundred kilometers from Taraco.

For the next five months, various preparations were made and 74 families committed themselves to the experiment. Chijnaya was a sparsely populated manor of 1,200 acres, which had been rented by the Church to an absentee landlord. This landlord brought serfs from her other estates to work its lands and graze livestock there. Only six serf families lived on Chijnaya.

In September 1963, the "brave seventy-four" families sallied forth toward their new destiny . . . The first task for the settlers was to build temporary sod houses, since there was no housing of any sort on the estate. With [Bolton's] constant assistance, the program went forward . . . [Bolton] helped the settlers to form a cooperative organization through which . . . loans could be handled, and the new houses constructed, school and community center erected, etc.

The settlers established under [Bolton's] direction a consumers' cooperative, a small retail store to cater to their immediate needs.

To cultivate the virgin land, the settlers formed a producers' cooperative to be able to rent a tractor and obtain fertilizers and seed. Thirty-five acres of potatoes, 90 acres of forage crops, and two acres of quinua were planted the first season, despite the relatively late arrival of the settlers and the initiation of agricultural activities in relation to the growing season. Subterranean storage silos were constructed to hold silage for cattle. In spite of the late planting and a severe drought which plagued the area that season, the people of Chijnaya enjoyed a better harvest than anyone in the surrounding area. . . .

In a parallel manner, the scrawny cattle belonging to the members of the new settlement were pooled, forming another cooperative organization. . . . One significant immediate result of cooperative cattle management is that children are no longer required to shepherd animals, allowing them to attend school.

. . . After a campaign of telegraming and petitioning the Ministry of Public Education in Lima, the community obtained recognition for its school, and the Minister dispatched three teachers to work in the new school.[35]

What was interesting about subsequent production in Chijnaya was that the cooperative structure of the community led to the disappearance of disguised unemployment and the appearance of a series of cottage industrial enterprises. The most important of these was the mechanized spinning of alpaca wool.[36] Curiously enough, the villagers did not have a stock of *auquénidos*. They bought their wool from peasants on neighboring haciendas.[37]

The most spectacular innovation of the Chijnaya peasants was the embroidery of little tapestries by the children, using bright colors and rudimentary designs on a plain wool backing. The tapestries have been sold in Peru and the United States with the help of the Peace Corps volunteers, and in 1965 they were put on display in museums in Brooklyn, Boston, and Washington.[38] Also, in the field of craft development, experimentation was being done in weaving, leather-working, and similar skills.

By April, 1965, construction had been completed on sixty new homes and the school, while a village plaza had been laid out and foundations dug for the community meeting hall and offices. A cattle-fattening center was built, with aid from the agricultural university, La Molina, in Lima, and new techniques were being experimented with.[39] The influence of the community was widespread. Delegations from other communities in the altiplano and elsewhere in the sierra

[35] Henry F. Dobyns, Paul L. Doughty, Allan R. Holmberg, *Peace Corps Program Impact in the Peruvian Andes: Final Report*, pp. 187–188.

[36] *Ibid.*, p. 188.

[37] Interview, Crispe Mamani, Corpuno employee in charge of liaison with Chijnaya, Puno, April 14, 1965.

[38] Dobyns, *et al., Peace Corps Program*, p. 189; interview, Ralph Bolton, Chijnaya, March 20, 1965.

[39] Ralph Bolton, "Chijnaya: A Peace Corps Success," *Pomona Today*, 63, no. 3 (October, 1965): 6.

visited Chijnaya to see the programs and to talk with the community leaders about their own problems.[40]

The total investment made by Corpuno and other governmental agencies in the Chijnaya project was $200,000.[41] By August, 1965, the tapestry business alone had earned over $10,000 and appeared to be expanding.[42] In 1966 it was reported that a school, a cooperative office, and an artisan center had been constructed, along with modern housing for each of the families. The economic prosperity of the enterprise was so striking, the report continued, that the community had arranged to purchase two adjoining haciendas with its own money.[43]

Chipana

The other project of importance begun by Corpuno, was in Chipana, near Ilave (province of Chucuito). Chipana is in a flat plain surrounded by thirteen villages, in which 23,000 peasants have a total of 5,000 hectares cultivated between them. Called a "Little London" by *Caretas*, this was the site of an experimental program in cooperative land consolidation, that is, the piecing together of tiny plots for mechanized cultivation.[44] As a pilot project for other consolidation programs around the lake, Chipana was intended to benefit almost 8,000 inhabitants through construction of a rural model city, in which cooperatively organized services, such as a school, medical post, store, artisan center, market, church, and a civic center, would be located.[45] The establishment of several of these services was to precede land consolidation efforts, so as to provide a basis of confidence among the peasants.[46] In 1965 it was reported that 532 peasants had affiliated themselves with the consumer cooperative, the first organism to be established in the area.[47] Subsequently, a school was installed, along

[40] *Ibid.*, pp. 7–8.
[41] *Peace Corps Volunteer*, 4, no. 3 (January, 1966): 20.
[42] Dobyns, *et al., Peace Corps Program*, p. 189.
[43] *LA*, August 8, 1966, p. 2.
[44] *Caretas*, no. 313 (June 25, 1965): 41–42.
[45] Romero, *Report for 1963*, pp. 42–44.
[46] *Ibid.*, p. 44.
[47] *Caretas*, no. 313 (June 25, 1965): 42.

with a technical training center, and a forage silo and cattle-fattening center.[48]

However, the plan to encourage land consolidation was slow to gain hold. *Caretas* reported in 1965 that between 1964 and 1965 only 50 hectares (of more than 5,000) in the pampa were "organically integrated" by the first volunteers for the project. Another 100 to 150 hectares annually were expected to be added to this first allotment.[49] Although the number of participants and the amount of land affected was limited, Oscar Espinoza, the manager of Corpuno, said that of the forty families who finally agreed to the consolidation program, thirty would be freed by the consolidation to go into full-time artisan work.[50]

CONCLUSIONS

Ironically, both the Chijnaya and the Chipana projects will owe their success to economic diversification and small-scale industrialization, not merely to improved systems of land tenure and cultivation. Both projects, by improving the division of labor among peasant families, and, hence, stripping the mask off disguised unemployment, have created needs for craft and industrial training, as well as marketing research, credits, and capital investments. But these additional services greatly increase the cost of the projects. In addition, it is not clear that producers oriented to markets and away from a dependence on the land will remain for long as members of the cooperatives in either Chijnaya or Chipana. The long-run impact of these programs, then, may well be the continued migration of peasants to the coastal, industrialized society, where markets for one's skills and products are better paying and living conditions superior.

Sweeping land expropriations under the Agrarian Reform law, unaccompanied by technical assistance or the promotion of economic diversification, might provide a social and political breathing space for the political system of the altiplano (at the cost, of course, of forcing many landowners to leave the area). Nevertheless, conditions for agropecuarian production, combined with population pres-

48 *Ibid.*
49 *Ibid.*
50 Interview, Espinoza, April 20, 1965.

sures, will eventually necessitate large-scale migrations, to either the selva or the coast. Not a single informant for this study felt otherwise.

The alternative to such eventual migration involves expenditures of money (for hydroelectric power, industrialization, communications, education, and other services) that stagger the imagination. In a country like Peru, where every sierra department can make virtually the same gloomy prediction about its economic future, and where national income and foreign credits are limited, the hope of any *one* region for such heavy investments is absurd. With the exception of scattered pilot projects of Chijnaya or Chipana types, the fundamental man-land relationships in the altiplano are certain to remain fairly unchanged for a long time to come, while the flow of migrants to the urban centers will probably increase.

In this setting, it seems likely that successful political movements in the area will be protest movements, based upon the dissatisfactions of those with rising expectations, yet unable or unwilling to migrate. If the literacy of the lower, *cholo* and peasant, classes continues to increase, these protest movements will be reflected more and more in voting results. Given these circumstances and the proven ability of the Cáceres brothers to exploit these circumstances, it is difficult to foresee their loss of power in the area for a long time to come.

CONCLUDING ANALYSIS

POLITICS IN THIS STUDY was defined as the moderated conflict of members of a social system over the different resources in which they have an interest. Prominent resources over which conflict occurred among groups in the altiplano included land, public works, air and road communications, welfare aid, industrialization projects, and political office. Conflicts also took place between the department as an actor and outside political forces, including the national government, interest groups, political parties, and other departments, over such resources as the national budget and services, foreign aid allocations, industrial enterprises, and preference in getting decentralized control over development agencies.

Conflict in the altiplano has usually been moderated by local political brokers (e.g., the nationally appointed prefects and other authorities, or the Corpuno Assembly and its officials). At other times, internal conflict has declined among system members as they organized a common front demanding greater resources from the national government and abroad (e.g., during the great drought). Local conflict has also been moderated by outside suppression (e.g., the show of national force during the Juliaca riots).

The altiplano system bears a close resemblance to the plural society type developed by M. G. Smith. The barely self-sufficient *colonos* and *comuneros* among the Indians clearly possessed distinct cultural institutions from those of the mestizo elite. The principal cross-cultural relationships that had existed until recent times were the economic dependencies of *colonos* on their landlords and the exploitation of *comuneros* by lawyers, landlords, and local authorities. The mestizo elite, living almost exclusively upon the various kinds of tribute exacted from the peasants, had evolved a rudimentary, but organic, division of labor.

Once their pre-Columbian institutions providing for adjustment to ecological uncertainties had been broken down, the Indians became exceedingly vulnerable to exploitation. Dispersed and isolated in barely self-sufficient units throughout a wide area, the peasantry had little access to its own various segments or to outside groups for action in defense of its interests. An attrition of its already meager resources thus occurred in the conflicts of its individual units with the more mobilized groups of the mestizo society, whose interdependency permitted a greater strategic sharing of resources. The result was that, except for brief anomic outbursts, the peasantry remained atomized and politically subordinate throughout the four hundred years in which this plural society has existed.

In recent times, however, with the opening of better communications from the more advanced (and socioeconomically differentiated) sector of Peru into the altiplano, this castelike system has been eroded by the steady growth of the *cholo* group from among the peasantry, and by the immigration of Peruvians and foreigners, who are less constrained by the mores of the mestizo caste and are attracted by the area's scattered opportunities. Thus, beneath the old, semifeudal organic network of the mestizos evolved a new, commercial organic network involving *cholos*, outsiders (*forasteros*), and peasants. The generation of resources in the second network is difficult to measure. Although it may not have averaged much in per capita terms, this growth has been significant relative to the productivity of the dominant social elite. In particular, the generation of new resources meant the rapid accumulation of considerable wealth for a few individual *forastero* merchants (e.g., the Cáceres family) and permitted the financing of the federation of peasant syndicates through which the elite's dominance could be challenged politically.

Obviously, the breakdown of old segmentary units and their reorganization around new, more specialized and productive interests is not being accomplished without great frustration and conflict. Bourricaud described the insecurity of *cholos* trying to adjust to the new Westernized world, and he also indicated the elite's anxiety and contempt for the *nouveau riche* among the commercial intruders. Similarly, we have seen the frustration and ultimate surrender of the *forastero* technocrat, Oscar Espinoza, whose political brokerage, after an initially productive stage, was increasingly impeded or rejected altogether. As the processes of socioeconomic differentiation are still in their early stages in the altiplano, tensions and unproductive competition and conflict may be expected to continue.

THE ALTIPLANO'S CLEAVAGES AND THE FUTURE

This study has highlighted the gradual emergence of a series of cleavages that accumulated in recent years between the two primary geographical centers of the altiplano: the cities of Puno and Juliaca. At issue were the location of such material improvements as an airport and an industrial park, as well as preferential treatment in a range of other economic and social development services. We have also argued that this geopolitical cleavage gave expression to the deeper socioeconomic cleavage between the subordinated peasant majority of the department and the dominant mestizo elite.

Across this cumulative issue-cleavage seemed to fall a number of other cleavages that could dissipate the potential explosiveness of the regional rivalry. These included (1) the three-cornered conflict between peasant communities and *hacendados*, between the *colonos* and their landlords, and between *comuneros* and *colonos* over the eventual disposition of hacienda lands: (2) the conflict between peasant union federations sponsored by the *caceristas*, the Communists, and, more recently, the *belaundistas*; (3) the party conflict between the AP, PDC, PAP, UNO, Communists, independent conservatives, and *caceristas*; (4) the inevitable geopolitical rivalries among other regions, towns, and villages within the department over scarce resources; and (5) the diffuse, departmentwide, social conflicts between the mestizo elite and the *cholo-forastero* upstarts, and between the latter and the tradition-oriented peasants and members of the urban lower class. In addition, the common interests of the entire altiplano area for investments from the national government would seem to act as a potential blanket to smother any individual conflicts that got out of hand.

The problem that requires analysis here, and further research as well, is the exact location and effect of these additional cleavage lines in relation to the Puno-Juliaca cleavage. If these other cleavages do not, in fact, substantially cut across or dilute the Puno-Juliaca, or underlying class, conflicts, we can predict a continued acute level of tension (accompanied by occasional outbreaks of violence) and the absence of internal brokerage capable of preventing or seriously moderating it.

The first potential cleavage (or network of cleavages) oriented to the man-land problem has the capacity to dilute peasant strength relative to specific agrarian reform issues and decision-making. Divisions among *colonos* and *comuneros* can be manipulated by the landowners to confuse national and even local decision-makers trying to determine the depth of sentiment of peasants toward expropriations. But in future elections, the greater number of *comuneros* and their control by the Cáceres brothers may lead to greater representative strength for *comuneros* in Congress. Conceivably, then, the depth of this crosscutting cleavage may be reduced considerably, and peasants may increasingly influence the outcome of legislative and administrative, as well as electoral, decisions.

The second potential cleavage, among competing political groups organizing the peasants, has so far been of negligible importance. For one thing, the member syndicates of the Communist-oriented FDC (which sided with Puno during the riots) are mostly on the haciendas.[1] In contrast, over five-sixths of the FSC unions are in free-holding villages.[2] The leaders of the FDC and other Communists in Puno argue not for a land reform but for improved conditions for the

[1] Interviews, Rosendo Aza and Roberto Bautista, Puno, April 14, 1965.
[2] Interview, Atalo Gutiérrez, Puno, April 12, 1965.

colonos on the haciendas.[3] Thus, the Cáceres brothers and the FSC
emerge as the only outspoken proponents of a sweeping land reform
benefiting the *comuneros*. Because *comuneros* greatly outnumber *colonos*, this cleavage, like the first, would seem to be of declining importance relative to the basic line of conflict. Moreover, nationally
based groups like the *belaundistas* and Communists must compete
among other sectors of the electorate, such as the slum dwellers, university students, and organized labor. Whatever funds are left over
for the peasantry must be dispersed on a nationwide scale. The Cáceres
brothers, by concentrating their resources locally, have had a clear advantage and are likely to hold it.

The related cleavage of party divisions in the altiplano remains of
minor importance, too. The phenomenon of party fronts (of all the
others) against the *cacerista* PITC in 1966 re-enforced the basic cleavage line. In the riots of 1965, this crosscutting party cleavage disappeared altogether. Not only was the *cacerista* radio station in Juliaca
accused of "fomenting rebellion" and closed, but the same fate befell
the AP-sponsored radio station there.[4] Also, the trip to Lima by Puno
leaders of the major parties to protest the Juliaca "revolt"[5] was preceded by a similar visit by Juliaca leaders of the same parties to defend
the Juliaca grievances before President Belaúnde.[6]

It may be that regional or local rivalries, the fourth potential crosscutting cleavage, will obscure or reduce the viability of the Puno-Juliaca cleavage as a dominant political polarization of altiplano politics.
Nevertheless, the PITC already controls many district and provincial
councils, and has the capacity to funnel some resources to them
(through the parliamentary activity of its congressmen, the economic
activity of the Cáceres family, and the special funds of the FSC). The
Puno elite, if it can continue to hold on to Corpuno (and if it can
keep the agency funded), may be able to do some resource-funneling
of its own to reduce the Cáceres hold on these areas. But if Corpuno's
resources are scant, or if they are directed to urban projects in Puno

[3] Interviews, Aza and Bautista, April 14, 1965.
[4] *La Prensa* (Lima), November 6, 1965, p. 2.
[5] *Los Andes* (Puno), November 20, 1965, p. 1.
[6] *La Prensa* (Lima), November 9, 1965, p. 2.

or to sympathetic areas only, then the polarization of the department along the basic cleavage line will be increased, not reduced. Even if Corpuno moneys are directed to uncommitted areas, the psychological battle to see who winds up with ultimate credit for such investments may be won by the *caceristas*, regardless of the source.

Finally, in the social conflict between the old elite and the *cholos* and *forasteros*, some of the latter two groups in the city of Puno apparently sided with the anti-Cáceres movement there. The Communist-affiliated Federation of Workers, composed largely of *cholo* artisans and laborers in the city of Puno, denounced the leaders of the riots in the same language as others in that city.[7] Many of the *forastero* technocrats, merchants, and employees interviewed for this study in Puno also expressed undiluted hostility for the *cacerista* demagogery and bafflement over the enthusiastic peasant response to their leadership. But, curiously, the highest number of votes obtained by either Róger or Néstor Cáceres in the 1962 elections (the only ones for which provincial returns were available) was in the province of Puno.[8]

In Juliaca, on the other hand, *Los Andes* reported that during the riots, "the troublemakers and Indians" made great trouble for the "conscientious element" among the Juliaca elite. Some of them complained they were obliged publicly to give cheers (*dar vivas*) for the "new department" and for the Cáceres brothers.[9] How many there were among this "conscientious element" is not clear. In the 1962 elections, from among the San Román electorate (which comprised 12% of the province's total population), Róger Cáceres got only two-fifths of the votes cast.[10] Luís Cáceres, in his 1963 campaign for mayor of Juliaca, received almost exactly the same percentage of

[7] "Comunicado de Prensa del Comité Ejecutivo de la Frente Departamental de Trabajadores de Puno," printed in *Los Andes*, November 8, 1965, p. 6.

[8] Hermogenes Vera Salazar, *El Proceso Electoral de 1962 en el Departamento de Puno*, pp. 23–24. Although the province of Puno also had the highest number of voters, only twenty-three of the fifty-six candidates for deputy in 1962 scored their highest number of votes in Puno. Therefore, it appears that the high Cáceres vote there reveals a fairly sizeable undercurrent of support.

[9] *Los Andes* (Puno), November 9, 1965, p. 3.

[10] Vera Salazar, *El Proceso Electoral*, pp. 23–24.

votes.[11] Therefore, it is obvious that some opposition to the Cáceres brothers exists within Juliaca. But, as the testimonies in *Los Andes* imply, during the conflict these hostile elements were cross-pressured into silence by the behavior of the nonvoting majority.

More research is clearly needed regarding the obvious differences between progressive and conservative elements within the lower classes (peasants or laborers bound in clientage relationships with members of the middle and upper class versus unattached *comuneros* and *cholos*; or tradition-bound versus innovative *comuneros*). Fatalism and fear of the unknown are definite forces to be played upon by political groups anxious to preserve the *status quo* in the department. The extent to which the anti-Cáceres groups in Puno use these devices—as distinct from their more obvious emphases on cultural heritage, radical oratory, and urban improvement—needs to be explored.

Common interests, which had served to unify regions, classes, and parties in the drought period and during other emergencies in the past, no longer seemed to provide a method for conflict moderation. One of the reasons for this was Corpuno's unprecedented success in generating resources for local use. Skepticism about any new reallocations of Peruvian resources may have been the result of this success, while internal conflict over the allocation of these new resources became more important than cooperative solicitation of still more. In addition, the expectations of peasant villagers and *cholos*, being awakened by the prospects of schools and other unprecedented investments in the rural areas, may have risen more rapidly than the resources to satisfy them.

Obviously, the challenges of Oscar Espinoza's job as a principal broker of the Corpuno resources became unmanageable, and his ambiguous role as critic of both sides of the Puno-Juliaca conflict served only to widen the breach. With compromise no longer possible, his abandonment of the brokerage role was not surprising.

Thus, although there are obviously cross-pressured individuals in both the Juliaca and the Puno camps, and elsewhere, who have attempted to seek a higher common interest, it seems that the major

<hr />

[11] *Los Andes* (Puno), December 20, 1963, p. 1.

socioeconomic cleavages in the altiplano are re-enforced and given expression by the rivalry between the two towns. If these conclusions are accurate, the outlook for political stability in the altiplano is bleak. In the absence of bountiful new resources and of political brokerage acceptable to both sides of the cumulative conflicts, one can expect a political war of attrition that will continue until migration (of one side or the other) and/or socioeconomic and cultural assimilation have reduced the gulfs of understanding and privilege that exist between groups today. The Peruvian government will have to play an increasingly influential role in maintaining stability in the area. But, if conditions in this department are true of others as well, the government may be hard pressed to maintain rural stability if at the same time it wishes to sustain its rate of industrial growth.

BIBLIOGRAPHY

Primary Sources

Corporación de Fomento y Promoción Social y Económica de Puno. *Memoria Anual Leída por el Presidente Andrés Romero Portugal*. Puno, 1965.

————. *Textos de las Memorias del Presidente Sr. Andrés Romero Portugal. Correspondientes a los Años de 1962–1963*. Puno: Edit. *Los Andes*, 1964.

República del Perú:
Cámara de Diputados. *Relación de los Pedidos Presentados, Conjunta y Separadamente por los Señores Diputados Róger y Néstor Cáceres Velásquez y Julio Arce Catacora, Durante las Legislaturas de 1964 Hasta la Fecha*. Lima, March 18, 1965.

————. *Relación de los Proyectos Presentados, Conjunta y Separadamente por los Señores Diputados Róger y Néstor Cáceres Velásquez y Julio Arce Catacora, Durante las Legislaturas de 1964 Hasta la Fecha*. Lima, April 2, 1965.

Comisión Ejecutiva Interministerial de Cooperación Popular. *Datos Distritales para Fines de Desarrollo*. Lima, 1964.

————. *El Pueblo Lo Hizo*. Boletín No. 1. Lima, 1964.

Congreso. *Legislación Sobre Reforma Agraria*. Callao, Peru: Imp. Colegio Militar Leoncio Prado, 1965.

Instituto Nacional de Planificación. Dirección Nacional de Estadística y Censos. *Primer Censo Nacional Agropecuario, 2 Julio de 1961: Principales Resultados Obtenidos por Muestreo*. Lima, 1963.

————. *VI Censo Nacional de Población*. Lima, 1965.

Ministerio de Agricultura. Universidad Agraria. *Estadística Agraria 1963*. Lima: Convenio de Cooperación Técnico, Estadística y Cartografía, 1964.

Ministerio de Hacienda y Comercio. Dirección Nacional de Estadística. *Censo Nacional de Población de 1940.* Lima, 1949.

―――. Dirección Nacional de Estadística y Censos. *Anuario Estadístico del Perú 1955.* Lima, 1958.

Ministerio de Trabajo y Asuntos Indígenas. Plan Nacional de Integración de la Población Aborigen. *Informe: Actividades Enero 1963–Junio 1964.* Lima, 1964.

―――. *Informe del Plan Nacional de Integración de la Población Aborigen.* Lima, 1963.

Oficina Nacional de Reforma Agraria. "Informe Técnico de la Zona de Puno para los Fines de la Reforma Agraria," by C. Bambi Díaz. Unpublished manuscript. Puno, [1965].

Plan Regional Para el Desarrollo del Sur del Perú. *Informes.* 29 vols. Lima, 1959.

Romero Portugal, Andrés. *Memoria Anual 1964.* Puno: Corpuno, 1965.

―――. *Texto de la Memoria Leída Ante la Asamblea Departamental de Delegados* (March 4, 1963). Puno: Corpuno, 1964.

―――. *Texto de la Memoria Leída Ante la Asamblea Departamental de Delegados* (March 3, 1964). Puno: Corpuno, 1964.

United States. Department of State. "Press Release 350" (May 26, 1961), *The Department of State Bulletin* 44 (June 12, 1961): 923.

SECONDARY SOURCES

Books

Adams, Richard N. *A Community in the Andes: Problems and Progress in Muquiyauyo.* Seattle: University of Washington Press, 1959.

Alexander, Robert J. *Communism in Latin America.* 2nd ed. New Brunswick, N.J.: Rutgers University Press, 1960.

Alonso, Isidoro, *et al. La Iglesia en Perú y Bolivia: Estructuras Eclesiásticas.* Madrid: Centro de Información y Sociología de la Obra de Cooperación Sacerdotal Hispanoamericana, 1962.

Arnade, Charles W. *The Emergence of the Republic of Bolivia.* Gainesville: University of Florida Press, 1957.

Basadre, Jorge. *Historia de la República del Perú.* 6 vols. Lima: Ediciones Historia, 1961–1962.

Bolo Hidalgo, Salomón. *Cristianismo y Liberación Nacional.* 2nd ed. Lima: Ediciones Liberación, 1962.

Bourricaud, François. *Changements à Puno: Étude de Sociologie Andine.* Paris: Institut des Hautes Études de l'Amerique Latine, 1962.

Cáceres Velásquez, Róger E. *Puno: Universidad y Corporación.* Lima: Ediciones de Divulgación Popular, 1961.

—————. *Mensaje a los Puneños.* Arequipa: Cuzzi Impresores, 1962.

Carter, William E. *Aymara Communities and the Bolivian Agrarian Reform.* University of Florida Monographs, Social Sciences, no. 24. Gainesville: University of Florida Press, 1964.

Castillo, Hernán, *et al. Accopata: The Reluctant Recipient of Technological Change.* Translated and edited by Eileen Maynard. Cornell Peru Project. Socio-Economic Development of Andean Communities, report no. 2. Ithaca: Cornell University [1964].

Cuentas, J. Alberto. *Chucuito: Album Gráfico e Histórico.* Lima: La Opinión Nacional, 1929.

Díaz Bedregal, Florencio. *Apuntes Para una Reforma Agraria en el Departamento de Puno.* Ediciones del Centro de Estudios Jurídicos, no. 12. Cuzco. Editorial Garcilaso, 1960.

Diez de San Miguel, Garci. *Visita Hecha a la Provincia de Chucuito por Garci Diez de San Miguel en el Año 1567.* Lima: Ediciones de la Casa de la Cultura del Perú, 1964.

Dobyns, Henry F. *The Social Matrix of Peruvian Indigenous Communities.* Cornell Peru Project Monograph. Ithaca: Cornell University, 1964.

—————, and Carrasco R., Ella. *Un Análisis de la Situación de las Comunidades Indígenas en el Ambiente Nacional.* Folletos del Proyecto Perú-Cornell, no. 1. Lima, 1962.

—————, Doughty, Paul L., and Holmberg, Allan R. *Peace Corps Program Impact in the Peruvian Andes: Final Report.* Cornell Peru Program. Ithaca: Cornell University, 1966.

Durkheim, Emile. *The Division of Labor in Society.* Glencoe: The Free Press, 1964.

Escobar M., Gabriel. *Organización Social y Cultural del Sur del Perú.* Serie: Antropología Social, no. 7. Mexico City: Instituto Indigenista Interamericano, 1967.

Flores, Edmundo. *Land Reform and the Alliance for Progress.* Policy Memorandum, no. 27. Princeton: Center of International Studies, 1963.

Ford, Thomas R. *Man and Land in Peru.* Gainesville: University of Florida Press, 1955.

Galdo Pagaza, Raúl. *Economía de las Colectividades Indígenas Colindantes con el Lago Titicaca.* Plan Nacional de Integración de la Población Aborigen, Serie Monográfica, no. 3. Lima: Ministerio de Trabajo y Asuntos Indígenas, 1962.

———. *El Indígena y el Mestizo de Vilquechico*. Plan Nacional de Integración de la Población Aborigen, Serie Monográfica, no. 9. Lima: Ministerio de Trabajo y Asuntos Indígenas, 1962.

Garcilaso de la Vega, El Inca. *Royal Commentaries of the Incas*. Translated by Harold V. Livermore. Austin: University of Texas Press, 1965.

Herring, Hubert. *A History of Latin America*. New York: Knopf, 1956.

Hirschman, Albert O. *Journeys toward Progress: Studies of Economic Policy-Making in Latin America*. New York: The Twentieth Century Fund, 1963.

James, Preston E. *Latin America*. 3rd ed. New York: Odyssey Press, 1959.

Kubler, George. *The Indian Caste of Peru, 1795–1940: A Population Study Based upon Tax Records and Census Reports*. Smithsonian Institution, Institute of Social Anthropology, Publication no. 14. Washington, D.C.: G.P.O., 1952.

Lanning, Edward P. *Peru before the Incas*. Englewood Cliffs, N.J.: Prentice-Hall, Inc., 1967.

Lasswell, Harold. *Politics: Who Gets What, When, How*. New York: Meridian, 1958.

Markham, Sir Clements. *The Incas of Peru*. London: Smith, Elder and Co., 1910.

———. *Las Posesiones Geográficas de las Tribus que Formaban el Imperio de los Incas*. Lima: Imprenta y Librería Sanmartí y Cia., 1923.

Martínez, Héctor. *El Indígena y el Mestizo de Taraco*. Plan Nacional de Integración de la Problación Aborigen, Serie Monográfica, no. 8. Lima: Ministerio de Trabajo y Asuntos Indígenas, 1962.

———. *Las Migraciones Altiplánicas y la Colonización del Tambopata*. Plan Nacional de Integración de la Población Aborigen, Serie Monográfica, no. 1. Lima: Ministerio de Trabajo y Asuntos Indígenas, 1961.

Mason, J. Alden. *The Ancient Civilizations of Peru*. Harmondsworth, England: Penguin Books, 1957.

Matos Mar, José. *La Propiedad en la Isla de Taquile (Lago Titicaca)*. Instituto de Etnología y Arqueología, Publicación no. 13. Lima: Universidad Nacional Mayor de San Marcos, 1957.

Montalvo V., Abner, and Galdo P., Raúl. *Análisis Estadigráfico en Seis Localidades Seleccionadas en la Zona Circundante al Lago Titicaca*. Programa Puno-Tambopata, Sección de Investigación Antropológica, Serie de Monografías, no. 2. Lima: Instituto Indigenista Peruano, 1959.

Neira, Hugo. *Cuzco: Tierra y Muerte*. Lima: Populibros Peruanos, 1964.

Ortiz V., Pedro. *Hacienda y Colonato en Villurcuni*. Plan Nacional de Integración de la Población Aborigen, Serie Monográfica, no. 12. Lima: Ministerio de Trabajo y Asuntos Indígenas, 1963.

————, and Galdo P., Raúl. *El Indígena de la Isla de Amantaní*. Plan Nacional de Integración de la Población Aborigen, Serie Monográfica, no. 11. Lima: Ministerio de Trabajo y Asuntos Indígenas, 1963.

Owens, R. J. *Peru*. London: Oxford University Press, 1963.

Pareja Paz-Soldán, José. *Derecho Constitucional Peruano*. 2nd ed. Lima, 1951.

Pike, Frederick B. *The Modern History of Peru*. New York: Praeger, 1967.

Polsby, Nelson W. *Community Power and Political Theory*. New Haven: Yale University Press, 1963.

Ramsöy, Odd. *Social Groups as System and Subsystem*. New York: The Free Press of Glencoe, 1963.

Romero, Emilio. *El Descentralismo*. Lima: Companía de Impresiones y Publicidad Editores, 1932.

————. *Historia Económica del Perú*. Buenos Aires: Editorial Sudamericano, 1949.

————. *Monografía del Departamento de Puno*. Lima: Imprentas Aguirre, 1928.

Schaedel, Richard P. *La Demografía y los Recursos Humanos del Sur del Perú*. Serie: Antropología Social, no. 8. Mexico City: Instituto Indigenista Interamericano, 1967.

Schattschneider, E. E. *Party Government*. New York. Farrar and Rinehart, 1942.

Schultz, Theodore W. *Transforming Traditional Agriculture*. New Haven: Yale University Press, 1964.

Smelser, Neil J. *The Sociology of Economic Life*. Foundations of Modern Sociology Series. Englewood Cliffs, N. J.: Prentice-Hall, 1963.

Sociedad de Propaganda del Sur del Perú. *Guía General del Sur del Perú*. Cuzco: Librería Imprenta H. G. Rozas, 1921.

Stein, William W. *Hualcán: Life in the Highlands of Peru*. Ithaca: Cornell University Press, 1961.

Tschopik, Harry. *The Aymara of Chucuito, Peru, I: Magic*. Anthropological Papers of the American Museum of Natural History. Vol. 44, part 2, pp. 133–308. New York, 1959.

University of California, Latin American Center. *Statistical Abstract of Latin America, 1964*. Los Angeles, 1965.

Vera Salazar, Hermogenes. *El Proceso Electoral de 1962 en el Departamento de Puno*. Puno: Editorial los Andes, 1963.

Articles and Manuscripts

Adams, Richard N. "The Community in Latin America: A Changing Myth," *The Centennial Review* 6 (Summer, 1962): 409–434.

Beals, Ralph L. "Social Stratification in Latin America." In *Contemporary Cultures and Societies of Latin America*, ed. Dwight B. Heath and Richard N. Adams. New York: Random House, 1965.

Bennett, Wendell C. "The Archeology of the Central Andes." In *Handbook of South American Indians*, ed. Julian H. Steward. New York: Cooper Square Publishers, 1963.

Bolton, Ralph. "Chijnaya: A Peace Corps Success," *Pomona Today* 63 (October, 1965): 6–8.

———. "The Peasant Transformation," *Pomona Today* 62 (July, 1964): 6–9.

Brown, David. "Monthly Report." Iowa State Agricultural Mission. Puno, January, 1965.

Carroll, Thomas F. "The Land Reform Issue in Latin America." In *Latin American Issues: Essays and Comments*, ed. Albert O. Hirschman. New York: The Twentieth Century Fund, 1961.

Castro Pozo, Hildebrando. "Social and Economico-Political Evolution of the Communities of Central Peru." In *Handbook of South American Indians*, ed. Julian H. Steward. New York: Cooper Square Publishers, 1963.

Delgado, Oscar. "Revolution, Reform, Conservatism: Three Types of Agrarian Structure," *Dissent* 9 (Autumn, 1962): 350–363.

Dobyns, Henry F. "An Outline of Andean Epidemic History to 1720," *Bulletin of the History of Medicine* 37 (November–December, 1963): 493–515.

Gall, Norman. "Letter From Peru," *Commentary* 37 (June, 1964): 64–69.

Gomez, Rosendo A. "Peru: The Politics of Military Guardianship." In *Political Systems of Latin America*, ed. Martin C. Needler. Princeton: D. Van Nostrand, 1964.

Hirschfield, Robert Carl. "Passing through Juliaca," *The Minority of One* 8 (March, 1966): 25.

Kubler, George. "The Quechua in the Colonial World." In *Handbook of South American Indians*, ed. Julian H. Steward. New York: Cooper Square Publishers, 1963.

Kuper, Leo. "Plural Societies—Perspectives and Problems." In *Pluralism in Africa,* ed. Leo Kuper and M. G. Smith. Berkeley and Los Angeles: University of California Press, 1969.

La Barre, Weston. "The Aymara Indians of the Lake Titicaca Plateau, Bolivia," *American Anthropologist* 50, no. 1, part 2 (January, 1948): 1–227.

Lasswell, Harold. "Integrating Communities into More Inclusive Systems," *Human Organization* 21 (Summer, 1962): 116–121.

Lofchie, Michael. "The Plural Society in Zanzibar." In *Pluralism in Africa,* ed. Leo Kuper and M. G. Smith. Berkeley and Los Angeles: University of California Press, 1969.

Mangin, William P. "The Role of Regional Associations in the Adaptation of Rural Population in Peru," *Sociologus* 9 (1959): 23–36.

Mishkin, Bernard. "The Contemporary Quechua." In *Handbook of South American Indians,* ed. Julian H. Steward. New York: Cooper Square Publishers, 1963.

Murra, John. "Una Apreciación Etnológica de la Visita." In *Visita Hecha a la Provincia de Chucuito por Garci Diez de San Miguel en el Año 1567.* Lima: Ediciones de la Casa de la Cultura del Perú, 1964.

Nuñez del Prado, Oscar. "Aspects of Andean Native Life." In *Contemporary Cultures and Societies of Latin America,* ed. Dwight B. Heath and Richard N. Adams. New York: Random House, 1965.

Parsons, James J., and Denevan, William M. "Pre-Columbian Ridged Fields," *Scientific American* 215 (July, 1967): 93–100.

Patch, Richard W. "How Communal Are the Communities?" *American Universities Field Staff Newsletters, West Coast South American Series* 6, no. 5 (Lima, June 12, 1959): 16–17.

Peña, Carlos. "Problemas Socio-económicos del Departamento de Puno," *Perú Indígena* 6 (July, 1957): 37–45.

Rowe, John Howland. "Inca Culture at the Time of the Spanish Conquest." In *Handbook of South American Indians,* ed. Julian H. Steward. New York: Cooper Square Publishers, 1963.

Schaedel, Richard P. "Land Reform Studies," *Latin American Research Review* 1 (Fall, 1965): 75–122.

Simmons, Ozzie. "The *Criollo* Outlook in the Mestizo Culture of Coastal Peru." In *Contemporary Cultures and Societies of Latin America,* ed. Dwight B. Heath and Richard N. Adams. New York: Random House, 1965.

Smith, M. G. "Institutional and Political Conditions of Pluralism." In *Plu-*

ralism in Africa, ed. Leo Kuper and M. G. Smith. Berkeley and Los Angeles: University of California Press, 1969.

————. "Social and Cultural Pluralism," *Annals of the New York Academy of Sciences* 83 (January, 1960): 763–777.

"Stealing from the Starving," *Time,* April 7, 1961, p. 36.

Tschopik, Harry, Jr. "The Aymara." In *Handbook of South American Indians,* ed. Julian H. Steward. New York: Cooper Square Publishers, 1963.

Waggener, John G. "Army Civic Action in Southeastern Peru," *Peruvian Times,* March 5, 1965, pp. 4–8.

Periodicals and Newspapers

Los Andes (Puno), 1960–1966.

El Campesino (Puno), 1965.

Caretas (Lima), 1963–1966.

El Comercio (Lima), 1956–1965.

Hispanic American Report, 1960–1964.

Oiga (Lima), 1965.

Peruvian Times (Lima), 1940–1965.

La Prensa (Lima), 1965.

El Tiempo (Puno), 1963–1965.

La Voz de Puno (Puno), 1964–1965.

INDEX

access. SEE political access

Acción Popular. SEE political parties, AP

Acción Popular Rebelde. SEE political parties, Acción Popular Rebelde

Accopata, Peru: 61, 71, 75

Acora, Peru: 43

AD. SEE political parties, AD

Adams, Richard N.: 68

affaire sequía, la. SEE drought, the "drought affair"

agrarian reform: in Bolivia, 9–10; opposition of hacienda administrators to, 67–68; complicated by differences between *comuneros* and *colonos*, 78, 186, 187; called for by FSC, 129, 136, 170, 171, 172, 188; as land consolidation, 151, 181–182, 183; defined, 169; conflicting interpretations of, among groups, 169, 170, 171–174; as resettlement, 178–181, 182–183; impact of, on altiplano, 182, 187. SEE ALSO Agrarian Reform Bill; Agrarian Reform Institute; Corpuno, agrarian reform program of; ONRA

Agrarian Reform Bill: Congressional debates on, 171–172; promulgated into law, 172; provisions of, 173. SEE ALSO ONRA

Agrarian Reform Institute: 118

agricultural credit: 34. SEE ALSO Agropecuarian Development Bank

agricultural extension: 34, 71. SEE ALSO SCIPA (SIPA)

agricultural labor: wages of, 60, 61; traditional forms of, 71, 72, 73

agriculture: traditional system of, 20; periodic crises in, 39–40; livestock production, 40, 47, 57; intensive lake-and riverside, 40, 57; crops, 45, 57; as obstacle to education, 56; technology and, 71–72. SEE ALSO drought; floods; frosts; landholdings; landowners; land use

Agriculture, Ministry of: 34, 97 n. 60, 99, 105, 113, 117, 146, 171, 173

Agropecuarian Census (1961): 71

Agropecuarian Development Bank: 34, 74, 106, 113, 122

airports. SEE Juliaca, airport in; Puno, airport in

alcoholism: 75, 80, 82

Alemán, José: 89

Alianza Democrática. SEE political parties, AD

Alliance, AP-PDC. SEE political parties, AP-PDC Alliance

alpaca. SEE *auquénidos*

altiplano: political jurisdiction over, 18, 19, 23, 24; altitude of, 35; physical description of, 36, 39, 40, 41. SEE ALSO Puno, department of

Alva Orlandini, Javier: 160–161, 162, 164

Amazon River: 36

Andean Program. SEE Puno-Tambopata Program

Andes Mountains: 35, 41

AP. SEE political parties, AP

APRA. SEE political parties, APRA

apristas. SEE political parties, AD; APRA; APRA-UNO coalition; *apropradistas*

Arce Catacora, Julio: 137, 177

Arequipa, Peru: seized in Pumacahua revolt, 23; trade from Puno to, 26, 84; migration of Indians to, 40 n. 9, 90, 113; status for Puno mestizos in,

62, 83; food rotting in, 93; endangered by Puno development, 98; proposed Cuzco road to, 99–100; Puno road to, 99–100; effort to get meat-freezing plant in, 106; effort to get cement plant in, 107; and division of Puno Department, 151, 158, 159; plan for industrial park in, 157; Municipal Council of, to pay legal expenses of Luís Cáceres, 164. SEE ALSO transportation, railroads

Arequipa, department of: 25

Arguedas, Julio Jesús: 89

army, Peruvian. SEE military, Peruvian

Arnade, Charles: 24

artisan production: 48, 63, 93–94, 116, 180, 182

Asillo, Peru: revolt in, 28; irrigation project in, 108

assault guards. SEE guardia republicana

Association of Agronomy Engineers: 118

Association of Civil Engineers: 118

Association of Industries and Commerce: 118, 164

Astete Abril, Antonio: 100

auquénidos: importance of, in pre-Conquest times, 20, 40; British trade in wool of, 26; native to altiplano, 41; numbers of, 46, 47; economic advantages of, 57, 58; wool tax and, 117, 123, 170; and artisan production, 180. SEE ALSO artisan production; textile production; wool; wool-processing plant

Ayacucho, Peru: seized in Pumacahua revolt, 23; battle of, 24

Ayaviri, Peru: 43, 105. SEE ALSO Melgar, province of

Aymará language. SEE language, Aymará

Aymará peoples. SEE Colla tribe; Indian cultural group, Aymará-speaking Indians; Lupaca tribe

ayni: 72, 73

Azángaro, Peru: 43, 161

Azángaro, province of, Peru: revolt in (1945), 29; location of, 36; statistics on, 43; oil exploration in, 47; languages in, 53–55; literacy in, 56; Asillo irrigation project in, 108; effect of frost on (1960), 113; land-owner-peasant disputes in, 136, 158; municipal elections in, (1963) 139, (1966) 166

Basadre, Jorge: 25

Beals, Ralph: 61 n. 27

Belaúnde Terry, Fernando: develops Cooperación Popular, 72; and national elections, (1956) 88, 89, (1962) 127, 130, 131, 133, (1963) 134, 135, 137, 147; and cement issue, 108; municipal elections and (1963), 139; tie of, with Oscar Espinoza, 144; refuses to create Puno airport, 154; supports Puno-Moquegua road, 158; declares state of siege in San Román Province, 162; his neglect of Juliaca criticized, 163; and agrarian reform, 171, 172; and peasant union organization, 174, 175, 178; receives delegations from Puno and Juliaca, 188. SEE ALSO political parties, AP, AP-PDC Alliance

belaundista. SEE political parties, AP

Belgium: 156

Beltrán, Pedro: 127

Benavides, Oscar: 31

Beneficencia Pública: 117, 173–174

Bolivia: revolution in (1952), 9–10; independence of, 23, 24; attempts of, at federation with Peru, 25–26; trade for, through Puno, 26, 31, 84; and Peruvian-Bolivian Commission, 98–99; cement imports from, 107; observers from, to FSC Convention, 136

Bolton, Ralph: 178–179

Boston, Massachusetts: 180

Bourricaud, François: on social use of wealth, 65; on lawyers' exploitation of peasants, 66; on Indians' nonuse of Spanish, 76; on colono-hacendado relationship, 76–77; on social conflicts in altiplano, 78–79; on cholifica-

to; Puno, Arequipa road to, bypass road near, Moquegua road to; San Gabán Valley road; Tambopata Valley road
Treasury, Ministry of: 97, 105, 123
tribute: extracted by Incas, 18–19; extracted by Spanish, 20; as cause of Pumacahua revolt, 23; abolished by Castilla, 27
Trujillo, Peru: 99
Túpac Amaru II: 22–23

UNESCO: 34. SEE ALSO Puno-Tambopata Program
Unión del Pueblo Peruano. SEE political parties, UPP
Unión Departamental Puneñista. SEE political parties, UDP
Unión Nacional Odriísta. SEE political parties, UNO
United States: tourists from, attacked, 93; Peace Corps from, 116, 178–180; State Department, 122–123
—foreign aid: through SCIPA, 34; emergency program (1956–1957), 87–95 passim, 100, 104, 108, 109–111; scandal over, 92–97 passim, 109–111, 113, 122–123, 184, 190; later programs, 109, 113, 114–115, 120, 136, 153; Communist harassment of, 128

universal suffrage: proposed by Cáceres brothers, 138
Universidad Católica: 85
upper class. SEE mestizo cultural group, upper class
Upper Peru: 23, 24, 26. SEE ALSO Bolivia
Urubamba River: 115. SEE ALSO Machu Picchu hydroelectric project

Venezuela: 107
Ventilla Bill: 154, 155. SEE ALSO Puno, airport in
vicuña. SEE auquénidos
Vidangos, Darío: 138
Villarán, Mario: 134
Vilquechico, Peru: 75, 82
voting. SEE elections

wages for agricultural labor: 60, 61
War, Ministry of: 117
Washington, D.C.: 180
white-collar employees: 63, 67, 118
wool: 92, 94, 104–105
wool-processing plant: 105, 116, 121, 125

Yunguyo, Peru: 84

Zea Gonzales, Juan: 95, 129, 132, 133, 137, 161